Leading with their Hearts

Leading with their Hearts

The Story of St. Coletta of Wisconsin

Christina J Goldstone

Author of
Come to the Window
Life with Daniela - our Child from Romania

Foreword by
Ted Behncke - President of St. Coletta of Wisconsin

Published by St. Coletta of Wisconsin

Cover (and many interior) photos and design by Noah Smith
Communication and Design Specialist, St. Coletta of Wisconsin

Front Cover (and back) photo were taken on May 11, 2022

Front row:
*Daniela Goldstone -7 years (Time living in St. Coletta community)
*Ralph Derucki - 86 years

(L-R) back row:
Craig Buker - 32 years
*Candace Lilleeng - 6 months
Greg Burrill - 5 years
Barbara DeCleene - 1 year
Joe Shackelford - 40 years
Kathy Held - 37 years
Jenny Hood - 40 years
Sue Johnson - 57 years
Tawana Mettlach - 5 years
Michelle Prete - 33 years
Anne Weirick - 3 months
Mary Ann Tryon - 38 years
Andy Gengler - 10 years

Back cover photo*

For the St. Coletta Community

- The Sisters of St. Francis of Assisi, whose faith and hearts began a revolution

- The dedicated and compassionate staff, volunteers and supporters

- The remarkable St. Coletta children, adults and families who have been cared for, educated, respected and loved since 1904

The Original St. Coletta Mission Statement

"Recognizing the human dignity and spiritual worth of all persons, regardless of race, creed, or national origin, St. Coletta School attempts to provide a community with a homelike atmosphere of acceptance and respect. Within this atmosphere, individuals of all ages, particularly those who are mentally retarded, participate in programs designed to enhance their quality of life by contributing to each person's highest attainable level of independence, productivity and integration into society.

All persons are created by God to fulfill a unique purpose on this earth, to bring special gifts into the lives of all they touch. It is the goal at St. Coletta School to prepare individuals for their special mission and our privilege to be able to do so."

Updated and Revised St. Coletta Mission Statement 1995

"In keeping with Franciscan values, St. Coletta promotes an environment of respect, acceptance and teamwork by supporting each individual's God-given potential, realistic hopes and dreams."

Current Mission Statement

"Inspired by the Franciscan Values of compassion, dignity and respect, we support persons with developmental and other challenges to achieve their highest quality of life, personal growth and spiritual awareness."

St. Coletta of Wisconsin's Vision

"St. Coletta of Wisconsin will be the premier provider of support services for adults with developmental disabilities and other challenges throughout their lifespan. Through dynamic partnerships, exceptional customer service, a demonstrated commitment to quality and spirituality, we will work with persons receiving services to achieve their best life possible."

Foreword

As a group, having a disability is something we are all just one accident away from. Indeed, according to the Centers for Disease Control, it is estimated that over 25% of the American population, some 61 million people has a disability of some type or another. The past one hundred years have witnessed many victories for persons with disabilities like health care benefits in 1967, the Federal Fair Housing Act of 1968, and the Persons with Disabilities Act of 1996. All of these initiatives have advanced the quality of life and greater access to the communities persons with disabilities live in. They are more accepted, respected, and heard. This was not always so, and many organizations across the country and globe work tirelessly to make things better. More voices and more action make a difference.

At the turn of the 20th century, there were few that had taken up the cause for persons with disabilities. In fact, most were misunderstood, uneducated, experienced little or no health care, and often banished to institutions or a dark corner of life. Enter the Sisters of St. Francis of Assisi of Jefferson, Wisconsin. They were humble teachers, devout in their beliefs and like St. Francis servants of those in need. In 1904, with no background in special education, they embarked on a dream, the St. Coletta School, to change the lives of persons with disabilities one child at a time—and changed the world. Franciscan volunteers for the cause.

Christina Goldstone, like the Sisters is the embodiment of a Franciscan volunteer for the cause. In her case literally. In 1992, she along with her husband and daughter adopted Daniela, a daughter with a disability from Romania, and set out to make her life everything it could be. She is tireless in her work. I had a first chance meeting with Christina and her husband in 2016 near the history wall in our corporate headquarters. It was a pleasant introduction not unlike hundreds of others with family members served by St. Coletta of Wisconsin. Her passion for her daughter was very strong like mothers can be expected to be. But, I was unprepared for her undaunted passion to make a difference in the disabled movement. She is well read, patient, and vocal about causes. She is constant and steady, always looking for more ways to make a difference.

When she shared she was writing a book about St. Coletta, I was curious how serious she was about the project. St. Coletta of Wisconsin has never really had a full history chronicled, and there is a lot of ground to cover. More, many of the Sisters that were part of the journey have passed on. Only bits and pieces remain, some written, some remembered, and much more to be filled in between that scholarship. Simply, it would be a considerable effort to capture the story, but it is a story that needs to be captured and told while it can be. The mission is still active and the present challenges leave little time to think long about the past.

Of course, this book necessarily begins with the Sisters and the founding days of the early twentieth century. It was a period largely devoid of resources. There was no governmental money in those days, you had to do it yourself. Self-sufficiency and stewardship were more common than now but the Sisters had to use their Franciscan values to prevail. Christina captures that period, it is essential to understand the St. Coletta brand as it is today. Structure, faith, work as ministry, and independence at work and on display. The heart that made these women successful and the strides made early that set a foundation to build on are well displayed.

The emergence and evolution of special education is also told. In 1904 there were only two schools, the Vineland School in the east and St. Coletta of Wisconsin in the Midwest. The origins of what exists today in America and indeed the world, has DNA that comes all the way back to the initial work. It was pioneering work and the story of the pioneers is also told. Critical intellectuals like Sister Mary Theodore Hegeman who not only actively wrote and traveled to share the successes and educate families about the feelings they were experiencing with their disabled children. By the 1950s St. Coletta had grown into a large school and endeavor with an international reputation. Families from across the country and beyond were sending their children to learn, grow, and return home to successful lives.

Perhaps the most famous person to become part of the fabric of St. Coletta was Rosemary Kennedy, the eldest and favorite sister of John F. Kennedy.

When people hear St. Coletta of Wisconsin they most naturally connect her with the organization. When Rosemary came to St. Coletta in 1949 it was not to attend school but to live an active life away from the public. Often this story is not told accurately and is regularly distorted. Rosemary lived a life that included all of the normal relationships and activities of a woman during her time. This too, the Sisters accomplished in stride and Christina accurately covers that story and the larger impact the Kennedy family provided for. Mainstreaming and the closure of the successful school is a story that still offers debate about whether it was the right thing to do and the impact that is still felt. Christina takes you right there to the times, covers the pertinent sides of debate, and the emotions at the time.

Christina does an excellent job of capturing not only the story but the personalities including families. At the heart of every disabled person is their family and their struggles in the quest for the highest quality life. And, there are those that have helped along the way, those people that love the work and are glad to be part of it. Christina covers it all. You are going to like this book.

It is at the same time, a personal story of Daniela and the Goldstone family but also a still evolving story of a vibrant, active organization engaged in the effort to provide the dream of the Sisters—a full life of compassion, dignity, and respect.

Ted Behncke
President
St. Coletta of Wisconsin
April 2022

Introduction

"St. Coletta" - Two simple words in a book that changed my family's life. In the summer of 2015, I read those words in a newly published book about the challenging and mysterious life of Rosemary Kennedy, one of President John F. Kennedy's younger sisters. St. Coletta was the community where Rosemary lived for over fifty years of her life.

I am the mother of a young woman named Daniela. My husband John, our nine year old daughter Marcy and I adopted Daniela in 1991 from a Romanian orphanage. She was fifteen months old. Like Rosemary, Daniela has lived her entire life with intellectual and developmental disabilities. Her disabilities were caused by prenatal alcohol exposure, severe neglect and abuse. Since her adoption and even before, I have been drawn to reading about people with disabilities and their families - families who either supported, mistreated or abandoned them. I feel a strong connection with families who have fought to find a place in the world for their child - a place for them to be included and to be treated equally and humanely. For thousands of years and across the globe, society has made that effort extremely difficult.

Throughout years of research, I had come across other books that mentioned Rosemary and her family. Some of those sources said that, after experiencing her tragic lobotomy at age 23, she lived her life in "an institution" or a "mental institution". The first time that I read about St. Coletta in 2015, I wondered if the book was going to describe Rosemary's institutionalized life. It didn't seem logical, with their history of supporting disability legislation and creating organizations like the Special Olympics, that the Kennedy family would have allowed that to be her life for over fifty years. What was St. Coletta?

Was it a hopeful place? Had it always treated people with intellectual disabilities with respect and compassion? I wondered to myself, "Does this place still exist?"

My interest quickly became more than just a passing curiosity. For me, for my family and for our daughter, these questions became very personal.

During that summer when I first read about St. Coletta, my husband and I were desperately seeking to find a community where Daniela, then age 25, would be able to live her best independent life - for the rest of her life. Since adopting her from Romania she has been diagnosed with multiple disabilities. Her history is complicated. Suffice it to say, it would be almost impossible for Daniela to ever live anywhere entirely on her own. We had many requirements for her residential setting which did not make our search an easy one.

In 2015, Daniela was failing miserably in a residential setting where she had lived for less than a year. It was totally inadequate for her needs and we

1

wanted more for her. We dreamed of a place where she could live in a community atmosphere. A place that would give her as much independence, acceptance and happiness as possible. It also needed to give her the support she would need to stay safe as she made mistakes and found her way in the world. We were certainly not unique in our search for a safe haven for our adult child. We're among millions of families who have a loved one with intellectual and developmental disabilities. Countless families across the country - and the globe, are on this same frustrating odyssey.

Just as important to us was for Daniela to be included in the search and, in fact, let her lead us in this critical decision. She loves and respects us and she enjoys spending time with her sister, my husband and me, but she has always wanted more than that. Like any young woman in her mid-twenties, she wanted her own life, not a life in a boring house with two people approaching retirement. The most important goals for her have always been to continue to learn and to have an active social life with friends. We knew that was never going to happen in our small southern town, no matter how hard we tried to facilitate it.

In 2015, and for most of Daniela's life, my husband and I lived in Virginia. (We have recently moved to Washington state.) Like many other states, it was sorely lacking in programming and housing for individuals with disabilities. The major reason for this is funding. In 2015, the waiting list for state disability funding in Virginia was agonizingly long. This has sadly continued even after a lengthy investigation by, and ultimate settlement with, the Department of Justice in 2012. Before the settlement the situation was even worse. Many individuals with disabilities had been unable to leave the institutions where they had lived for decades. The DOJ judgement rightly prioritized closing institutions in Virginia and finding residential options for those people in their communities. But this meant that everyone else had to wait and wait and wait. Many are still waiting.

To complicate our situation, Daniela was no longer a resident of Virginia. She had moved to Wisconsin for postsecondary schooling in 2011 and had established residency there. There was no waiting list at the time and she was fortunately able to receive state waiver funding. If she had moved back to Virginia in 2015, she would have lost her Wisconsin funding as soon as she reestablished residency in the state. That would have put her back at the very bottom of Virginia's waiting list. Our guess was that she might have been in her forties before she came to the top of the list. (In January 2019, the intellectual disabilities waiting list in Virginia was over 13,000 persons long.[1]) We feared that my husband and I might not even be alive at that point. We did find out that having no parents could move people onto the "urgent" list, but that brought us no comfort. Our worst nightmare would be for her to have to face our deaths and also have to move into a possibly ill-fitting and strange new living situation - all while she was grieving. This is a tragic circumstance that happens across the country on a daily basis and it's a situation that haunts parents' dreams. It certainly haunted ours.

We decided we just couldn't bring her back home. Daniela didn't want that and it wouldn't have been good for her. She had finished three years of postsecondary schooling where the goal was for her to live and work as independently as possible. Coming home would have been a sad defeat for her and Daniela wanted her own separate life. It's what she had been striving for. She wants a good job and opportunities to participate in activities and sports. She wants to keep learning. She wants to attend concerts, dinners out and go to the movies - and not always with us. She wants a life with friends, love, and inclusion. In short, she wants a life that all of us want and deserve. We certainly want that for her as well.

We weren't naive. We knew that helping her to find the life that she wanted was going to be an epic challenge. How on earth would we find this utopian place in the world where she could have all of her dreams?

We thought we had already found that place only a year before. We were wrong.

When Daniela graduated from her postsecondary school in southeast Wisconsin, she had optimistically moved an hour away to her first residential community. It became quickly and painfully obvious that the situation was a disaster. Daniela, who is on the autism spectrum, started to regress. She was depressed, angry and acting out in ways we hadn't seen since her childhood. Our hearts sank. We were back to square one, or even further back than that.

By some form of a miracle, it was at this horrible moment in time that I had just begun to read "the book"[2] that mentioned this mysterious place called St. Coletta. I had searched across the country the year before for a solution for Daniela's future. It seemed very unlikely that we would find our answers in this previously unknown place. Like anyone else, I put down the book and googled - St. Coletta in Wisconsin. Their website had lots of information. It sounded intriguing. It sounded fantastic. Too fantastic. I was wary. My husband and I had become skeptical, even cynical, about this search. If this organization was that wonderful, then the costs and waiting list surely had to be astronomical. Despite my doubts, something deep inside of me, in the middle of a worry filled night, told me to explore further. After a long night, at 5:06 am, I shot off an email. I thank God, and the stars in the universe that I did.

This book is a culmination of the past six years exploring St. Coletta of Wisconsin, the place that has become home to our very happy, and now incredibly independent, daughter. She is so proud of being part of their welcoming community. This story is about St. Coletta's unique and inspiring history. It is also about the present and the community's bright future. The book includes some disability history and the sometimes heartbreaking journey of individuals and families trying to find the dignity and respect that they deserve.

Leading with their Hearts is about St. Coletta's people - hearing their stories, exploring their programs and giving readers an insight into a place where generations of families have found solace and hope. It is about the many things that St. Coletta was, and is - a family, a sanctuary, a community. It is an oasis, a blessing, a loving and warm home. It is lifelong learning. It is fun and laughter. It is research. It is advocacy. St. Coletta is a continually innovative and groundbreaking leader that is showing the world that people with disabilities should be educated, included and respected. They can work and live the lives they want - just like everyone else.

Chapter 1

Jefferson Wisconsin is a small, lovely farming town located an hour west of Milwaukee and an hour east of its Capitol - Madison. In 1842, word spread to German immigrants that the soil in Jefferson County was fertile. They heard that the climate and landscape were much like their former homes and they began to flock to the area to create their new lives. In that welcoming atmosphere in 1864, a small, resilient band of German Catholic Sisters arrived in Jefferson with purpose in their hearts. They founded a small convent, and eventually, a girl's boarding school. Then in 1904, they were inspired to create something completely new and unheard of. Despite their naysayers, these strong Sisters persisted. With faith, stubbornness and determination they founded a school like no other in the world.

My daughter Daniela and I first drove into Jefferson in the late summer of 2015. At first glance it reminded me very much of Eaton - the small Ohio farm town that I grew up in the fifties and sixties. My county had also been settled by German immigrants. Some of them were my ancestors.

Jefferson is surrounded by lush farms with dairy cows and rolling green fields. The smell of freshly cut hay that day brought back memories of my rural childhood. Daniela and I looked at each other and smiled as we made our way out of the center of town and drove closer to our destination. Though we had both been extremely nervous about what was to come next, we began to relax a little. We shared that we both already hoped this could be her home. Still, Daniela's hands were trembling.

As we drove down the shady main drive of the St. Coletta campus that first day, there was nothing readily apparent that would indicate the unique things that had transpired there since 1904. Across the road we saw the much larger campus, which had once been the bustling center of St. Coletta's past. I knew that those old buildings had all been sold. They looked lifeless. They were now only a memory for those who still remembered all that had happened within their walls.

Nothing could have prepared Daniela and I for the open-hearted welcome that we would soon receive. We were greeted like long-lost family. Daniela was shy and overwhelmed by the attention. Soon though, she was caught up in the glow created by everyone we met. We didn't know it then, but it was the first day of her new life.

We came to learn that we were experiencing the same warm welcome that had been given to every family who had come looking for miracles since

1904. Since St. Coletta's opening that first year, thousands of families have traveled to Jefferson Wisconsin. They traveled in all manner of transport - from every part of America. For over one hundred years all of us have come to this place, hoping against hope that, in this place, there might lie the answers to our prayers. I thought about all of those other families on that warm day in September as we explored the surroundings of both Jefferson and St. Coletta and I felt a kinship with them. I hoped that we also had found our child's place in the world.

I knew that those families must have had some of the same worrisome questions -

"Will this be another disappointment?"
"Will my child be accepted?"
"Will my child be safe?"
"Will my child be happy?"
"What on earth are we going to do if this place isn't the answer to our prayers?"

And then -

"Please God, please. Let this be the answer."

I pictured each family's heartaches and the sacrifices that they must have made for their children to get them to this place. I wondered, how on earth, they had even found St. Coletta in the early 1900s. When parents had been told to hide or institutionalize their "defective" child, how did they have the strength to find this needle in the haystack? What bravery and fortitude those pioneers must have had.

A short history of disability -

In the early 1900s, and in all the centuries before, having a baby with a disability meant having to make terrible decisions about whether to keep that child within the family. Keeping a child with disabilities was highly discouraged by doctors, clergy, extended family, and especially, by society. Even the wealthiest families had this dilemma. For a child with an intellectual, developmental or physical disability, even a very mild one, there were almost no educational programs in the US that would even consider them for admission. There was no effort made to educate the "crippled", the "moron", the "idiot",

6

the "imbecile" and the "feebleminded" child (only five of the many disparaging terms that were used).

The few options that were available for families were mostly in state institutions that were large, dismal and poorly staffed. The objective of the state and federal government was to hide away these children in "warehouses", "asylums" or "colonies" until they miserably died after a lifetime of being abused and neglected - lives that were usually shortened by their lack of care. Almost without exception, they were alone and unloved. Even those with minor differences were shunned within the tight constricts of society. They were considered a blight or a scourge, not worth living. Families were shamed and blamed for giving birth to them. It was thought that children with disabilities were only born from incest, from criminals, and from other unworthy parents. Their deaths were considered a blessing. This was the era that bred "Eugenics" - the forced sterilization of undesirables so that their children would not weaken the quality of society and not bring disease, crime and shame to their families. (Hitler based many of his ideas about getting rid of "undesirables" on the concept of Eugenics.) Marriage was also forbidden to the other children of those families who had a person with disabilities in their midst.

Perhaps money might buy wealthy parents a place in nicer, cleaner institutions where they could still hide away their child. They could afford institutions with better food and clothes for their child. In their minds, this was the best they could do. What other choices did they, or anyone else, have? In reality, this was all just a facade. It was still custodial care at its worst, all behind closed doors. Secreting these children away was the chosen, and much preferred, way to deal with an issue that many felt polite society should never have to look at, think of or deal with. Out of sight, out of mind. It was a time of disappeared children. Siblings were told their brother or sister had died or they were simply told nothing at all.

These inhumane and cruel ideas had become normal over the previous centuries. They had existed for all of human history. In ancient times, children who were blind, deaf or who were physically or intellectually disabled, were drowned, abandoned in the woods or used as beggars or slaves. Royal courts often bought them and used them as "fools" to entertain themselves with. The rise of Christianity initially encouraged some compassion and better treatment of those who were disabled. Infanticide was discouraged in the early teachings of the Christian faith. The good will didn't last long. For most of the world, and for most of history, brutal treatment continued unabated for the next two thousand years. Even the early efforts of reform were fraught with questionable motives and ideas.

In the Middle Ages, many religious beliefs considered the disabled "children of God" but they were still never deemed to be a normal part of

7

society. In Italy, in 787 A.D., the Catholic Church founded the first asylums for abandoned children. They were rudimentary and most who lived in them did not survive. In this time period, "idiot cages" were built in town centers, where people could laugh and disparage the poor souls inside until they died from exposure, disease, and starvation.[3]

In the late 1500s, Queen Elizabeth of England began to pass laws to take care of the poor, many of whom were disabled. Almshouses and workhouses were built to house those unable to work and feed themselves. As has been written in history and literature books, the places were filled with disease, cruelty and death.

From that time period until the beginning of the twentieth century there were some kind and compassionate people who tried to make a difference. There were pioneering individuals like the French psychiatrist, Philip Pinel. In 1793, he tried to create better understanding of the causes of intellectual disability and mental illness. He tried to encourage better treatment and training. Unfortunately there were also those like the clergyman, Thomas Malthus, who in 1798 believed that the population should be limited and thus, those who act differently and could not contribute to society, should be eliminated.[4]

One prominent American social reformer was Dorothea Dix who lived in Massachusetts in the 1800s. She wrote a passionate speech on behalf of those with disabilities that she wanted to deliver to the U.S. Congress. She was unable to do that, solely because she was a woman, so she asked her friend and fellow reformer Samuel Gridley Howe to do it for her. The speech requested 5 million acres be designated for housing. It was surprisingly passed by both houses, but ultimately vetoed by President Pierce. It was through her growing advocacy, exceedingly well meant, that some of the first institutions were eventually planned and built to house those with disabilities in the United States. Little did she know the pain and horror that would be contained within their walls.

Governments, doctors and anyone else who has tried to force their solutions (well-intentioned or not) on society at large, continued to prevail through the centuries and even into life in the twenty-first century and the new millennium. It's hard to believe that places like "Willowbrook"[5], the horrific institution brought to light by Robert Kennedy and Geraldo Rivera in the 1970s, could have existed so recently in America. From my research, I was shocked to learn that places like Willowbrook were the norm in the first half of the last century and some persisted even into the end of the last century.

I discovered a television show from the 1950s, well-intentioned in that time period, with the host portraying a visit to a state institution in Iowa.[6] Various types of adult "imbeciles" and "morons" were brought on stage. They called the adults "children" and then pointed out their physical and mental characteristics right in front of them. This demonstration was to show what "type" they were. These "specimens" could fully understand what was being said about them. They answered questions correctly when asked. As I watched the show I cried for them and for all that they had to accept and endure.

The plight of individuals with disabilities in this country continued into the very last part of the 1900s. When the world and my own family watched, in horror, television images of the callous treatment of children in Romanian institutions in late 1989, Willowbrook State School had only been closed for 2 years. Forest Haven, another horrific institution in Maryland, didn't close until October 1991. These were but two of many. While the world was shocked about what was happening in Romania, (including my family - it was what led us to adopt Daniela from her abusive institution) we as a country had continued to choose to be blind to the abuse that went on right under our noses.

What has finally turned the tide of major disability reform has been the rise of disability rights activists - most of them being individuals with disabilities themselves, their loved ones and supporters. It has only been because of these brave warriors, and their undaunted courage and strength, that public policy and society began to initiate real systematic change.

This very short history of the treatment of people with disabilities highlights the miracle created by the small band of the Sisters of St. Francis of Assisi on a gentle hill outside of Jefferson Wisconsin. They had begun their own fierce social activism and reforms back in the 1800s, even before St. Coletta's creation. I find their story fascinating, inspiring and, at times, unbelievable. The constant transformations that have occurred since that time could never have happened if it wasn't for the ferocious belief in their mission and the undying faith of many, many people. Their dedicated efforts miraculously have come together to create a dynamic community - a place that those first brave sisters might never have imagined.

There were innumerable times over the past 117 years when it all could have, and should have, fallen apart. That fact that it didn't, is one of the truly magical parts of St. Coletta's history. Their story has captured my heart and imagination and each new revelation pushed me to learn more.

Chapter 2

In exploring the history of St. Coletta we have to look back further than 1904, when the school for children with disabilities first opened. We need to start the story in 1848 in the village of Ettenbueren. The village is located in Bavaria, Germany's largest state. The creation of the Order - The Sisters of St. Francis of Assisi - was featured in the book "By God's Providence - The Sisters of St. Francis 1849-2001". The book was written in 2007 by one of the Sisters - Sr. Doris Pehowski, OSF. The author passed away two years later at the age of 84. I was enchanted by the existence of these strong, determined and defiant women. These were not the angelic, soft spoken nuns that I watched in movies growing up. They were spirited activists whose faith propelled them to choose a very different life than most other women in their place and time.

In the beginning, the original Ettenbueren group were not nuns or Sisters. In fact, the first group was comprised of six women and five men. They were Franciscan lay missionaries (not ordained or consecrated by the Roman Catholic church) who modeled their lives of charity and devotion to the ideals of St. Francis of Assisi. They had heard the call for missionaries in America. Their pastor was Father Francis Keppeler at the parish of Our Lady of the Assumption. Father Francis responded to the requests of Bishop J. Martin Henni who was in charge of a new diocese in Milwaukee Wisconsin. German immigrants were pouring into the Midwest. Bishop Henni needed help with this growing population.

The devoted group of men and women spent the rest of the year getting ready for their long journey and new life in America. In December of 1848 they drew up a document dictating all of their plans and rules. They took vows of chastity - unless married. They agreed to split their time between manual labor and prayer. They had many other rules to guide them. The document was sent to Bishop Henni who was very pleased. One of his main goals in Milwaukee was to create a seminary for young men in his diocese.

With everyone in agreement, the band of missionaries departed for the U.S. in the spring of 1849, arriving, after traveling across the Atlantic on the ship "the Herman". With donations and their own money, they were able to buy over 35 acres of land in an area called Nojoshing, four miles from downtown Milwaukee. They immediately built small huts to live in while they planned and began to build a convent for the women and a house for the men. The women made extra money teaching school for German speaking children in a mission station.

Once the groups became established, the focus changed somewhat from their original plans. The community was supposed to include sisters, brothers and married couples. Despite the Rt. Rev. Bishop's desire that the whole group should remain together, the women in the group decided to create a religious community amongst themselves, including the wife from the one married couple who had traveled with the group. The men, to include the husband of the couple, remained pious and hardworking, but never formalized into creating their own religious order. The Bishop acquiesced and decided to assist the women with their wish to create their own community. The women moved from their huts into their convent and the men into their newly built house. Their lives became increasingly separate.

In 1850 the women received, and started wearing, simple black habits with a white Franciscan cord. They wore black bonnets with white bonnets underneath. They changed their names to reflect their devotion to the Order. They elected their youngest member, named Aemiliana, to become their superior. Their lives as Sisters began.

Despite their desire to create a religious order and become missionaries, in reality their life became overwhelmed by backbreaking days of cultivating their land and simply trying to survive. The money that they had brought with them was quickly depleted. The local priest, Father Keppeler, who had encouraged them to travel to America, took over the pastorate in 1850 and built a new church and school. In an effort to help the new Sisters, he hired two of them as teachers. Sadly, all of these efforts came to a halt in the fall of 1851 when Father Keppeler and the priest of another local parish died in a cholera epidemic.

This became the first of many crises that could have thwarted the eventual creation of St. Coletta of Wisconsin. The group of Sisters and their efforts to move forward could have easily disbanded. For a year after the priests' deaths, there was no source of income and no one to administer the sacraments. Besides having to try to physically survive, the women also had to deal with language and cultural differences. Most people in their dire situation would have given up, but not this strong group of women. Guided by their faith and St. Francis, they persisted. They did whatever they had to do, offering tutoring and seeking employment as domestics. I can only imagine how disheartening this period was as they saw their dreams in such tatters.

Seeing how devoted these women were to staying together and following God's wishes, Bishop Henni sent them a new priest. This priest, Reverend Michael Heiss, would be instrumental in helping in the development of the community. He gave them three new basic rules for their order.

Heiss began by making the distinction that the Sisters of the Third Order were "non-cloistered with simple vows". The "works of Christian love" to which they were called were three-fold:

1. To carry out the ordinary women's tasks for the seminary of St. Frances de Sales.
2. To dedicate themselves to care and instruction of orphans - first at St. Aemelian Orphanage and then in other places.
3. When they find among their members a sufficient number who were qualified, to give Christian instruction to the young, especially through schools in rural areas."[7]

With these goals in mind during the next four years, both the Orphanage and Seminary were built. This small group of women were expected to not only work in the seminary and orphanage, but also live by strict religious rules of prayer, fasting and silence. Father Heiss was a "hard taskmaster". He referred to himself as the founder of the congregation. He wrote to a friend that the convent gave him trouble in following the rules of the order. While the survival of the community as a whole may have depended on the Father, what he created was not what they themselves had desired. Their Superior however was very well liked. The Sisters trusted Mother Aemiliana and she kept their spirits high despite their struggles. By the time the seminary opened they had expanded to seven Sisters with three new candidates.

As the seminary started to grow however, so did the work. The director of the seminary, Father Salamanca, was very frugal and the women began to become overwhelmed with their workload. The labor involved in keeping the seminary running fell to them, including harvesting crops, cooking, laundry and cleaning and managing daily operations. Tensions began to grow, especially between the original older German women and the new younger American women. The German women were used to a much heavier load of work than their younger counterparts. Mother Aemiliana tried her best to intervene. The sisters were paid very little and their convent began to fall in disrepair. This crisis seemed insurmountable.

Feeling that they had failed to achieve the goals of their mission, the original six Sisters disbanded and left the convent in June of 1860. These older women, broken-hearted, remained in Milwaukee, determined to live quiet lives of prayer and service. A local priest who was sympathetic to their plight, oversaw their care and housing. In a solemn moment as she was departing, Mother Aemiliana called out to one of the remaining postulants, indicating to her her own habit which she had removed. She said, "Behold this holy garb, my child you will soon wear it. I loved it. I tried my best to establish the community upon a firm foundation and to instill into it a truly religious spirit. I have failed. God grant that you may succeed."[8]

From a book called "A New Assisi" came this passage - "When the Sisters who remained saw the senior Sisters heavily veiled disappearing around the bend of the road, they turned to one another and said, 'What will become of us? What shall we do? We are abandoned. We are orphans.' "[9]

The following Sunday, Father Heiss addressed the remaining eleven Sisters and postulants, encouraging them that their mission could continue. He rededicated himself to acting as their spiritual director and continued to stress the rules by which their order was created. The Sisters and postulants returned to their duties. A new Mother, Sr. Seraphine Sanders, was appointed. It was decided that the order could no longer live in the original little convent and a new one was built for them (which they had to repay by receiving only a $200 stipend for the next two years for all of their service at the seminary.)

As the remaining band of Sisters began to try again, there was still the same continuous hard work and many struggles. Mother Seraphine was abrupt and not well received by the other Sisters. After two years they held an election and unanimously chose Sr. Crescentia Nondorf as the third Superior General. This was a huge disappointment to Sr. Seraphine and she shortly thereafter left the community. Mother Crescentia was young, only 32. The rector was skeptical and only allowed this selection to be valid for one year. She was devoted to the Sisters but unfortunately did not have the knowledge or experience to handle the financial aspects of the community. Debts started to accumulate. At the end of the year there was to be another election. By this time there were more Sisters who had taken their vows. The younger Sisters tipped the vote to elect the Sister who had been their mistress of novices - Sr. Antonia Herb. This choice was a monumental one and one that would eventually impact the creation of St. Coletta.

Sr. Antonia's journey to join the Order was quite different than her fellow Sisters. She had been born in Bavaria and emigrated to Ohio at the age of 19 with her family. She had married, but her husband was an alcoholic and the marriage was a disaster. They separated and the church, because of her circumstances, granted her a dissolution of the marriage in 1858. She decided after that to follow her heart and join the convent in Wisconsin. She became a part of the community in 1859 at the age of 32. When she was elected as Mother four years later, she was surprised, but she had become not only a kind, generous Superior General, she was also very independent and headstrong. She took the reins with vigor and immediately made plans to increase the membership of the order and to make plans for the Sisters to become teachers. She petitioned (then Archbishop) Henni to proceed with both requests. He turned her down twice before she went to see him in person. Surprisingly, he then agreed to her request. Father Heiss was also surprised but he decided to help her choose students among the Sisters who showed that they would have

13

the aptitude for the program. New postulants were sought and admitted to the order.

Though Father Heiss was initially supportive of the education program, his main goal and purpose was the seminary. He expected the Sisters to devote almost all of their time to this endeavor, leaving little time for classes and study. Mother Antonia was not happy with the circumstances and began a new campaign. She decided she wanted the order to be completely separate from the seminary. She wanted to relocate the Motherhouse to a place where the order could be wholly independent in the way it was governed. She again petitioned Archbishop Henni to fulfill her plan and also to be allowed to teach in Wisconsin schools. Twice again the answer came back no. This amazing woman would not back down.

She enlisted Father Heiss to be an intermediary and he, quite unexpectedly, agreed. Mother Antonia prayed diligently and, taking another Sister with her, returned to again visit the Archbishop to make her request. This time before saying no, he told her that they had no qualified teachers. She, with much heart, told him they they would study diligently and that the professors at the seminary had agreed to teach them. Seeing their level of hope and dedication, Archbishop Henni finally agreed. He even gave them a parting gift along with his blessings. I choose to believe that, though no one involved knew it at the time, there was a greater power and purpose that was directing this cause - one that would eventually lead to changing the lives of thousands of individuals with disabilities.

With the permission to proceed with their plans secured, Mother Antonia focused on beginning the studies for teacher education for the Sisters and postulants. Father Heiss took time out of his busy schedule to teach classes, along with a professor from the seminary. One lay Sister who was also a teacher came from Austria and joined the teaching staff. Mother Antonia also increased her efforts to bring in more postulants. Not everyone was supportive of their efforts and thought the Sisters should do more farm work to pay for their upkeep. The Sisters agreed to this request while spending every free moment studying. Another teacher joined the community and the members of the order were encouraged that their plan was succeeding.

Knowing that there was always going to be a conflict about their reluctance with the seminary work they were expected to do, Mother Antonia decided to press forward to secure a new Motherhouse away from St. Frances and the seminary. Some of the older Sisters were not happy about this idea and the staff of the seminary also fought against this plan. Sr. Antonia went to Father Heiss and Dr. Salzmann, who directed the seminary, for support of her idea. She was, as always, very persuasive and they ultimately agreed to let her proceed. Dr. Salzmann unfortunately, refused any financial support for the

14

move. The convent had very little money of its own, which would have seemed to dim the chance of the plan succeeding. Still, Father Heiss and Dr. Salzmann started pursuing possible sites for the new convent. One rector that they knew offered a free piece of land that his parish could not use. It was a wonderful offer, but the land was found unsuitable for its required purpose.

The pastor, Father Jansen of St. John's church in Jefferson Wisconsin, 50 miles west of St. Frances, decided to offer a place for the Sisters there. A another local parish, St. Lawrence, located on a hill outside Jefferson heard about the search for the new Motherhouse. They came forward and petitioned Bishop Henni to allow the order to be sent to them. Bishop Henni, remembering a long-forgotten promise to these same parishioners that he would someday build a convent near St. Lawrence, told Father Heiss, "If the sisters want to go to Jefferson, let them build near St. Lawrence."(from the Providence book). There became an ensuing argument about where the convent should be built.

Dr. Salzmann and Mother Antonia came to St. Lawrence for the Patron Feast day of the parish and the parishioners implored them in their cause. Father Jansen was still against the plan. Thinking of a way to thwart their plan, he told the St. Lawrence parishioners that, if they were serious, they had to buy the Methodist farm at the foot of hill next to St. Lawrence and sell it to the sisters at half price. Much to his surprise, a committee of parishioners came back that evening telling him they would buy the farm for $4000 and sell it to the sisters for $2000. Father Jansen was shocked that Mother Antonia immediately agreed to the offer. She made this decision while knowing how difficult it would be to pay that large amount of money. Father Heiss decided to intervene in the matter and bring some civility into the disagreement with Father Jansen and the St. Lawrence parishioners. He made several conditions including that the Sisters would not be required to teach without compensation in return for the $2000 gift. If the Sisters could not succeed and had to leave, then they would not have to continue their payments for the property. The Parish would also not get their own pastor. Father Jansen would be the pastor of both St. John's and St. Lawrence.

Though their hopes had been to acquire their own pastor, the parishioners agreed to the offer, hoping with time that they would be able to have a separate pastor. A contract was drawn up and the Sisters had to pull together $1000 to make the initial payment. They did this by joining together their dowries to make the payment. Father Jansen, who was still unhappy with the plan, took his time transferring the deed of ownership to the Sisters of St. Francis. Back home in St. Francis, when word of the plan spread, there was much protest, even declaring the idea unholy. Many thought the idea was a folly and would never succeed. Mother Antonia was undeterred. Her faith and will were limitless. She would not even wait until the following spring as Father Heiss advised (so that they wouldn't have to meet that first winter unprepared).

Without wasting time, Mother Antonia and five Sisters set off for St. Lawrence on September 29th, 1864. When they arrived at the farmhouse which would become their new home, they were touched that the family who had owned the farm had left them a large barrel of apples. They started their lives there with straw beds and almost no other furnishings. Besides the apples, they survived for the first few days on tea, potatoes and salt. Some of their neighbors then kindly brought them some bread, ham and eggs. Despite the hardships, the Sisters were excited to finally have an independent Motherhouse. Bishop Henni suggested the name - St. Coletta. It was named for a saint who was known as a great Franciscan reformer. What name could be more fitting for this group of women, who set themselves up to transform the congregation and children's lives who they sought to serve. The name would go on to have even more meaning when, many years later, the purpose of the Motherhouse and other buildings that would gradually be built, would transform the lives of individuals with disabilities.

The coming winter for the Sisters was not easy and it continued to be filled with dissent and wavering meager support from Father Jansen. They continued to live with very little food and supplies. There quickly came a point when they discussed giving up the project and moving back to St. Francis. Bishop Henni encouraged them to persevere. When the local community heard about their struggles they rallied around them, bringing them firewood and food. The local farmers offered to plant and cultivate their crops. One even came forward and served as their farm manager. With spring came hope and resolve. There was continued   disharmony with Father Jansen. They prayed continuously for him to bring the Blessed Sacrament to their chapel. He finally relented.

Once they decided to stay, the Sisters moved forward to build a new convent. With the bishop's permission, they went throughout the diocese asking for money. They raised $3000 and Mother Antonia's brother was hired to build the convent. By the fall of 1865, the building was completed. (A chapel was built three years later). The Bishop appointed a chaplain to be designated for the new convent. The Sisters were very happy not to have to continue to deal with Father Jansen, whose negativity towards them continued. The new pastor, Father Flasch, was exceedingly kind and supportive. His tenure was short, only a year, but he invigorated the community. The pastor who replaced him, Father Obermueller, was also a boon to the Sisters. He was considered an experienced teacher and helped the Sisters with their studies. Rapidly the number of Sisters and postulants grew over the next four years. By 1869, they numbered over

100. The Sisters had begun teaching and they spread out into the local communities.

Despite the progress and successes, there continued to be dissent among the community. When in the early 1870s, Father Heiss was promoted to the office of Bishop to serve in La Crosse Wisconsin. He wanted to have the Motherhouse of the Sisters in Jefferson moved to La Crosse. He approached Mother Antonia. She quickly agreed without informing Bishop Henni. She faced criticism for this but decided to move forward. During the move, St. Coletta was stripped of much of its furnishings. The Sisters remaining in both Jefferson and St. Francis were given the choice to either move with her or stay where they were and be separated from the new community in La Crosse. Many chose to remain and not go with Mother Antonia. Those thirty-seven Sisters became the remnant of the original Sisters of Francis of Assisi. On March 13th, 1873, after this third great crisis, they began yet again.

For the rest of the nineteenth century, the Sisters of St. Francis worked diligently to rebuild, reorganize and rededicate their order and their purpose. They slowly started to grow again and find ways to use their faith and skills to serve others. Through that period, there were several Mother Superiors who added their strengths to the order. In 1877, Mother Catherine Murphy, already an experienced assistant Mother, served for the next three years. That year a new Motherhouse was established in Jefferson, along with a novitiate and a school, St. Lawrence. This arrangement lasted only a year. The Sisters begged Mother Catherine to return the Motherhouse to St. Francis. She agreed. In 1878, they returned to the place where they began. And there the Motherhouse has remained over 140 years later.

In 1880, a new Mother Superior was elected. Mother Helen Wagner was considered very modest and pious. It was during her leadership that another crisis was narrowly averted. It was suggested (by the spiritual director of the convent) to Archbishop Heiss that the 42 Sisters combine with two other Franciscan orders. Fortunately the rector of the seminary, Father Zeininger, knowing the struggles and determination of the Sisters, strongly objected. He felt they deserved to remain their own entity. The idea was abandoned. In 1884, he was appointed their spiritual director. During Mother Helen's leadership, she brought many needed new members into the order. She was able to establish several new mission schools in both Wisconsin and Illinois. She also was there to bring the Sisters into service with the already established St. John's Deaf School in Milwaukee.

In 1886, Mother Helen was ready to step down. She continued to be well-loved and to serve in missions until her death. The next two Mother Superiors were familial sisters. With their very strong leadership, they would go on to make the Sisters of St. Francis of Assisi into the secure and dynamic

17

order that it became. The order would thrive for the rest of the century and well into the twentieth century.

The oldest of three Sisters who were in the order, Mother Antonine Thecla, served as Mother for twelve years. Under her leadership she rapidly increased the membership. She doubled their number from 60 to 128 in her first two years. These women came from the U.S. and also from Bavaria and Poland. To meet the needs of the growing population, Mother Antonine greatly added to the convent building and also built the beautiful St. Francis Chapel. She seems to have been a brilliant financial administrator as well. She paid off the debts of the order and in 1896, she finally gained independence from the seminary. She was kind, but also a strict and demanding leader. She was most demanding of herself. Besides being a dedicated leader, she was a wonderful cook and would create new recipes in the kitchen. Not content to be idle, she spent her spare time sewing habits for her fellow Sisters. She continued to serve after a stroke and until her death in 1898.

Mother Antonine's death was a great loss, but as with all their other losses and challenges the Sisters, as always, persisted and they gathered in the weeks after her death to choose her successor. The choice came down to a tie between two Sisters - Sr. Mary Martha and Mother Antonine's sister, Sr. Mary Thecla Thren. In the end, the choice was Sr. Mary Thecla. She was only 29 when she was elected and she would go on to serve as Superior General for the next 27 years. She was known as a "monumental builder". She built and improved the Motherhouse campus with many new buildings, including a guest house and barn. She had too many achievements during her tenure to name them all. During her tenure she increased the membership of the Sisters of St. Francis from 186 to almost 500. She was insistent on having professionally trained teachers and created St. Catherine Normal School and a Teacher's Institute. She opened 57 schools in seven states.

The school in St. Lawrence had remained since the Motherhouse moved to St. Francis in 1878. The St. Coletta buildings were used to house the children. During this twenty year period, the property was called "The St. Coletta Mission". In 1898, a new boarding school for girls was established on the property, the St. Coletta Academy. The academy very quickly outgrew the property and a decision was made in 1903 to move the school to the site of the Motherhouse in St. Francis. With this move the school was renamed St. Mary's Academy. The St. Coletta property became vacant again.

After the St. Mary's staff and students left, the little St. Coletta school did not remain silent for long. The blessings from the Sisters continued to echo. It stood waiting and ready for new beginnings. And so the next chapter begins.......

Archbishop Sebastian Mesmer

Mother Thecla Thren

Father James Feider

Sister Anastasia Mueller

Chapter 3

The story of how St. Coletta of Wisconsin began its revolutionary mission to serve children (and eventually adults) with intellectual and developmental disabilities is still a little bit of a mystery. The most accepted version of the story was told by the Right Reverend Monsignor George Meyer. In 1904, he was simply Father Meyer. He had been the chaplain of the St. Coletta Boarding School for Girls before the students were transferred to the new St. Mary's Boarding School in St. Francis. He was still the chaplain for the Sisters who remained in Jefferson after the students left St. Coletta. The school now was vacant and there were no concrete plans about what to do with the empty buildings.

After the school closed, Father Meyer decided to travel south to the state of Tennessee for a vacation. During his travels he was introduced to a wealthy family (name unknown). When they found out his former connection as the chaplain of the boarding school, they told him about their child, a young girl who had intellectual disabilities. They lamented to him as they told him about their struggles in finding a Catholic school program where their child could be educated. They especially wanted a religious education for their child. Even those parents with a great deal of money could not find good educational programs of any kind for a child who could not manage a regular school curriculum. The norms of who could be educated were very narrow and differences were not tolerated. The family must have touched the priest's heart. He promised them that he would see what he could do.

On the long trip back to Wisconsin, Father Meyer pondered the issue with some seriousness, thinking about two particular students who had been at the St. Coletta school. "There had actually been two students with disabilities at the St. Coletta Academy who were there to receive religious instruction. It is said that they did well and were able to receive their First Holy Communion. With that in mind, and with his poignant discussion with the family, when he arrived at St. Francis, he approached Mother Thecla with the issue."[10] From this point in the story, the history of St. Coletta becomes more clear and well documented. Knowing that St. Coletta was now vacant, he suggested to Mother Thecla that it could be well used as a new school for "backward" children. It is not surprising that this bold idea took Mother Thecla aback. His suggestion was an unusual one. The idea that "backward" children would be capable of school and religious education was a radical idea. With some hesitation, Mother Thecla agreed to explore the priest's request. She was quite worried that it might be too heavy a task to ask of the Sisters. She decided to ask for volunteer teachers amongst them. Father Meyer spoke to the Sisters as well. In speaking to them he was quoted as saying, "It is noble work to train the normally fit and to educate them, but it is greater work to awaken a dormant and darkened mind to the knowledge and love of God."[11]

Much to Mother Thecla's surprise, a large number of Sisters were enthusiastic and signed up for this experimental and pioneering new project. It was in her sixth year as Mother Superior, that she began this new endeavor. Archbishop Sebastian Mesmer of Milwaukee was also an avid supporter of this venture. It was to be the first program of its kind in the Midwest. There is a list of 25 Sisters who became involved with the new school that first year.

Before the school began, Father Meyer traveled to Wisconsin state institutions and also to private homes where individuals with disabilities resided. He could painfully see how few efforts were made to help these individuals to function more independently, much less provide them with actual training to develop their minds to their greatest potential. He became even more determined to make a difference.

The original name for this new program was "The St. Coletta Institute for Backward Youth". In that time period, it was considered as an accurate medical description. To advertise the new school, a circular was printed about its upcoming opening and was sent across the country.

It is written that the opening of the school was a joyful occasion and that Mother Thecla was delighted that her Sisters had so nobly taken on this new challenge. Religious education was to become the most important part of the new program. This idea was something new and untried.

On September 10th 1904, Sister Superior Theophila Nussbaum, the Principal of the new school, welcomed four young girls to become the first students of St. Coletta. I can only imagine the fear and excitement that they, their families and the Sisters experienced that day. Along with their big dreams, there must have been so much uncertainty about whether this grand experiment would be a success. They were operating on a wing and, most definitely, a prayer.

As the school days progressed that fall, and the Sisters started to figure out the curriculum they wanted to establish, they began to add new students. By December they were up to ten students, including boys. It was at the time of the first boy's enrollment that a new and longstanding tradition was created. From that point on, every time a new student enrolled, the chapel bell joyously rang to welcome them into the fold.

For the next few years, (and continuing to this day) fundraising became a major effort and concern. In the beginning there was no set fee for tuition and boarding costs. The Sisters made all types of efforts to support the school and expand its buildings and grounds. They created crafts for sale and held a bazaar in 1906. They were thrilled when Archbishop Messmer attended that event. Many of the local people spoke only German and it is said that the Archbishop helped to translate for the auctioneer. This event and others helped to create goodwill and understanding within the local community. Later that year, the school held a benefit Thanksgiving dinner in which local people not only attended but assisted at. Thus began regular events to include ice cream socials, auctions and entertainment for the public by the students of St. Coletta.

Father Meyer continued to be a staunch supporter. When he was called back to St. Francis in 1907 he remained vigorously involved and provided guidance and supervision. The local fundraising events did not bring in sufficient sums to help provide for the continuing growth of the school population. Father Meyer traveled widely to help gather funds. He also found new students in his travels. Some of the families had unrealistic expectations in the early years. They thought that the Sisters might be able to "cure" their children. A few families withdrew their children in disappointment.

Despite those early withdrawals, enrollment continued to grow. The small school building was soon unable to hold everyone. In 1905, St. Coletta bought a farm next to the school which added acreage to build a dormitory. Until they could finish its construction, they rented the local St. Lawrence School Hall for the boys of the school. In 1909, the school had grown to around 40 students. There were twelve Sisters providing care and education. The boys' dormitory, St. Anthony Cottage was finally built and housed the boys with more severe disabilities. Also housed there were the needed farm and maintenance workers. A German man named Thomas Schwaninger (Mr. Thomas), who had some medical training, provided care for the boys. He also created a woodworking class for the boys who were capable of attending. The buildings contained a laundry in the basement and in 1910, a "power house with a tall smoke stack" was added.

On August 18th 1909, a new Sister arrived in the community who would become a very important person to St. Coletta's story. Only a young novice at the time she entered, Sr. Anastasia Mueller would come to be one of the most influential people in the history of the school and the community. Her lifelong service and devotion to all of those she served impacted the mission in groundbreaking and life changing ways. Her life and work continue to inspire everyone who is involved with St. Coletta.

From the very beginning, the emphasis was to create a homelike atmosphere. Not every child in the early years was deemed capable of attending the classes that they taught. In 1910, a fee was set and families who could afford to pay were charged $15.00 a month if their son or daughter attended classes. If they could not attend class the fee was reduced to $10.00 a month. The next goal, especially important to the families whose children had

22

never been able to participate, was to have the students begin religious training. With patience and grace, the Sisters began to instruct the children to pray and learn about God. Academic, non-religious education was not a high priority in the beginning. Besides religion classes, loving custodial care was provided to all, along with life skill classes and crafts. Slowly the idea that these children might be capable of more began to crystallize in some of the Sisters' minds.

In 1912, St. Coletta welcomed a new chaplain, Father Adolph Kline. He is remembered as being devoted to the Sisters and their work. In 1913, the St. Coletta Institute for Backward Youth was incorporated under the laws of Wisconsin and the first seal was cast in 1914. In 1915, a historic event in the American Catholic Church occurred for the first time. Seventeen intellectually impaired Catholic children prepared to receive their First Holy Communion. This was unprecedented and was a great cause of celebration within the St. Coletta community. (St. Coletta, even in its early years, accepted children of all religious creeds. They were not required to receive the Catholic training.)

The population of the school continued to expand as more and more families found out about this unique program. A decision was made in 1915 to build an administration building. Plans were drawn up and construction began. Local farmers brought stones from their properties to lay the foundation. The city of Jefferson extended their electric lines to the compound so that the community could teach with modern lights. By 1916, the new building was completed and dedicated to the Sacred Heart of Jesus. A statue of the Sacred Heart of Jesus was placed in the middle of the circular driveway of the building. On May 31st, 1916, a celebration was held and all of the stores in Jefferson closed so that everyone in the town could attend. A bazaar was held to raise money to go towards the costs of the new building. Almost $1000 was raised and the event was considered a wonderful success.

The large new building served many purposes. The first floor held a kitchen, dining room and a bakery. On the second floor were "day rooms". One for the boys and one for the girls. On that floor there were also Chaplain's quarters, classrooms and a reception area and parlor. The main entrance was located on the second floor. Outside near the entrance was a chicken coop and an orchard (They were very practical.) On the third floor the administration office was located, also a dormitory for the Sisters, another classroom, and rooms for visiting guests. In addition, there was a sewing room and medical area that included an infirmary and dental office. On the fourth floor, the younger "Sacred Heart" girls and boys had dormitories. (The older girls stayed in the original St. Coletta building and the older boys were in the St. Anthony Cottage.) Doors separated the girls from the boys. There were small rooms for the Sisters in each area to provide care and supervision. The continual

23

development of the program and the physical growth of the buildings in the twelve years since the school's humble beginnings was quite remarkable.

Being the first (and eventually the largest) Catholic residential school for children with developmental disabilities meant the Sisters had to create their program with no professional guidance. They were constantly looking for ways to help the young people who had been lovingly entrusted to them by their families. They adapted a system of calisthenics called the "Ralston System". Many of the students also had physical disabilities which hindered them in their development. The Sisters thought that a physical activity program would help to lessen these disabilities and also assist in the development of their minds. These activities included sensory training which was well ahead of its time. Sensory integration therapy is now considered essential in educational programs for children with developmental disabilities, and especially for those on the autism spectrum.

Early on it was decided to introduce music as a way to stimulate the young minds. They decided to create an orchestra which was mentioned for the first time in the local newspaper in 1916. Performing at fundraisers and other events not only gave the students a sense of pride but surely helped to change the perception of the citizens of Jefferson regarding the capabilities of the children. The Sisters made the band members uniforms of dark blue with dark trim. Music and theatrical performances would be a hallmark of St. Coletta in the years to come.

Sister Emerentia Ozar had been in charge of the school programming since its beginning and, in 1910, she was appointed the Director of the Institute. Sister Anastasia became her secretary. In 1916 they traveled together to Washington D.C. to attend the National Conference of Catholic Charities. They became the first Sisters to be appointed committee members. They spoke to the gathered attendees about St. Coletta and encouraged them to treat those with "mental retardation" with empathy. They should certainly be considered early activists in the humane treatment of individuals with disabilities.

In 1917, a new chaplain, Father Julius Wermuth, was appointed. He brought fresh ideas and improvements to the community, including landscaping to make the school more aesthetically attractive. He was not a fan of having the chickens and the orchard being one of the first things people saw when they visited, so they were promptly moved to the farm area.

In 1919, a new Sister was appointed as the Institute Director. At that time the school was still considered more custodial than academic. Sister Spes Knott made sure that the residents maintained good habits such as respect, cleanliness and courtesy. Some older, more severely disabled individuals were accepted into the program and they were treated with loving care in a home-like environment. A large barn was added to the farm in this year and in the

24

next year, buildings were erected to house both hogs and hens. They also added a smokehouse. The Sisters wanted to be as self-sustaining as possible to both keep costs down and to provide healthy food for everyone.

The beginning of the 1920s brought tremendous changes to St. Coletta. Its expansion and focus on an actual academic school program were influenced by a number of factors. News of the Institute had began to spread nationwide. By word of mouth, the Catholic community and from other sources, the program started to get inquiries and applications from desperate families all over the country. Because they were operating at capacity most of these applications sadly had to be declined. A decision was made to expand again to meet the demand of this obvious need. The tuition was raised to $25.00 a month for students. None of those fees were to be used for building purposes.

In May of 1920, a meeting was held that was open to everyone in Jefferson and the surrounding area. The Sisters explained their mission and program in the hopes that, again, they would help to raise the funds they needed for St. Coletta to be expanded to help more children.

Their efforts in reaching out were very successful. A group of local businessmen decided to create a committee to raise funds by a voluntary subscription. They hoped to reach a goal of raising ten thousand dollars of the expected two hundred thousand dollars needed for expansion. This was a remarkable amount of money to raise in 1920. Ten thousand dollars then is the equivalent of over one hundred and thirty thousand today (and two hundred thousand is equivalent to two million, six hundred thousand). How a rural town in Wisconsin and this band of Catholic Sisters had the faith, hope and gumption to be able to achieve such a lofty goal is almost beyond imagination.

The local newspaper, the Jefferson Banner, published a story on May 27th about the meeting, letting people know about the fundraising effort and imploring them to give. The article finished with this line - "We have given much for foreign charity; now let's all give a little for this great institution which we have in our midst." The community was both inspired and generous. Within a month, the committee had raised over nine thousand dollars. By the next March, the goal had been surpassed. The Banner wrote about the triumph of the effort in May 1921. "This event will always be remembered as one of the greatest and noblest charitable undertakings in the history of Jefferson." For anyone reading this book who lives in Jefferson Wisconsin now, they should remember and be proud that their town has such a noble history of empathy and charity.

As I previously wrote, the original goal of the school was to provide a homelike, loving program and to provide its students with a basic religious education and training in life skills that would improve their lives and give them

25

dignity and purpose. That was no small goal in that time period and far more than almost any other program in the United States.

Mother Thecla, the longtime creator and administrator of the Institute, thought that this achievement was enough and was satisfied for St. Coletta to continue in its current efforts. However, some of the Sisters thought that the young individuals in their care were capable of so much more. In 1920, Sister M. Madeline Herman joined the staff of the school as a teacher and group mother. In the next couple of years she and Sister Anastasia spoke often about how much more many of the children were capable of. They bravely decided to approach Mother Thecla on the issue of creating a true academic program for those students who they felt could benefit. Mother Thecla, bluntly, was not enthusiastic. The two Sisters were persistent. They had done research before speaking to her and asked Mother Thecla to be given the opportunity to spend the summer at the Vineland Training School in Vineland, New Jersey.

At that time Vineland was considered to be the premier institution working with individuals with "mental retardation". The two Sisters had come to know about the school and thought they might better be able to develop an academic program by spending time there and receiving training. The Sisters made a strong case to be granted permission for this opportunity. With a great deal of reticence, Mother Thecla gave the Sisters her permission. (The history of this exchange is still well remembered by current Sisters of St. Francis of Assisi who related this story to me.)

Sisters Anastasia and Madeline were thrilled they would have the opportunity to learn more about education for children with disabilities. They wanted to give all of St. Coletta's children a more enriching future. "Academic education for the retarded was practically unknown at that time. There was opposition and even scorn as Sister Madeline and Sister Anastasia pioneered in developing an educational program for retarded children that was both scientifically and psychologically sound.[12]"

The two Sisters decided their pupils should have their intelligence formally tested in some way to better know what they were capable of accomplishing. They found out that Dr. Henry Goddard, who practiced at Vineland, had translated the Stanford-Binet Scale from French. It was a tool that would give them the ability to measure the children's intelligence quotient.

They also learned about a merit system that was successful in giving positive feedback and rewards. Students would start off with five merits each month. By doing the things they were supposed to do each month, they would keep all their merits. Serious infractions would cause them to lose a merit. Every month, each student would be able to choose prizes according to the amount of their merits. Those with no merits left knew that they could start off fresh the next month and hope to do better. Yearly awards would be given for those with the highest amounts of merits. This would include a special outing. The system was a very progressive way of educating those with disabilities. Positive reinforcement is still used in special education. It is also in ABA (applied behavioral analysis) a successful therapy in educating children with disabilities .

The Sisters returned to the St. Coletta campus full of enthusiasm and new ideas. Before the new building was built (whose construction had been enabled from the generous donations) much research went into creating a structure that would enable all of those new goals that the Sisters now hoped to accomplish. The staff also visited state schools for the disabled to gather ideas for their planning. They wanted to build the most modern and best equipped school possible. It was to be named for St. Joseph.

The building was annexed onto the Sacred Heart building for easy access across the campus in harsh winters. They were excited to build a new chapel on the ground floor. This meant that the old chapel could be transformed into a new dormitory for the older girls. They built big day rooms on the first and second floors. They built large dorm-like rooms on the third floor for the older boys that the school would accept. There were also rooms for the Sisters on night duty. With this new building the school was soon able to enroll more children and enlarge the educational program. It became a school that, thanks to Sisters Anastasia and Madeline, would in the next few years develop a solid progressive academic program.

Early classroom at the St. Coletta School

1st class to receive Holy Communion

Early classroom at St. Coletta School

Early photo of St. Coletta Band

Chapter 4

In 1926, on a train from the St. Francis Motherhouse, Mother Thecla arrived. Traveling with her were four other Sisters. For one of the young new Sisters, Sr. Mary Theodore Hegeman, the plan was for her to live at St. Coletta while spending the next four years teaching at the adjacent St. Lawrence School. That was the plan. What eventually happened to that plan was something quite different.

Like Sr. Anastasia, Sr. Mary Theodore was to become an exceedingly important part of the St. Coletta community in the coming decades. She would become a much loved leader. She would become an author and a sought after source on the subject of education of children and adults with disabilities. She would tour and teach throughout the US, and in many other countries. Her guidance and compassion were life changing, not only for the students who passed through St. Coletta's doors, but for thousands of other children and adults with disabilities, many who are still living today.

With the assistance of current Sisters and St. Coletta staff, I was given several books to assist me in writing this book. Three books that I have found through them, and through my own research, were authored by Sr. Mary Theodore. I felt lucky to have been able to find these treasures and consider them my greatest source in creating this book. Two of Sr. Mary Theodore's books, "The Challenge of the Retarded Child" published in 1963, and "Developmental Disability - A Family Challenge" published in 1984, were published for both educators and the general public. "The History of St. Coletta Jefferson Wisconsin 1904-1994" was a volume authored by the Sister in 1995. This, I believe, was created as a resource for the St. Coletta community. Without being able to use the volume that St. Coletta kindly let me borrow (it is one of the few remaining copies), it would have been extremely difficult to tie together the dates, places and names of all of my other resources.

As I move forward with this story of St. Coletta, it is with a voice heavily influenced by Sr. Mary Theodore. I was overjoyed when someone at St. Coletta copied a television interview with her from the 1950s on to YouTube so that I could view it. To be able not only see her, but to actually hear this trailblazer's voice meant so much to me. She spoke as someone within the disability community who was far ahead of her time in both her beliefs and actions.

As Sr. Mary Theodore started her teaching career at a school for students who did not have disabilities, she became intimately aware of the St. Coletta School and its activities. Because she was living with the St. Coletta Sisters, she was able to keenly observe all that went on around her. One of her earliest memories included sharing a first anniversary cake for Sister Anastasia who had become the Sister Superior and Superintendent in 1925. She also noted a new chaplain Father Francis Sampson.

By 1927, the school was beginning to attract attention from the main source of news for that time period - local and regional newspapers. In the fall of 2019, I had decided to add archived newspaper research to my efforts to present a broader and more impartial insight of St. Coletta through the years. Each article that I found added a new layer to my depth of understanding. The stories that I located went back to 1927. That very first article was enlightening.

I could not stop thinking about that oldest story. It was published on December 11th, 1927, in the Wisconsin State Journal (headquartered in Madison). I knew that I wanted to share it, in its entirety, in this book. I reached out to the current publisher of the newspaper since I wasn't sure who to approach about an article written almost 100 years ago.

In my letter I briefly wrote about my plans to write this book and also about my connection to St. Coletta. I expressed my appreciation for all of the supportive and informative stories about St. Coletta that had been written by the WSJ over so many years and asked that my request be forwarded to the proper person so that I might receive the needed permission to reprint the 1927 article. I included my intention to use quotes from a number of other articles written in the past century. Within a few hours, I was extremely surprised to get a reply from John Smalley, the editor of the Wisconsin State Journal. His email was gracious and positive. He fully granted me permission to use any of the articles I wanted to use, including reprinting the entire 1927 article. (His only request was that I attribute the newspaper and writers as the source which, of course, I had already planned to do). I was, and am, so grateful for his permission.

The article gives an objective perspective, written by an journalist of that time period. This was a time when children with disabilities were generally thought of and written about as subhumans. The language in the article is definitely not written in terms that would be used today, but the writer and the Sisters were using the terminology and the prevalent attitudes of that era. I am sharing the complete article, exactly as it was printed, without editing any grammar, capitalization, spelling or missed words.

Wisconsin State Journal - December 11, 1927 -

- Jefferson Nuns Guide Stunted Child Minds Toward Normal - by Catherine Colburne

- Continent Sends Backward Youth to School -
Home-Like Atmosphere Brings Placidity to Troubled Brains; Wealthy Families Represented -

Tucked under the brow of one of the hills that surround the little town of Jefferson, Wis., is the St. Coletta Institute, unlike any other place in the United States. Yet comparatively few people beyond that immediate vicinity know of its existence, so quietly does it carry on its work.

Back of its commonplace gray stone walls is a home and training school for subnormal children, where gentle, placid-eyed sisters are devoting their lives to these backward youngsters. Here, from all corners of the country and from Canada, come those whose young minds are so low, so stunted, or so warped that they cannot keep up with their classmates in public school. To give the children a congenial, peaceful home, a Christian upbringing, and as much education and training as they can grasp is the aim of the sisters who conduct St. Coletta Institute. They overcome the double handicap which the abnormal child often suffers in contrast to the carefully reared and educated normal child.

- Is Non-denominational -

St. Coletta's most decidedly does not limit its admission to Catholics, those in charge assert. It accepts any child deserving of what the home has to offer, regardless of the religion of its parents. Neither could the religion which these children are taught be called Catholicism; it is described as a simple non-denominational Christianity composed of chapel every morning and longer services on Sundays. Some of the cases, of course, are too low on the scale of mentality to grasp anything at all of the significance of religion, but for a large number it is an important factor in shaping their lives in the way the home intends.

"We strive to make the children happy and to create a really home-like atmosphere for them here, which is often more than their own families can do for them," said Sister Marguerite, the soft-spoken woman who led the way through the institute. "This requires loving treatment and endless patience. To give them that, along with healthful living conditions, instructions by trained teachers, and a Christian education, is our entire aim."

With what success these aims are realized is indicated by the immaculate, modern rooms, all flooded with sunlight. The children were invariably smiling and apparently contented.

"The children are not dressed alike, don't you believe in uniform?" she was asked.

"No, that would seem to much like an institution. Besides, most parents prefer to send clothing."

Many of the boys and girls are very well dressed, she pointed out, indicating several attractive Sunday costumes hanging ready, beside the little white beds. Some wealthy families are represented there, as well as middle-class and poor ones, since the institute attempts to keep the charges as low as possible. A fund, which will grow as the school becomes stronger financially, is being established to take care of charity cases.

- Has Four Dormitories -

Four dormitories, one each for small boys, small girls, large boys and large girls, provide hygienic sleeping quarters for the youngsters. The rooms are large and airy, with individual clothes trees, and the infirmary rooms, all completely modern in equipment, were shown with the added information that a dentist from Jefferson, less than a mile away, paid regular visits and were available for emergency calls.

The classrooms on the first floor were like ordinary public school rooms, with their regulation desks, blackboards and walls hung with the pupils' work. Sister Marguerite explained that boys and girls are classes together, but that the groups have to be much smaller and could be less definitely graded than in public schools.

"All the sisters who teach hold a degree either from a normal school or a university and all are especially trained to deal with sub-normal children", she said.

Each child receives special attention, because each an individual problem. Some cannot grasp even the fundamentals of reading and writing. These are taught to make things with their hands out of colored paper and raffia, in order that they may learn a manual art or trade when they are older. In this way they will not, as adults, be dependent upon the state for support. It is a psychological fact that being able to support themselves goes a long way toward sustaining inferior persons' self-respect, said sister Marguerite. One such child was pointed out.

"She is almost an idiot we find." she said "We cannot teach her much of anything. She will have to enter a public institution when she comes of age. But with St. Coletta's background she will go into it with the habit of a happy disposition, as healthful an attitude toward life as possible for her, and the knowledge of a craft, by which she may become a useful human being."

Many are helped

A sweet-faced little chap came up to talk to sister Marguerite.

"He is typical of another kind of pupil" she told us. "Notice his slant eyes, short fingers, and sallow skin. He is what is called the Mongolian type of sub-normality. Despite his appearance, there is not a drop of oriental blood in his veins. He comes from apparently normal parents and his retarded mentality is due to some irregularity in the pre-natal period. It takes the form of these physical traits, a very affectionate and docile disposition, besides extreme difficulty in learning."

32

Like many others of the cases, hope is held out for his eventual cure. Many leave the institute, after various periods of training, partially or entirely cured.

An isolated and independent little community is St. Coletta's. A farm of 120 acres surrounding the building supplies the institute with fresh fruit and vegetables, eggs, milk and meat. In large immaculate kitchens all meals are prepared, and huge ovens bake all the bread and pastries. The larger boys do much of the agricultural work, and the girls, under sisters' direction, perform all the domestic duties so only one family of outsiders is employed. A 20-acre wood lot and large rolling slopes of grass provide places for the children to spend their recreational hours out-of-doors at wholesome games and exercise.

Many of the boys and girls are musically inclined. The St. Coletta band frequently is requested to give concerts in Jefferson. [13]

I have thought about this journalist, Ms. Colburne, who wrote this story. How was she affected by what she saw at the school that she had toured? Were her attitudes changed towards children with disabilities after her visit? Those of you who read the article may be repulsed by some of the language used not only by the writer, but also Sister Marguerite. I certainly was when I first read it. "Idiot, Mongolian, sub-normal". These were the actual medical terms used in that time period - just as the term "retarded" was used most of the last century until it gradually became an ugly term of derision.

Although what struck me more than those terms, was the underlying compassion of the Sisters, and their deep desire to create lives that were previously unimaginable for children with disabilities in the early part of the twentieth century. Initially, like the families, they hoped they could find ways to "cure" the children in their care.

My guess is that in some of the cases in which they said they had "cured" the students they were teaching, those students might have been affected by a combination of learning disabilities, mild autism or ADHD. As I wrote about earlier, in that time period most public and private schools did not accept students with any type of learning differences. With the individually dedicated attention that they were given, those students might well have been able to assimilate successfully back into regular schools later in their education.

Even in its early days, St. Coletta strove for all of the children in their care to reach their maximum potential. I wonder how many families who read this article on that cold December Wisconsin morning in 1927, felt hope for their own struggling children for the first time in their lives?

After Sister Anastasia became the Superintendent at St. Coletta, a new statue of St. Therese was created. The Sister had promised to honor the Saint if her prayers to Therese made possible the new school building. The building was also named in honor of St. Therese. The statue was placed in a special niche on the second floor. Along with the new building, St. Mary's Infirmary was added to the main building. The old infirmary became a community room for the Sisters. The children must have been very excited that the new infirmary included an indoor swimming pool. The two new buildings were dedicated on May 10th, 1928 with many dignitaries, prayers and much gratitude.

The new building included an auditorium, complete with a stage with a heavy velour curtain and gold fringe. There was an area for calisthenics and other exercises. The auditorium was put to great and varied use over the coming years. The building had two rooms for domestic science (home economics) and a printing room. Upstairs on the second floor was a new library, two classrooms and a teachers' study. There was also a kindergarten room for the youngest students and a sewing room. On the third floor were art, music and a basketry room. In a clever design move, French doors from the music room opened up into the auditorium. Regular band concerts were scheduled to entertain the children both inside and outside on the playground.

St. Mary's infirmary would come to serve many purposes as well. Besides the indoor pool (and dressing rooms) on the first floor, they also included several small dining areas. The second and third floors were designated as separate infirmaries for boys and girls. Also included on the third floor was a laboratory and even a dental office for a local dentist's weekly visits. Providing specialized dental and medical care for individuals with disabilities is still very much of a problem across the United States. St. Coletta was certainly - again - a pioneer almost 100 years ago in offering this service. In hearing from current staff, and from reading Sr. Mary Theodore's words about the school, it continually amazes me how forward thinking the administration was so many years ago.

They tried everything within their abilities to be as self-sufficient and to save money whenever possible. They installed a water softener and filter, a tank to catch rain water, an ice machine and an ice cream freezer. The comfort and care of their students and staff were always paramount in their decisions, no matter the cost.

As St. Coletta moved close to its 25th anniversary, the two new buildings were their largest improvements and projects. On September 22nd, 1929 they opened their doors to the public for a large Silver Jubilee, inviting everyone from Jefferson and the local community. The local newspaper featured a front page spread with neighboring businesses offering their hearty congratulations. Two days later, a Solemn High Mass was held to thank God for all of his blessings. Families of the students must have been amongst the most grateful.

In 1930, Sr. Mary Theodore requested and was granted a transfer to join the staff of St. Coletta. In her book on the history of St. Coletta, she describes her new journey (in the third person) in simple, straightforward terms. "This term began her life work as group mother, teacher, principal, writer, lecturer, superintendent and finally the director of public relations. After retirement Sister offered volunteer services in charge of the Archives and Gift Shop." [14]

This was truly a woman who dedicated her life to the service of others. In talking to the many staff and some St. Coletta clients who knew and loved her, they continue to speak about her with love, respect and awe.

As a new decade began at the start of the Great Depression, St. Coletta moved bravely and strongly forward. In 1931, a big step was to incorporate under a new name, "The St. Coletta School for Exceptional Children". Everyone had begun to understand that calling its students "backwards" was an insult to them and to their families. It was said that one student remarked, "We don't walk backward." It was their belief that the term "exceptional" was a much more positive reflection of who the students were.

In 1932, the Sisters had a chance to purchase another 44 acres to expand their farm operations. They miraculously always found the means to fund these opportunities to keep growing and improving. In late July of 1933, the St. Coletta community suffered a setback when their large barn was destroyed by a fire caused by a lightning strike. They were fortunate to save all of their cattle (except for a crazed bull which had to be shot.) They lost all of their stored feed, hay and some equipment. Immediate plans were made to recover and rebuild. Because of their strong faith, willpower, and the blessings of friends and the local community, they were able to rebuild in time for a fall festival in late September. A large radio station in Chicago provided live music and approximately 2,000 people attended. All of these events continued to bring new attention and supporters.

As the school gained attention, the staff created a "Touring Visitor's Guide". The guide emphasized what St. Coletta felt the students needed to succeed. "We believe that the children must be healthy, happy and secure - with a sense of being wanted and loved - if they are to derive full benefit from the complete program of St. Coletta School." I can say with confidence that this philosophy has carried on to serve the current adult clients. My daughter's confidence has blossomed from her sense of being secure and wanted within the community.

One of the major questions for the community, as it was for the families of the children in the school, was "What would happen to their students as they finished the school program?" Most students moved back to their own families and communities, returning with much better living and working skills to cope in the real world. Some students, unfortunately, would move on into the dreary state institutions available in their home states.

35

There was sadness for everyone that students were moving from the joyful, invigorating atmosphere of St. Coletta's to the horror of the neglect and abuse that was rampant in institutions. The Sisters were very distressed. When they began to hear about deaths occurring to their much loved former students, they knew they needed to take action. These were new and difficult decisions to be made at a time when St. Coletta was also surging in popularity as the singularly unique school that they were.

In the early days of St. Coletta the Sisters prayed for students to come to them. In 1904, getting the word out about their innovative new program for children with intellectual disabilities was a challenge. Despite the difficulties presented in that time period, the word did spread. Through word of mouth, churches, newspapers and radio, families heard about St. Coletta and began to travel to Wisconsin to find educations for their struggling children. By the 1930s, applications were flooding into the office of admissions. They often received, in a week, enough applications to fill the yearly admission quota. Families even began to uproot their families, at the height of the depression, to move to Jefferson. They had hopes that their children could at least be admitted as day students.

The Sisters hated to turn down the desperate families that pleaded for admittance to the program. They created a waiting list but it grew to such a large size that another residential school could have been built with just these students. The admissions office could only offer these sad, departing families a slight chance that their children would, at some point, be granted a golden ticket - a chance to be a part of this remarkable community. Many, if not most of those children, would wait in vain until they were too old to be admitted (between the ages of 6 to 15).

One of the Sisters' greatest fears was that the school would grow too large and, in doing that, they would not be able to provide the deeply individual care that they wanted to provide each student. It was certainly a dilemma that they faced year in and year out for years to come. Adding to this problem was their newest challenge - what to do with those graduating students whose lives were ending up in places that destroyed all of the gains that they had so lovingly learned.

The Sisters had sleepless nights wrestling with how to manage these almost insurmountable problems. Their current financial accounts simply did not allow them to make another expansion. Fortunately their chaplain, Father James Feider, rallied to help the school. He was assisted with the kind help of Father Anthony Nickel in raising the needed funding.

In 1937, on their recently purchased farm, they built a new building which was to be named the Alverno Cottage. It would be located down the road about a quarter mile from the main campus. This beautiful shady new campus, which included its own chapel, dining room and kitchen was to be used specifically for the now adult men who had finished the school program. Some now adult women were moved into St. Anthony Cottage which had already been used for some of the new adult population. Other women lived in the St. Coletta building.

In February of 1938, the Wisconsin State Journal wrote about the Alverno addition and what it would mean to the school. It said this, "Charges are taken into the school from a large waiting list whenever room is available. The motto of the school is 'To give the mentally handicapped child the maximum opportunities for developing his limited powers in an atmosphere of confidence and joy that will stimulate him to his best efforts.' After training in the school a good percentage of the charges are enabled to return to normal life under the guardianship of parents or guardians."[15] The article went on to say that the housing would be the new residence for those who couldn't return to their families, those who "had outgrown the school but cannot be returned to normal life."

By having housing available for those adults in need, it happily freed up more room to add more school aged children. The tuition, for those who could afford it, was increased from $35.00 to $50.00 a month. That was a huge amount of money in 1938. It must have been a tremendous sacrifice for families to raise that kind of money.

The new clients and students added practical issues like an increased laundry load. Funds were designated to enlarge the laundry room. When it was finished everyone was very proud of their modern new laundry. It had the additional benefit of offering vocational opportunities for the resident women who could fulfill their days in useful purpose, knowing they were contributing to the community. As they worked, a wing was planned and built onto the Alverno building just for them. This freed up the St. Coletta building so it could be used for the Sisters.

Much thought always went into these moves so that everyone could live and work in the most useful and comfortable circumstances. The Sisters were happy when a new dedicated space was built for devotion and communion. Sr. Mary Theodore stated "The real presence of Jesus became the center of devotion once more." "Daily prayers were offered for the children and adults whose mental retardation brought them to the care of St. Francis of Assisi."[16]

While the education and care of the children and, then the adults, of St. Coletta were of supreme importance, their religious education was always a priority. The school accepted children of all religious affiliations and never pressured any of them to become practicing Catholics. (Some of those children did, however, express an interest and would request rosaries and prayer books from their parents.) The chaplain of St. Coletta, Father Feider presented a paper at the 1939 National Conference of Catholic Charities titled "The Objectives and Methods of Religion to Subnormal Children."

In 1939, religious education for children with intellectual disabilities was still as rare as academic education. The efforts to open the minds of the public in respect to the capabilities of children and adults on the disability spectrum was, and is, an ongoing effort of St. Coletta. It is only through consistent efforts of disability advocates that the wheels slowly turned. Families, the general public and the state and federal governments of the U.S. finally began to regard these individuals as humans who deserved lives like everyone else.

In 1963 in her book, "The Challenge of the Retarded Child" Sr. Mary Theodore, wrote this, "The term "mental retardation" replaces such terms as idiot, imbecile, moron, or feeble-minded which are no longer considered acceptable. Personally I am grateful that the unfeeling terms just mentioned are no longer in general use. Society, becoming more understanding of the retardants, avoids causing unnecessary pain to parents and to others who love these children. It is easy to understand the crushing defeat of parents who, before the growth of tolerance and understanding, were forced to "put away" their retarded children in institutions bearing such names as "Custodial Asylum for Unreachable Idiots". Such an insignia above the door would extinguish all hope that their small ones could expect any help in this world."[17]

Of course, that term "mentally retarded" has now also become one of those unacceptable terms used to describe individuals with developmental disabilities. We are now encouraged to use "people first" terminology, such as an individual with autism, or a person with intellectual disabilities, rather than - an autistic or disabled person. Some people get frustrated with, and make fun of, this attention to semantics. For those of us who are or who love someone that can be categorized in cruel ways, it is important to make the effort. In the end it is all about basic human respect.

The 1940s would bring on many new opportunities to help more children. As the campus of St. Coletta was making an effort to not become too large, they decided that a branch campus to serve children from the western states could be a solution to the huge waiting lists of families across the country. St. Coletta-of-the-Rockies opened its doors in Longmont Colorado in 1941. The former girl's high school, St. Joseph Academy, was to be the school's new home. They retained the Principal of the high school, Sister Humiliana Mueller, to be in charge of the new program. Sister Inez Wagner, from the main campus of St. Coletta, became the new Superintendent.

Another wonderful new program at the campus in Jefferson was created in 1943. This program continued for the next thirty years and would revolutionize special education teacher training in the Catholic school system.

Monsignor Edmund Goebel, who was the Archdiocesan Superintendent of Schools in Milwaukee, observed the St. Coletta program for a day and decided that one teacher in each parochial school in the Diocese should be trained to teach the children in the school who were "slow learners".

Sr. Mary Theodore said that Msgr. Goebel deserved the credit for creating, naming and providing moral support for their new summer training program. It was named "The Psychological Institute for the Study of the Mentally Handicapped". The program operated under the St. Clare College in Milwaukee, (which is now Cardinal Stritch University) which was also operated by the Sisters of Saint Francis of Assisi.

The new program offered six week residential sessions, including courses and laboratory schooling. A number of courses were created and taught, including The History of Mental Retardation, Psychology of Exceptional Children and Intelligence Testing.

Sister Mary Theodore, who had received her Master's degree from Catholic University, researched clinical types and the history of mental retardation to create two lecture courses on those subjects. The lab portion of the program, actually working with the students, included observation, administering tests and all sorts of training in teaching crafts such as woodwork and machine sewing. The end of the summer session featured the crafts created. All of the extra hands and new enthusiasm were beneficial for all of the children involved.

It was a very full and fulfilling six weeks. It must have been eye opening for the teacher trainees. It brought them much insight to take back to their schools. With pride, Monsignor Goebel presented certificates to the newly trained teachers.

Besides training these teachers, another goal was to interest other religious communities across the country. They hoped this innovative new training program would encourage training teachers in their community school programs to create special education programs of their own. This occurred in the time period before special education was mandated in public schools. Most children with intellectual and developmental disabilities were still not being educated to any degree of regularity. St. Coletta, as always, became a game changer and strove to change the world in a very creative and dynamic way. It's striking to think of what they were accomplishing then and continue to accomplish today.

Chapter 5

In 1944, the 40th anniversary of the founding of St. Coletta, Sr. Mary Theodore took stock of the personnel and students on campus. She noted that there were 22 consulting persons who assisted with education and medical needs, two chaplains, 67 Sisters, and five lay persons on staff. She didn't separate students from the adults but listed 325 total individuals that they were now serving. This was a monumental growth from their original 5 students. She said their total enrollment over 40 years stood at 1678. So many lives enriched and improved.

St. Coletta had not only survived and thrived during the Great Depression, they also weathered the severe shortages and rationing during World War II. Learning from their challenging early days when the Sisters survived on potatoes, they knew that the only way to provide the proper nutrition was by continuing to be as self-sufficient as possible. At every opportunity, they bought additional acreage for their farming operation. The houses on the farms were used for the workers' families. In the 1940s, they bought several small farms and immediately put the land to good use, for not only crops, but also for their animals, including a dairy and beef herd. In 1945, they installed a large deep freeze. With this, a root cellar and a steady canning operation, they made sure the long freezing winters of Wisconsin would not prevent them from providing nutritious, warm meals.

In 1946, a new diocese was founded in Madison. It was decided that St. Coletta would now be part of this diocese.

In 1947, the monthly fee (for those who could afford it) increased to $65.00. Many of adult clients were wholly dependent on charity and the Sisters provided for them free of charge. That year another branch school was created in Hanover, Massachusetts. It was named St. Coletta-by-the-Sea and would be under the patronage of the well-known Richard Cardinal Cushing. Now the families of New England also had their own school. Very quickly, large amounts of applications arrived. There became a rush to prep the school for opening and some of the Wisconsin Sisters traveled to Massachusetts to offer their assistance.

With the large number of students and adult clients now living in the small town of Jefferson, the Sisters decided it was time to solve another dilemma. Many of the families of these residents lived far away. The Sisters thought it was very important for those in their care to continue to nurture their family connections. Jefferson had only one small hotel and it was insufficient to welcome everyone who visited. This created an expensive hardship for traveling families who then had to travel over an hour back to Madison for lodging each night so that they could spend time with their children. It was uncomfortable and strange for the children, who thrived on their regular routines and surroundings.

The solution was Serra House, a warm and friendly guesthouse built in 1948 on the St. Coletta campus. Families were relieved to finally have a place where they could enjoy their children's company without stress and additional travel. An unexpected benefit came with creating new friendships among the families. They, perhaps for the first times in their lives, met others who could understand what it was like to raise a child with disabilities. There was a large lobby to gather in, along with the dining room and recreation room. There were plenty of opportunities to meet up and compare stories. Families living today who have children with disabilities can find themselves isolated. Sharing the challenges of living with a disability, with other families who are facing these same issues, can be comforting and provide an outlet to relieve stress and loneliness. In the 1950s, when shame was still a factor in raising children with disabilities, finding others to share their joys and challenges with provided a true lifeline.

Another development that was decades ahead of its time, Serra House, served as a vocational training opportunity for older students. Six girls were chosen to live at Serra, where they served as waitresses and assisted with cleaning. Some of the young men working there proudly dressed up in red caps and jackets and served as porters to assist with luggage. In January of 1951, the Wisconsin State Journal wrote about the Serra House. "Parents who come to the beautiful guest house and see their boy in a bellhop's outfit may suffer a pang when they think of the plans they once had for him. But the grief is their own. The boy is so proud the shiny buttons are nearly bursting off his smart jacket; the privilege of being a bellboy at the guest house is awarded only to pupils on the honor roll."[18]

Many other students and adults trained and worked on the farm, harvesting the fruits of their labors and caring for the animals. Their families were filled with pride as they came to visit and saw their children being productive members of their community. Some of the students then moved on to successful job placements within the local community with some eventually became self-supporting.

While we are fortunately living in an era where we are seeing coffee houses and other employment opportunities for young adults with disabilities can train in them and be employed, St. Coletta was fifty to sixty years ahead of them.

As St. Coletta has evolved over the years (due to changes in special education laws and societal progress in disability practice) many of these innovative programs transitioned or were discontinued. However, the focus of

St. Coletta has never wavered. Their original goal of substantially improving the lives of these people who were marginalized in society has remained. The St Coletta community continues to create new opportunities for everyone that it serves.

Students excited to meet Cardinal Cushing

Helping with the corn harvest

Student Redcaps welcoming families to Serra House

Enjoying a snowy Wisconsin day

Chapter 6

Rosemary Kennedy and her life at St. Coletta (from 1949-2005)

There is no question that every single person who has been served by St. Coletta over its long history is equally loved and valued. Each one has been welcomed into the community with open arms and treated with respect. As the 1940s were coming to a close, St. Coletta gained a new member whose life made an impact not only on her family and the St. Coletta community, all over the world.

Rosemary Kennedy was the sister of the future President John F. Kennedy and was a member of one of the most well-known and documented families in America. In 1949, she moved into her own home at St. Coletta, which was designed and built specifically for her needs.

Rosemary struggled with challenging disabilities since birth. She was deeply loved and lived amongst her large family, attending various day and boarding schools in the U.S. and overseas. As Rosemary reached adulthood, her behavioral challenges grew, as did her family's efforts to find a safe and happy life for her.

In the hopes of helping her to live a more settled life, in 1941 her father, Joseph P. Kennedy, arranged for her to receive a frontal lobotomy at the age of 23. The procedure had been first performed in the U.S. in 1936 as a way to treat mental illness and intellectual disability and became more common during the 1940s. The results for Rosemary were disastrous and her disabilities thereafter became much more severe and permanent.

After the lobotomy, Rosemary spent some years at a private hospital in New York but it did not provide her with the life her family hoped she could have. Joseph Kennedy decided to reach out to his friend, Archbishop Richard Cushing, to find a compassionate place where he could build a home for Rosemary. He wanted her to be able to live her life happily and privately. The Archbishop determined that St. Coletta, a community that he was very familiar with, would be that ideal place. The home was promptly constructed and arrangements were made for staffing and programming. Rosemary blessedly found peace and joy in her new setting. St. Coletta became Rosemary's home, second family and community until she died in 2005. She enjoyed many visits from her family over the years and traveled to see them in their homes. She was, until the end of her life, a much loved member of both the Kennedy and St. Coletta family. Her sister Eunice became her champion and, inspired by Rosemary, became a champion for all individuals in the world who were living with disabilities.

Although her father's decision to have Rosemary lobotomized was drastic and certainly a tragedy for her, I have great empathy for her family. They were like so many other families who had a child with disabilities who for years and years tried to find ways to include their child, and help them find their way in life. Yes, the Kennedys were very wealthy and influential, and they had many more options that others did not have. It is significant to me that even this esteemed and wealthy family had struggled to find compassionate options for their child. She, like so many others, lived her life in a world that did not accept her or treat her with respect.

Individuals with disabilities have often been the first to be subjected to radical, and often, failed experiments to treat and "normalize" them. The outcome for Rosemary was incredibly sad. She and her family had to live with the choice her father made for the rest of their lives. What I care most about in this saga is this, St. Coletta made the decision to come to Rosemary and her family's aid. They were determined to protect her as they did all of the children and adults in their care. They provided her with a dignified, long and happy life.

Rosemary's life, living in a separate home on the campus, was, in some ways, different than the other St. Coletta adult residents. The family's concerns about her being photographed and exploited by outsiders and the press were legitimate. The staff were very mindful of this and were extremely protective of her privacy. They were ultimately successful in those efforts. The press never descended on them. This is surprising, especially since during her brother's presidency, Eunice wrote about Rosemary and her disabilities openly for the first time in an article in the Saturday Evening Post. At the end of the article, published on September 22, 1962, she said this -

"My mother found an excellent Catholic institution that specialized in the care of retarded children and adults. Rosemary is there now. She has found peace in a new home where there is not a need for "keeping up", or for brooding over why she can't join in activities as others do. This, coupled with the understanding of the sisters in charge, makes life agreeable for her."[19]

I don't agree that St. Coletta was an "institution". And perhaps Eunice used that term as you would say a college or a hospital is and institution. In its entirety, the article was moving and beautifully written. It was an eye opener for the public and created quite a splash. This was still an era when most well-known people did not publicly admit to having a family member with a disability.

In my newspaper research I was able to find only one article about Rosemary at St. Coletta while she was still alive. It was written in the Chicago Tribune in January of 1976. In the article St. Coletta was identified as her home. Rosemary at that time was 57 years old. Sr. Sheila Haskett, who was the administrator of St. Coletta in 1976, was quoted in the article -

"Retarded people generally feel undervalued and unesteemed." "In God's eyes, Rosemary knows she has worth and value. She is a wonderful, remarkable woman." She goes on to say, "Her whole life is wrapped up in doing things she likes, like taking trips into town". The article noted that no one recognized her as she went with one of the Sisters on walks through the town of Jefferson or when she went to the airport to fly out to visit her family. The article also said that the reporter was told that Rosemary wasn't given special treatment at St. Coletta. Sr. Sheila said, "We treat everyone the same." "Everyone is equal in God's eyes." The reporter continues by saying, "Visitors to St. Coletta aren't allowed to see or talk to Rosemary, as expected." "But Rosemary visits many of her retarded friends whom she has known for years."[20]

Rosemary was able to enjoy the social atmosphere and activities of the community. Several of the older members of the community have volunteered to me (I never asked them about her) that Rosemary was their friend and they miss her very much. Even today, staff are very protective of Rosemary and her privacy.

My daughter Daniela feels a strong affection for, and connection with, Rosemary. She knows we found St. Coletta because of the book I read about her. It is Daniela's book now and she has read it more than once. She remarks fondly on "Rosemary's house" whenever we pass it. It is located next to the Alverno building on campus. Daniela and I were able to tour the home in 2018 during St. Coletta's Family Weekend. There are no visible letters signs of Rosemary in the house anymore. Still, Daniela and I both could clearly feel Rosemary's spirit in the house that day. It was heartwarming to see just what a welcoming and simple home it was. St. Clare is currently vacant, patiently awaiting its new mission.

Rosemary's life was absolutely valuable, in and of itself, (as are the lives of my daughter and everyone's sons and daughters). Her life, however, was also important in many other ways. Her disabilities influenced, and continue to influence, her family to create new programs, and even laws, for people with disabilities. Special Olympics (created by Eunice), Best Buddies and Very Special Arts, which have served millions of individuals across the world, were created and overseen by Rosemary's siblings and their children. The Joseph P. Kennedy Jr. Foundation was founded in 1946. It became the first foundation to focus on the needs of individuals with intellectual disabilities. Its early focus was on the causes of intellectual disability and ways to prevent it. It also came to focus on the treatment of individuals of intellectual and developmental disabilities and mental illness.

When John Kennedy became President, his sister Eunice urged him to focus on this neglected population. He created a panel which produced a report called "The National Action to Prevent Mental Retardation". This report also provided guidance for developing special education guidelines. It encouraged new and specific federal funding for education, personnel training and residential care.[21] In 1963, President Kennedy created the Maternal and Child Health and Mental Retardation Planning Act. This was amended to the Social Security Act and became the first legislation to specifically address, not only intellectual disability, but also mental illness. (These were created and enacted right before his assassination.) Eunice Kennedy Shriver and her family's love for Rosemary impacted the world in profound ways. They are still creating positive change for individuals with disabilities all over the globe.

Daniela ties her love of the Special Olympics and Best Buddies to Rosemary and her family. In 2018, she was thrilled to have the chance to meet Dr. Timothy Shriver, Rosemary's nephew and Eunice's son. He is also the International Chairman of the Board of Special Olympics. At the 2018 St. Coletta's Annual Lead the Charge - Believers and Achievers Gala, he was the keynote speaker and accepted the Lifetime Achievement Award on behalf of Special Olympics. Before his speech, Daniela presented him with a signed copy of the book I wrote about her. She also asked him to sign her copy of his book, "Fully Alive: Discovering What Matters Most." Dr. Shriver was incredibly kind to Daniela. She was star struck. She later proudly joined the other St. Coletta Special Olympians up on stage with him.

Every single individual at St. Coletta, from those first few young children in 1904, to the ones who just now are entering this loving community, receive the same privacy, compassion, love and dignity as Rosemary and Daniela have received. Whether they are mildly or profoundly disabled, poor or wealthy, well-behaved or extremely challenging, all are treated with the same care and diligence needed to give their lives independence, acceptance and meaning.

Meeting Dr. Tim Shriver and sharing books

A stage full of Special Olympians

Chapter 7

Before the start of the 1950s, a big change came for the satellite program in Colorado, St.-Coletta-of-the-Rockies. It didn't seem to have the same kind of support as the Wisconsin and Massachusetts programs. When Cardinal Stritch requested the Sisters create a program for boys in Chicago (there was already a school for girls with intellectual disabilities in the city), they made the decision to transfer the Colorado program to Palms Park, Illinois. It became St.-Coletta-of-the-Plains. Almost all of the residents from Colorado transferred to the new program, with some transferring to Jefferson. The Sisters secured another farm near Jefferson and created a group home for sixteen boys who had milder disabilities. It was called Capistrano Cottage.

In 1949, a woman named Lena Sell died at the age of 99. Lena had been one of the original adult residents at St. Coletta, along with her three sisters. She moved to the community at the age of 67 in 1917. Her long, happy life at St. Coletta showed the success of the care that the community provided. The long range care of adult residents has now continued for over 100 years.

In Sr. Mary Theodore's "History of St. Coletta" book, she updated the number of individuals served in 1950. The total people served in the community was 432. There were representatives from 33 states and one person from Canada. 301 members were Catholic (or became Catholic while living at St. Coletta). The youngest person in the community was four years old and the oldest resident was 77.

The Sisters served a great range of ages, interests, and disabilities. The average IQ was listed as 54. They served at least one person whose IQ was 28, considered to be in the severe intellectual disability range. Some of their students' abilities seemed to be in the learning disability range. That fact is backed by a statement in the update saying the upper level of IQs went to 95 (which is in the average IQ range). Most schools, both public and private, were still not serving children outside of a narrow range of abilities and behaviors.

The teachers at St. Coletta were determined to educate each student to the maximum measure of their ability to learn. The students who were not capable of attending academic classes were taught classes and activities within their capabilities. They tried to teach these students to read and write at a very basic level. From an article in the Wisconsin State Journal in January 1951, writing about life at the school, "Every child at St. Coletta School writes to his parents every week." (There is an accompanying photo of a Sister helping several students writing letters.) "Sometimes they need quite a bit of help - like Sister Frances Borgia is offering here - but they are proud to send and receive mail." The article speaks about life at the school, including little boys gathered around a TV set watching a puppet show while little girls are nearby playing cards. I was touched to read about another little girl in the article. "And in the sewing room a child is working earnestly on a gay knitted Afghan for her grandmother's birthday. 'Her IQ, the teacher tells you softly, is 36.' 'Her grandmother will be very proud of that laboriously worked Afghan'"[22]

St. Coletta has a wonderful newsletter/magazine named "St. Coletta Homelights" that shares the good news, progress and plans for the organization. When Daniela was preparing to join the community, I received my first copy of the magazine. Homelights has a long history at St. Coletta. Its first edition came out in late 1951. That issue shared the news of another new building to be built. As the population grew, so did the need for a new chapel and gymnasium. Construction of a double-duty building began and it soon began to serve this purpose.

In 1952, the community decided to welcome fourteen of the adult residents to become "Tertiaries". A Tertiary is a lay member of a religious order, in other words, not a priest, Brother or a Sister, but given a special designation within the order. Tertiaries were able to be "sharers in the prayers and good works of nearly three million members of the Franciscan family." These residents aspired to be like the people in their lives whom they looked up to. When I have been to services at St. Coletta and the nearby Catholic Church, I have witnessed the full inclusion and acceptance of members of the St. Coletta community in its services.

Also during this period, it was decided to purchase a vacation home for residents who had no other family or home to visit. They bought a place on a lake which they named Padua Point. The Sisters were also able to take vacation days at this large home. After a period of time it was decided it was a little too far away. It was sold so that they could purchase a property on a lake nearer to the campus. Construction and improvements to the campus continued. New playrooms were added along with new dormitories. When a barn was destroyed by a tornado in 1953, a new activities building was built on its foundation. The new chapel was also completed that year and was celebrated and dedicated with the attendance of two Archbishops, Cardinal Stritch and Cardinal Cushing. Also in attendance were three other Archbishops, five abbots and many Monsignors and priests. Hundreds of family members, friends and supporters were included in the celebration.

A reporter from the Wisconsin State Journal was in attendance and wrote a moving article about the event, including parts of Cardinal Cushing's speech. From Cardinal Cushing - "This chapel was built in glorious gratitude to God by the friends and relatives of these children here.....when to the unbelievers God's benevolence might seem least in evidence."

Cardinal Cushing continued his speech saying "It is fair to say that the best index to the civilization of a community is what is done for the 'exceptional children', for they are usually least in so many ways; least in years, least in endowments, least in privileges; least in all the things people covet for their children."

Cardinal Cushing ended his speech saying these words, "Against the background of such a standard of civilization, what a civilized, what a humane, what a divine place is St. Coletta's!...We meet to dedicate a new chapel, a tribute of love to our loving God and of praise to the Lord of Life; to Him whose power is manifest in our little children, Him whose might works are done by the least of us who try to be good to His least 'exceptional ones'."[23]

The article speaks about the mass being sung by both the Sisters and children from the school. It describes the luncheon in which the children entertained with songs and that the school band "vehemently" played "McNamara's Band".

In 1954, St. Coletta celebrated its monumental 50th anniversary. There was so much to acknowledge and be thankful for. There was now an enrollment of almost 500 individuals being served. With 700 acres and multiple buildings, the efforts of so many dedicated servants of God had achieved something the world had never before seen.

The celebration had to be equal to the moment. There was a Solemn High Mass of Thanksgiving to start the festivities, followed by a homemade dinner. Then everyone gathered to watch a 125 member cast present a pageant, titled "A Rosary of Divine Love". It wound the meaning of the Rosary with five memorable moments in St. Coletta's illustrious history.

1. The founding of St. Coletta in 1904
2. The building of the Sacred Heart in 1915
3. The dedication of St. Terese Hall in 1927
4. The creation of the Psychological Institute in 1943
5. The dedication of the new Chapel in 1943

The event ended with a young actress playing St. Coletta receiving a crown of Triumph, which she then gives to the Queen of Heaven. There were many tears shed watching the students and adult clients presenting this tableau of love. The Sisters surely remembered this day for the rest of their lives.

That same year marked the development of a new way to raise funds for the community. New governmental restrictions on fundraising meant that some of the previous ways of raising needed funds were no longer allowed or

50

practical. The Sponsor Club was created to meet the huge shortfall in funding that was being taken in from tuition payments. Monsignor Feider developed the club and went to families and benefactors with his idea. He asked that members of the club sponsor a child monthly for a year, or as long as they could afford. Within one year there were 700 members of the club. This effort helped raise much needed funds for many years.

Always looking for new ways to serve and educate their clients, Monsignor Feider, Sr. Anastasia and Mother Madeline made a ten week trip abroad to visit various organizations and institutions that cared for individuals with disabilities. Because the school had an innovative approach in creating new programs and opportunities, the Sisters were always searching for new ways to teach the children they loved. They visited programs in Italy, Switzerland, Germany, France, Belgium, Spain and Portugal. They were able to have an audience with Pope Pius XII while in Rome and visited Assisi, the home of the patron saint of the Sisters. As they gained knowledge in their travels, they also shared their own. Sr. Anastasia later created a report about the trip, noting the similarities and differences between American ideology and that of European programs. One issue the Sisters knew they needed to emphasize and broaden was an increase in specialized training in special education.

From the results of the report came the development of their original short-term training program at the Psychological Institute. They then expanded their program to a more formalized multi-year certificate program conducted over five summers. The students/teachers came from all over the U.S. and Canada. There were both lay and Sister teacher representatives among the 57 participants. They earned 30 credits over the five summers, with three years spent at Cardinal Stritch College and two years working with the students of St. Coletta. After its first two years, the program received accreditation to become a Master's degree program. There was one center at Cardinal Stritch and one in Boston at the Cardinal Cushing Educational Clinic. The St. Coletta School in Boston served the Massachusetts program for practical training.

The teacher training program continued for forty years before it gradually ended. The program ended due to changes in national policy, laws regarding special education and the rights of all children to receive a public education. (This also led to the gradual changes in the focus of St. Coletta's School and the programming for children. As more students were being educated in their local public schools, the demand for St. Coletta's school program lessened.)

One of the activities the community focused on in the 1950s was creating theatric and musical events for the residents to participate in. Everyone enjoyed these performances including parents, friends and all of the Sisters of St. Francis of Assisi. They were very ambitious in creating these productions, even producing a production of the operetta, Amahl and the Night Visitors. One popular big event was the annual Christmas pageant honoring the Feast of Saint Anastasia. That production had a cast of 150 members. The staff, students and residents made all of the costumes and sets for the performances. There were usually festive dinners for everyone in attendance after the event.

Christmas was always the highlight of the year for everyone. Starting in 1954, there was a new attraction outside of the administration building. A large life size group of Nativity figures and a stable were placed so that the community could also enjoy them as they drove by the campus. It was lit by spotlights at night. People would often stop to admire them, in the same way that people now view neighborhoods filled with Christmas lights. This same group of figures is brought out annually, now in front of the current main campus. The ritual of traditions is important to all of us who treasure St. Coletta's history. Because Wisconsin winters and Christmases generally involve lots of snow, sledding and building snowmen were popular activities over the years. Some of my favorite St. Coletta photos from the past are of children sledding down hills with the Sisters close behind them.

Occasionally fame would visit St. Coletta. In 1955, William Boyd, the star of both movies and TV productions of the very popular character "Hop-along Cassidy" made a grand appearance at St. Coletta, bringing along his famous horse Topper. One student even got the chance to climb on Topper's back. Hop-along made an effort to travel across the country visiting children in orphanages and hospitals. When visiting the smaller girls' dayroom, he exclaimed "What greater reward could I ask than to have little children run up and kiss me!"

There was always a demand for updates to buildings and operational systems. The heating system was enlarged and changed to a system that would use natural gas, instead of the smokier oil furnaces that had been previously used. One of the farms which had been used to house the retired Sisters was converted and enlarged into a large homelike cottage for girls. Twenty-four girls and Sisters happily moved in to "Villa Rieti", which was named for the town in Italy where St. Francis sought refuge for prayer.

In 1956, Sr. Anastasia, still the Superintendent, received a lifetime award for her contributions to individuals with disabilities at a ceremony at Marquette University. Her life indeed deserved recognition for all that she had accomplished in service to those in her care. Sr. Mary Theodore, who was then the supervising teacher, traveled with Sr. Magdeline Mueller to Salzburg Austria in the summer of 1957. They gave a presentation at an international workshop, spreading their knowledge and the results of their many years of work and research.

In the 1950s, St. Coletta day schools had been opened in locations in Wisconsin, Illinois, and Massachusetts. Teachers from five different schools collaborated to create their own curriculums. These curriculums were published and offered at the bookstore at Cardinal Stritch College. They featured many different subjects involved in educating children with intellectual disabilities.

In 1958, a parent brought members of the Milwaukee Braves to visit the children and residents. Since that time period, St. Coletta has continued to enjoy a long tradition of involvement with Wisconsin's professional and college sports teams. It continues to be a highlight for everyone in the community, including staff. Another long held tradition began in 1959 when a pilgrimage was planned for some of the children and Sisters to visit the holy shrine at Lourdes in France.

(Since 2015, (with travel canceled during the first 2 years of the pandemic) an annual pilgrimage trip is now scheduled to visit Assisi in Italy, the home of St. Francis. It has quickly become a tradition that is cherished each year by selected members of the community, both clients and staff. During the pilgrimage, holy water is brought back from various holy sites for the spring opening of the St. Coletta fountain. These places include - in Assisi - San Rufino (the baptismal font for St. Clare and St. Francis) , the St. Francis Basilica, the St. Clare Basilica, and San Damiano. Water has also been collected from St. Mary of the Angels in the Umbrian Valley near Assisi and from St. Peter's Basilica in Rome.)

Sr. Mary Theodore continued to broaden all of the ways in which she could serve and advance the St. Coletta community. Her knowledge was becoming well known and sought after. She traveled and spoke at conferences in the U.S. and abroad. Monsignor John O'Grady, the Executive Secretary of the Conference of Catholic Charities, decided a book needed to be written to assist families in their search for help and answers as they were navigating life with a child with disabilities. Sr. Mary Theodore rose to his request and somehow managed to find the time to write a book that was sorely needed.

"The Challenge of the Retarded Child" quickly sold out of its first printing and before 1959 was over, a second printing was requested. I was very excited when I found a used copy of the book available on Amazon. My copy had been originally owned by the Southern Connecticut State College Library so it was evidently used for educational purposes, as well as families. It was even translated into Braille. My copy was an updated revised edition published in 1963. Eunice Kennedy Shriver wrote a beautiful introduction. This edition was also translated into French.

Sr. Mary Theodore, in writing the book, had a goal of desperately wanting to help the thousands of families who didn't have access to St. Coletta, or any other educational or residential programs. The book has some concepts which no longer apply in current educational programs, though much of the book is still relevant. For the time period in which it was written, it was incredibly progressive and useful for families who were trying to access help for their children. Many of the stories in the book were written about children at St. Coletta. (In doing so, the Sister mentions in her introduction that she took great care to protect their personal information.)

In 1959, Sr. M. Anastasia celebrated fifty years working with St. Coletta, and Father Feider celebrated twenty-five years as St. Coletta's Chaplain. The community produced an operetta in their honor. The Wisconsin State Journal, which had written about the school for many years, wrote an article about Sr. Anastasia, honoring her dedicated service since the day she arrived as a novice at the age of twenty. They described her arriving on August 18, 1909, in a horse drawn buggy. They wrote about her life at the school for next fifty years. They quoted her as saying happily, "I loved it from the first." "I think the Lord wanted me here with these poor little kiddies." "Every child is a challenge, an individual, and you learn to study what you can do for each one and how you can win him over." She said she personally interviewed all of the families that were hoping to enroll their children and it was her sad duty to sometimes tell them that St. Coletta could not accept their child. She described advances in society's acceptance of retarded children but also said "There is a long way to go." "Even today, how many neighbors refuse to let their children play with the retarded child down the street! People who don't understand and can be so cold." "That's why we are so happy when people want to come and visit our school. When they see our children - and they are such sweet children - and our happy Sisters, they feel differently."[24]

Sr. Anastasia was honored to be appointed to the Committee for the Study of Standards in Residential Institutions for the Mentally Retarded. St. Coletta was well regarded for raising the standards of institutional care. (Though it seems many institutions miserably failed those standards). One of Father Feider's greatest accomplishments during that period was expanding the farm. His motivation was led by a desire to provide occupational opportunities for the older boys and men. He wanted to provide them with a sense of self-worth. Father Feider was very proud of the community's cattle. In 1960, He sent a registered Holstein Friesian bull named Laddie to Pope John XXIII for his papal farm in Italy - The Pope sent back his blessings.

Lunch at St. Coletta School

The children received in house medical and dental care.

Music was always central to life at the school.

Independent living skills were part of the curriculum.

Sewing and knitting gave the students work skills.

Chapter 8

The beginning of the 1960s brought a new era for people with disabilities. This decade was pivotal in the creation of new legislation and organizations designed to improve the lives of those families who were impacted by disability. The NARC (National Association of Retarded Children), which had been founded in 1950, expanded its reach with the opening of a Governmental Affairs Office in Washington D.C. They were represented on the first President's Panel on Mental Retardation. They advocated with other organizations in the enactment of Medicare and Medicaid. The National Down Syndrome Association was founded in 1960 by the mother of a child with Down Syndrome.

The President's Panel was created by President Kennedy in 1961. It had a twenty-six member panel that was comprised of outstanding professionals including physicians, educators and scientists. Six task forces were developed to create a groundbreaking report that was released in 1962. The report, besides setting guidelines for education, housing, and the treatment of the disabled, was the impetus for major legislation.

Families had started a movement that created tremendous social change for people with disabilities. That movement included the family of Rosemary Kennedy. Mental retardation was finally brought into the open. Centuries of secrecy and shame gave way to advocacy and pride. After President Kennedy's assassination in 1963, President Johnson carried the mantle to continue to create broad social changes for all Americans. His civil rights agenda and his "War on Poverty" positively impacted individuals with disabilities as well. The President's Panel on Mental Retardation ended with the death of President Kennedy. In 1966, President Johnson created the President's Committee on Mental Retardation. This committee is ongoing and is now called the President's Committee for Individuals with Intellectual Disabilities. The committee is re-appointed with each new President.

St. Coletta continued to attract accolades and positive attention for their work. In 1961, the Governor of Wisconsin attended the dedication of Saint Anastasia Hall. This new building would become the residence of thirty girls and fourteen Sisters. Sr. Mary Theodore was invited to speak on a TV program in New York about the work of St. Coletta and the subject of mental retardation. Her goal was to show individuals with intellectual disabilities could be educated and that they could advance in their abilities. A copy of the video tape was given to the National Association of Retarded Children (now the Arc).

In 1962, when only two in ten children with intellectual disabilities were enrolled in special education classes (with many states not providing any classes at all)[25], a workshop was hosted on the St. Coletta campus, co-sponsored by the National Catholic Education Association and the Office of Vocational Rehabilitation (part of the federal government). It was called the "Workshop on the Inter-relationship of the Education of the Mentally Retarded and Vocational Rehabilitation." St. Coletta was increasingly sought after as a critical source on the future of children with intellectual disabilities as they transitioned into adulthood. The community wanted their students, and all students with disabilities to have productive lives and to be a real part of their communities. This is still the main goal of St. Coletta's mission.

In 1963 because of their dedication and success over many years, Sr. M. Anastasia and Sr. Mary Theodore were invited to Washington D.C. for the First International Awards for Achievement in the field of Mental Retardation with President John F. Kennedy presenting the evening's awards. Later that fall, along with the rest of the nation, everyone at St. Coletta was devastated by the assassination of President Kennedy. They were affected by his loss for many reasons. Besides President Kennedy being Rosemary's brother, in the few short years of his administration, he had made great strides in the fields of education and treatment of individuals with disabilities. The loss to the community was a very personal one.

In 1964, a great change happened when Sr. M. Anastasia stepped down from her 39 year tenure as the superintendent. Her work, however, continued. She worked as public relations director, a business consultant and performed countless other duties. The reins were handed over to Sr. Mary Theodore who, simultaneously, directed the Cardinal Stritch Graduate Program and the lab school for the college practicum at St. Coletta. The School was reorganized into a six member team, with everyone sharing responsibilities for the efficient running of the school program.

A new school building, St. James Hall, was built and opened in 1964. They were proud of their shoe repair shop that adult clients ran with skill. Music continued to be emphasized and, after much demand, the 44 member chorus recorded an album playing the songs they loved singing. It was called the "Voices of St. Coletta". It was so popular that three more albums were recorded and sold over the years. I was able to find three used volumes on Amazon and decided to digitize them for the St. Coletta archives. Staff were able to send me the missing fourth album so that the entire set is now available for anyone who wants to listen. Hearing the chorus's enthusiastic voices from so long ago is a truly memorable experience.

Never content to rest on their laurels, in 1964, Sisters from the different school programs, including their superintendent, Sr. Mary Theodore, traveled to Denmark to attend a scientific workshop on the "Study of Mental Deficiency." Educating themselves on current disability studies was crucial in

58

making sure their own program continued to make advancements in care and education.

While the focus of St. Coletta in 1964 was still heavily invested in the school program, that year there seemed to be the beginnings of a sea change for the future. This change focused on what was happening to the students when they became adults. It was preceded and influenced by some challenges and decisions that were hard on everyone associated with the community.

One of the most agonizing decisions made by the administration in 1964 was to lower the numbers of elderly and most demanding adult residents living at St. Coletta. This decision was a very difficult and painful one. The main impetus for this change was because the community was still almost entirely run by Sisters. The Sisters were aging themselves and they physically could just not manage handling this growing population of aging adult residents. With the combination of the students and adults being served now numbering almost 500, a decision was ultimately and sadly made by the administrative board to decrease the adult population by 100 members.

Some of the residents had no family and those adults were promised lifetime care. For those who had families it was a different story. Some of the residents involved were transferred to a new residence in Illinois that was run by the Brothers of the Good Shepherd. Later the Brothers also opened a community in Ohio and elderly male residents were able to transfer there. The women involved also found compassionate placements. In 1964, with other residential options rarely available, it was a very stressful time for everyone, including the Sisters of St. Francis of Assisi. They had devoted their lives to the people involved.

This is a situation that has happened across the country for many years. I have personally seen it happen in the past ten years with other disability communities in Wisconsin. In the present, this situation is generally caused by state and federal funding shortages, sometimes necessitating reduction in programming and the closure of disability organizations. Sometimes closures are caused by the organizations involved not meeting state and federal guidelines. Disturbingly, sometimes closures happen because organizations have been abusing or neglecting their clients. (This was not a factor in the Wisconsin communities that I mentioned above).

With this situation in mind, the Sisters of St. Coletta and the administrative board decided they needed to re-evaluate their plan for their transitioning students. For most young adults with intellectual disabilities across the country and at St. Coletta, the plan for them was to enter a sheltered workshop program. Until quite recently, this was still overwhelmingly the only option for many adults with disabilities after they finished their education at age 21. Changes in federal and state laws are now strongly emphasizing moving away from this model. In those states that have not changed their laws, it is a common occurrence for capable disabled adults to spend their days in sheltered workshops. Vocational rehabilitation organizations continue to struggle, in 2021, to find acceptance for competitive employment for their clients.

I have mixed feelings about sheltered workshops. It would be ideal for every person, no matter the severity of their disability, to be able to find employment in the community and to be paid equitably for it. Practically though, it is highly improbable that this would be an option for everyone. For some individuals with severe disabilities, sheltered workshops - with no competitive pressures - might be the only solution for them to have a fulfilling experience. The matter of equitable pay is a complex and sensitive one and there are strong disability advocates on both sides of this issue.

St. Coletta's plan for their transitioning students, in 1964, was to create a program to try to get their young adults out of working in a sheltered workshop environment and instead working in the local community. This continues to be the plan for St. Coletta 57 years later. It is their goal, for all clients who are capable and interested, to be able to work in the local community. It is something the organization strives for every day.

The St. Coletta Habilitation Program began in earnest in January of 1965. They planned a wide range of services to help with social growth, independent living skills, and vocational training. They assisted with job placement and provided continuing support in those jobs. Each prospective participant was evaluated for their strengths and weaknesses. Sr. Sheila Haskett, who had assumed the responsibility of the school program the year before, headed up this new program and was instrumental in the coming years not only in the Habilitation Program's success, but also to the future of St. Coletta.

For the new trainees to be completely ready to enter the program, it was decided the focus of the St. Coletta School needed to change as well, with an ultimate goal of working and living the community. Some of the initial trainees came from St Coletta's own sheltered workshop. Those workers, who were evaluated and deemed the most capable of living successful lives in the community, were the first candidates. There were a number of other factors in play. Family support was considered crucial. Some families did not like the idea and preferred their children to remain in a more sheltered setting. The leaders of the new program knew that without family support as these young adults moved into the community setting, they would have a much greater chance of failure.

Forty sheltered workshop workers were chosen. The new trainees were well known by the Sisters and had proven themselves with their dedication to working within the St. Coletta community. They knew these individuals would do well in new job settings within the local community. The program also made a bold move in reaching out to young adults (over the age of 16) who had not previously been a part of St. Coletta. They admitted commuting clients, as well as the residential ones. Trainees from outside of Wisconsin were sponsored by their individual states. By the end of the first year, they proudly announced that 38 of their trainees had been employed in the community. Considering both the size of the rural community and the mindset of employers when it comes to hiring people with disabilities (even today), this was a remarkable and auspicious beginning.

St. Coletta was continually trying to think of new ways to engage the local community. This had so many benefits besides generating donations. It helped create jobs for the new trainees and also helped make the residents more welcome and accepted as they shopped and participated in local events. In 1964, a school auxiliary was formed to include welcoming local volunteers to assist in many different aspects. Volunteers helped in the classrooms, offices, and most importantly, in giving one on one attention to students and clients. This was especially beneficial to those without family close by. The volunteers were trained before working with students to make sure they treated the children respectfully and compassionately.

In 1965, Sr. Sheila Haskett stepped away from her many duties to pursue a doctoral program. She received a doctoral fellowship at the University of Wisconsin, Madison. She was given the fellowship in recognition of the many lay teaching students St. Coletta had trained for the state of Wisconsin since 1949. Special education teachers now continued their Master's degree education in correlation between St. Coletta and Cardinal Stritch College.

The University of Wisconsin created a three-year research program at St. Coletta that year to study and improve the interactions between people with disabilities and counselors. Sr. Mary Theodore was also called away to accept an assignment as a consultant in Washington D.C. at the Federal Office of Education. Her expertise was much sought after in helping to create a growing amount of public education programs and services for children with intellectual disabilities.

In helping to prepare the oldest St. Coletta School students to both live and work in the community, and to prepare for the Habilitation program, a "Buy and Learn Shop" was opened in the school. The students could act in different aspects as both customers and workers. These type of in school shops are now a common part of educational programs for students with disabilities. St. Coletta's shop was many years ahead of the current school programs.

St. Coletta programs, in their communities located in three states, had moved into serving individuals from preschool until the end of their lives. Their programs covered many different populations and services. Their highly trained staff were members of many different local and national organizations

61

involved in the disability spectrum. The early dreams of the first Sisters, to have specially educated teachers working with their students, had been realized and succeeded beyond all expectations. Besides the special education teachers, there were also speech therapists and counselors to provide group therapy to assist students with their social skills. Every aspect of life was considered and taught to help their students and clients live their best lives.

In 1966, in recognition of their lengthy and admirable contributions to individuals with disabilities, the Kennedy Foundation presented the Sisters of Saint Francis of Assisi the "Joseph P. Kennedy Jr. Foundation International Service Award". The Award came with a $50,000 prize and a trophy. The money was split between St. Coletta's different programs to be used for different projects.

Through the University of Wisconsin, a group from Pakistan came to observe and learn about St. Coletta's methods. Visitors from other countries became a regular occurrence as they came to learn more about providing better educations and services for their citizens with disabilities.

Despite their many efforts to engage the local community, donations and involvement were still not what St. Coletta hoped for. Unlike the early days of picnic gatherings, fundraisers and barn building, they knew they had to work harder to create more connections and support. To try to create more goodwill and support, the 40 member St. Coletta Chorus toured 6 local counties. It was arranged for them to stay with local families to create further opportunities for engagement. They were a popular group. In 1973 they were selected from 75 other groups to perform with Pearl Bailey at the Annual Meeting of the President's Committee on Employment of the Handicapped in Washington D.C.

It was during this time period in the U.S., and across the world, that the amount of women who were both becoming and remaining Sisters had greatly begun to decrease. This effectively meant the average age of the Sisters at St. Coletta increased and their numbers serving the community decreased. In 1967, there with 98 Sisters down from a high of 103 only 4 years earlier. This number would continue to spiral downwards over the next few decades. The aging Sisters worked extremely long hours, often working two shifts and more than one job. This forced St. Coletta to hire many more lay staff, up to 55 in 1967.

Hiring lay employees greatly increased the costs of running all of the programs. The Sisters had always worked without pay. This had saved an incredible amount of money and helped keep the tuition affordable. Because of the new lay staff, the tuition took a fairly large leap from $125 to $175 a month. The Sisters continued their work in teaching. Lay workers were hired for more general services, including child care and personal care workers, kitchen workers, etc.

In late 1967, as one of the most illustrious honors that St. Coletta has received over the years, Sr. Mary Theodore, as the Superintendent of the community, was invited to a ceremony at the White House for the signing by President Lyndon Johnson of H.R. 6430 (90th): "An Act to amend the public health laws relating to mental retardation to extend, expand, and improve them, and for other purposes." One of the purposes of this amendment was to provide money to colleges and non-profits for the purposes of educating teachers in the field of "mental retardation." This was an area in which St. Coletta was leading the nation. Sr. Mary Theodore received one of the pens used to sign the Act which now has a place of honor on St. Coletta's history wall at their Jefferson headquarters.

1968 brought renovations to the St. Joseph building. As a move towards individuals eventually living in community settings, the housing areas were transforming into less dorm-like settings. The new housing offered a much more homelike living style. This was also designed to give the residents more privacy and individuality.

That year also brought the anticipation of the very first International Special Olympics. The community excitedly prepared for the athletic events in their Physical Education department. Close to 140 students participated in the various competitions held at Soldier Field in Chicago. Special Olympics continues to be an important and well-loved part of St. Coletta. My daughter and her friends train each season for various sports such as swimming, bocce ball, bowling, basketball, skiing, and track and field. Many clients bring home regional and state medals every year. In 2018, a St. Coletta contingent, which included Daniela, traveled back to Soldier Field for a celebration of the 50th Anniversary of that first Special Olympics. They had an incredible day with lots of activities and events.

Sr. Sheila Haskett finished her doctoral program in 1968 and the next year she and two Sisters (Sr. Coletta Dunn and Sr. Gabrielle Kowalski) from Cardinal Stritch College created a new program to train Special Religious Educators. St. Coletta itself also developed a pilot program at the Madison Wisconsin Diocese for the religious education of children with intellectual disabilities. It was a rousing success with many participants.

After dedicated service for 35 years, Monsignor James Feider retired due to health issues. Monsignor Feider provided so much to the community over his many years of service. He loved the people at St. Coletta so much he chose to retire to a cottage on campus with his sister.

As the decade ended, changes to the school and its administration were necessary just as they had been at the beginning of the 1960s. In 1969 a planning committee did a study to determine the best plan to go forward in the changing atmosphere of special education. A new Corporate Board and a Board of Directors were formed. There was a majority of lay persons on the Board of Directors but there were also three Sisters. Sr. Sheila Haskett, Ph.D. took the initial position as the Chief Administrative Officer.

Sr. Mary Theodore, now the new Director of Public Relations, joined a delegation from the National Catholic Educational Association on a 1970 summer tour of facilities for individuals with intellectual disabilities. They visited several European countries. The goal was to gain and share knowledge in creating new ways to better educate children with disabilities. Later that year, Sr. Sheila represented the state of Wisconsin at the White House Conference of Children and Youth. This conference concentrated on studying the problems of all American children and how best to help them learn despite life's challenges.

One of biggest arguments in the area of public special education first began during the 1960s, and lasted into the 1970s and beyond. At issue was whether children with disabilities should be educated in their home schools, local special schools, or more distant boarding schools. This argument would continue and evolve over the next 4 decades. In the sixties there was no clear consensus, probably due to the fact that modern public special education was in its infancy. At least there was finally a growing consensus that these children mattered and were worthy of deserving an education that would work best for them.[26]

Remodeling of the residential areas continued, continuing to focus on creating a more homelike atmosphere, this time for the younger students. Since the living areas had been updated for the adult residents, it was directed that each child also had a right to live in a space conducive to their individuality and privacy.

In 1971, Sr. M. Anastasia Mueller was given a Governor's Citation for her lifetime service of 62 years. A new Olympic size swimming pool on campus was dedicated in her name.

1971 brought a large shift by hiring St. Coletta's very first lay administrator. Times were definitely changing. Thomas L. Atkinson became the Assistant Administrator with a background and emphasis in business administration and finance. Focusing on finances was a critical issue which the community felt was essential to the survival of the community.

That same year, in trying to find ways to help the most able of the oldest students to reach a higher level of independence, driver's education was offered. They enlisted the local high school for classes. The University of

Wisconsin provided simulator experience. I'm sure their families never imagined this would be a possibility for their children when they were younger.

The statistics for that year reflected the continuing changes to the community. In 1963, there were only 13 lay staff. In eight years that number had sharply increased to 72. The number of Sisters continued to steadily decrease and was now down to 83. The students and adults being served also grew smaller, down to 362 from 505 in 1959. As more public school systems began to embrace special education in a positive way, families were more inclined to keep their children at home and send their students to their local schools.

The next year St. Coletta opened its doors to host a large conference. The National Apostolate of the Mentally Retarded welcomed Dr. Jean Vanier as its keynote speaker. Dr. Vanier was internationally known for his ideas promoting inclusive living for those with intellectual disabilities. As a writer and a humanitarian, he founded L'arche in 1964. It is an international federation of inclusive communities which has now spread to over 37 countries. Dr. Vanier recently died at the age of 90, after devoting his entire life to changing the mindset of the world and its treatment of those with disabilities.

Since the community now had more living space with its lower census, a new pilot summer program was started and lasted until 1986 called ReCreation. The idea was to create "learning experiences" for up to 40 adults with disabilities who were not part of the St. Coletta program. It was open to all ages and religions and designed to give people a more independent living experience than they had living with their families. Along with the regular staff, the program employed people from colleges, seminaries and high schools. They were able to work one on one with the participants. This program also hoped to increase the students' interest in working with adults with disabilities.

In 1972, a parent conference was held called "Life Planning for the Retarded." Its focus was on the subject "What happens after I am gone?" Almost all families, who have a family member who needs lifelong financial, living and social support, consider this one of their greatest worries. The conference included vital information on estate planning and Social Security. In 1972, government funding solely focused on those individuals with disabilities who were living in hospitals and institutions. It wasn't until 1981 that the "Omnibus Budget Reconciliation Act" began to slowly offer funding to deinstitutionalize individuals with disabilities. It would take many more years for this to become a more widespread concept.

The school began some new learning paths with modular scheduling and team teaching. The goal was to provide a more individualized learning atmosphere to cater to each student's strengths and weaknesses. The school continued to be involved with the local community of Jefferson. In a nod to its heritage, Jefferson had (and still has) a lively annual German festival called Gemutlichkeit that has a parade with floats and they traditionally crown a "king" and "queen". The school had its own float which won the Mayor's Trophy in 1972. The St. Coletta band proudly rode atop the float playing German songs.

The state and federal government began to increasingly set new standards and certifications. As a non-profit who had not previously relied on government funding, St. Coletta had been exempt. This began to change. In order for out of state students to receive funding for tuition, in 1973, the school had to receive state certification as a licensed child care facility. In the coming decades when the government began providing funding for individuals with disabilities to live in the community, St. Coletta had to adapt to meet all the qualifications for that funding as well.

In 1973, the new indoor swimming pool named for Sister Anastasia was completed. This new addition was greatly enjoyed for the health and recreational benefits it provided, to not only the students and adult residents, but also to the staff. Several new lay registered nurses were added to the staff to direct the health services.

Later held that year was a grand celebration for the 125th anniversary of the Sisters of St. Francis of Assisi. The event featured photos of the earliest years. Everyone marveled at how much that small group of dedicated women

Celebrating a birthday with Sister Sheila Haskett

had achieved. Their inspiration was the bedrock for everything that had been accomplished since those challenging first days.

Swimming on a hot summer day - under the careful watch of a Sister

Mary Noone - one of the first students at St. Coletta School - is buried at the st. Coletta cemetery -

1967 - Sister Mary Theodore with President Lyndon Johnson at the White House

Sister Mary Theodore Hegeman - teacher, leader, author, humanitarian

Chapter 9

From its simple beginnings in the early part of the century, St. Coletta had become, by 1974, a complex organization with many different departments. While all of the departments shared the goals and ideals of the community, each one was unique. Sr. Mary Theodore listed all the current departments in her "History of St. Coletta" book. They were - Alverno, Health Services, Public Relations, Religion Program, Residence Program, School Program, Resident Workers, Habilitation, Business Office, Farm and Grounds, Food Service, Laundry, Maintenance, Social Services, and a new Fund Development Department. Each department had their own head and everyone met regularly to keep the organization cohesive. Since my daughter has been part of the community I have seen that same high level of diversity in departments and similar efforts to bring everyone together for their common goals. It is because of their ability to continue to come together, grow, transition and adapt that St. Coletta has been able to thrive while satisfying the ever changing requirements of the disability movement.

The school continued to make itself available to host conferences. They hosted the 2nd Annual Council for Exceptional Children Action Conference in 1974. This conference involved the Arc, as well as federal officials involved in creating legislation for children and adults with disabilities. They spoke about subjects ranging from marriage and sex, to insurance and the growing community living movement. By hosting these events the staff was always up to date on any current and future changes in policy.

In late 1974, there were four separate occasions to celebrate. The first was the resurgence of the annual St. Coletta Picnic. It had always been a much loved event. A staff member led the push to again make this gathering an annual tradition. The Annual Family Picnic continues to this day as a way for St. Coletta families, clients and staff to celebrate and reconnect.

The next celebration that year was the 125th Anniversary of the day when the Motherhouse of the Sisters of Saint Francis of Assisi was first located at St. Coletta in Jefferson. It was actually a double anniversary since it had also been 70 years since the opening of the school.

The third event to rejoice was the blessing of a new building, St. Francis Hall. This building had three separate living areas for men. The mission continued to emphasize creating a home-like atmosphere for all of the residents.

To round out the year of wonderful gatherings, in October, a special invitation was sent out to local community residents who had never visited St. Coletta. They were invited to attend an Open House. 400 people came and were treated to a concert by the Voices of St. Coletta, a tour by the older students, a slide show of the school and refreshments. The involvement and interest of St. Coletta's neighbors continued to be essential to the community's success.

During that decade, a new emphasis was placed on the organization of the library. The library was used by the students, residents and staff. Students from Cardinal Stritch helped to classify books and help provide new books and magazines.

In 1975, while the Voices of St. Coletta went on a concert tour, other adult clients joined six Sisters on a pilgrimage called the Allied International Faith and Light Pilgrimage. It was conducted by Jean Vanier for individuals with intellectual disabilities. Pope Paul VI had issued a "Holy Year call of renewal and reconciliation". The highlight of the tour was a visit to Rome with special ceremonies involving Pope Paul.

With the finances and viability of the community always (and still) a major concern, a new Sister joined the community as the Director of Development. Sr. Jeanne d'Arc Omilan created a series of projects designed to increase visibility and funding. The never ending efforts for non-profits to raise funds require ingenuity to highlight what makes them worthy of donations. St. Coletta has certainly proved, and continues to prove, its worthiness. Many of the staff belonged to local and national organizations that benefitted individuals with disabilities and these staff members did their part to raise awareness and funds by spreading the word of the organization's good works.

A very sad event occurred on July 25, 1975. Monsignor James W. Feider, who had devoted his adult life to serving God and St. Coletta, died. He was grieved by the entire community. His enthusiasm and support for the people that he served truly helped make St. Coletta the incredible achievement that it was, and is. He was fortunate to have celebrated his 50th anniversary as a priest just a few months before earning his eternal rest in Heaven. The next year, Sr. Anastasia Mueller finally left St. Coletta to live at the home for retired Sisters located in St. Francis. St. Mary Theodore said of her leaving, "Her leadership as superintendent, 1925-1964, was instrumental in developing programs, increasing enrollment, and providing facilities for the ever-growing number of children enrolled at the school. Her departure from St. Coletta's marked and end of an era".[27]

1975 marked a change that would impact both the St. Coletta School and the rest of the country. That was the year "The Education of All Handicapped Children Act (PL 94-142)" passed and was enacted by the federal government. This new law required free, appropriate public education for all students with disabilities in the least restrictive setting. (This Act was later renamed The Individuals With Disabilities Education Act (IDEA).) The law was a huge victory for families in their battle to get their children the educational services they needed, for no cost, and right in their local communities.

St. Coletta rejoiced that the population they cared about would finally be entitled to the same type of education as their non-disabled counterparts. They also knew this new law would drastically affect the St. Coletta School. The number of families who would seek an education for their child at St. Coletta, or at any other residential private school for children with intellectual disabilities, would gradually begin to decrease.

For the rest of the year, the staff conducted studies and interviews to determine the best path forward for the community. They focused the study on "normalization" for students and adults and emphasized residents' rights and freedom of choice. They had already been expanding their habilitation program for young adults and they knew this was a good direction to focus on moving forward.

As the 1970s continued, and the research from the studies were collated, they began to present their findings to others, including at an international symposium in Ireland. The community began to pay attention to creating more "normal" settings in all facets of the residents' lives. Allowing more interaction between men and women and more privacy and independence were key efforts in their initial plans. The residents moved freely in the local community and participated in adult classes and outside recreational opportunities.

On the special education front, with the U.S. beginning to expand services to every child, the Sisters began to increase their focus on the lives of children with disabilities who lived internationally. In 1978, Sr. Sheila Haskett gave a workshop in Africa (Sudan) to train teachers in special education. Sr. Rebecca Burke presented a paper at the "First World Congress on the Future Of Special Education" in Scotland. Her focus was on bioethics. The Sisters' goals were lofty. They wanted children all over the world to be treated with dignity and educated no matter where they lived and how impacted they were by their disabilities.

On the home front school life continued, even as services expanded and changed. Even with the new laws regarding public education, transitions took time and families only gradually began switching their children to public school settings, especially those families with older students.

That same year, Sr. Anastasia Mueller passed away and was buried at St. Coletta. I visited her there in 2019, seeing her simple headstone along with the ones of many former Sisters, students and residents. It was moving to see them all together in this special place that had been home to them for most of their lives.

In 1979, a committee was formed to plan the much anticipated Diamond Jubilee for the St. Coletta School. 75 years of dedication and service were worth celebrating in a big way. There were a number of events over the entire year for the staff, residents, benefactors and clergy. There were picnics, barbecues, dances and prayer services. Sr. Joyce Meyer, who was then the Director of the Sisters of St. Francis of Assisi, said this -

"A time of remembering and celebration, like this 75th Jubilee, enables us to acknowledge the entire history that is St. Coletta's. It allows us the opportunity to ask pardon for the shortcomings of the past, as well as to delight in the countless good that has been done over the years. It is a time to remember the many sacrifices made, as well as the joy experienced."[28]

As the next decade began, St. Coletta knew that to stay viable and relevant, as a community assisting people with disabilities, they would have to become an organization that followed all federal and state guidelines. New regulations and laws were evolving to set standards of care. The organization received their license to operate as CBRF (Community Based Residential Facility) in 1980. This license was required for all of the adult resident living spaces (for clients over 18). As some students were also over 18, their residential areas had to be licensed as well. The transition to meet all of these requirements was complicated, time-consuming and frustrating. That is true to this day. When Daniela moved to a different type of housing at St. Coletta a few years ago, there was endless paperwork and many meetings that were required by the state before her move could happen.

Nationwide in the early 1970s, a new movement grew out of the accelerating disability rights movement. "The Independent Living Movement" focused on a new paradigm stating that individuals with disabilities should be the ones to develop their own plans for their lives; this included education, rehabilitation and housing. Two of the leaders of the movement, Ed Roberts and Judith Heumann, had fought successful battles at their universities to be able to live in college housing, despite having severe physical disabilities. Through these two activists, and many others, a new collaboration was formed that emphasized the rights of all individuals, no matter the severity of their disability, in deciding what was best for themselves. Taken from the Independent Living Institute -

"Independent Living is a philosophy and a movement of people with disabilities who work for self-determination, equal opportunities and self-respect."[29]

In 1980, St. Coletta also began its own independent living movement by beginning a transition of adult clients moving into community housing outside of the St. Coletta property. In their first venture, they purchased a convent in Madison for young women within the community. Two Sisters were

71

in charge, including the last remaining Sister who still works at St. Coletta, the wonderful Sr. Grace Schauf. Everyone loves Sr. Grace and her long years of dedicated service continue to impact the community on a daily basis. The new property was considered ideal because it was central to local services, employment possibilities and entertainment. From this point on, the community moved slowly and cautiously into the new, and still sometimes controversial, adventure of having clients living out in the broader community. It would take another 20-25 years to fulfill the goal of having every client living off of the campus.

The year 1981 was proclaimed the International Year of Disabled Persons (IYDP) by the United Nations. This designation was given in hopes of promoting the ideals of better living conditions around the world for individuals with disabilities. It also had a goal of making them an equal part of society across the globe. The IYDP was fully embraced by St. Coletta and events were planned all during the year to celebrate and promote it. Sr. Mary Theodore wrote, "that it would create greater understanding and deeper respect for our handicapped brothers and sisters in Christ."[30] Within the Catholic community, there was also an emphasis on being more inclusive and bringing people with disabilities into the everyday life of the church.

In 1981, after providing her incredible leadership for over a decade of great transition and growth, Sr. Sheila Haskett stepped down as the School Administrator. In her time as administrator she had initiated a number of new programs, including the family camp program, the resident care program and the Alverno personal care program. She also opened the first group home for residential living in Madison for young women who had graduated from the school. After resigning, she went on a one year sabbatical to both travel and study. Sr. Elaine Weber, who had joined St. Coletta the previous year as an assistant administrator, took over her role. Sr. Elaine was a very experienced leader who had served in various roles in disability education.

A new job training program was added to the high school program that year. It was called, "Becoming Independent: A Living Skills System." This was designed to assist graduates once they left school to find competitive employment.

The appointment of more lay senior staff continued to grow. In 1982, the first lay Principal was hired. His name was Michael Weber. Carson Fixmer was also hired as the new Residence Director, both replacing Sisters who had held those positions.

With all of the transitions in programming, as St. Coletta moved towards primarily serving adults, a donation of one million dollars was made by Rosemary Kennedy's family and was extremely welcomed. The donation was made in honor of Rosemary's mother, Rose Kennedy's 93rd birthday. The funds were designated to be used "to facilitate a program that would serve as a national model of aging persons with mental retardation." As people with intellectual disabilities began to live much longer, due to better health services, having housing and programming for this population could not have been more timely and essential. The Wisconsin State Journal wrote about the donation and the new program in July of 1983. "Mary Bellis, an administrative secretary at St. Coletta said that over a year ago the school wanted to expand its program for elderly residents. 'We found that there just weren't any models around. The elderly, even those that aren't mentally retarded, are just a neglected part of society.' The article continued, "Instead of living in a dormitory, the older residents will share an apartment with one other person; instead of storing their belongings in lockers, they will have closets." Ms. Bellis said, 'It's all part of self-worth, self-image. You can't build those up if you don't have to make any choices.'"[31]

The community decided to purchase a new vacation home in nearby Genesee Lake. The previous vacation spot, Lake Beulah, was further away and not as convenient and safe for swimming. For some adult residents without families, this spot was their only chance to experience a holiday away from their St. Coletta home.

Transition services for older students with disabilities were beginning to be practiced in public school. Moving from a academically based program into the real world is a bit of a shock for all teenagers. For individuals with disabilities, learning to function as an adult in both their home and in any possible workplace was a critical challenge. In 1983, St. Coletta developed a new program to help their students make that transition process smoother and more effective. They wanted there to be a transitional step between the school and the Resident Worker program. Academic skills were focused on practical applications. For instance, math focused on measuring for kitchen skills and money management. They encouraged those in the program to be more mature in their interactions with staff and other students. This was and continues to be something that my daughter, and others with intellectual and developmental disabilities, struggle with. Recognizing physical boundaries and space are sometimes a challenge. Learning not to hug everyone in work situations is an important skill.

After the organization's hard work to meet all of the requirements for government funding, in 1983, St. Coletta was delighted to find out that HUD (Housing and Urban Development) had granted them the approval and funds to build thirty units for adult housing in the local community. The units were divided between three group homes and an apartment complex. All of the new residential units were to be built within the town of Jefferson. Community living was beginning to happen in earnest, and with it a new era as St. Coletta focused on independent living. This focus gradually developed to make them what they are today, an organization where every single client is living, and enjoying, their life amongst their local community.

Chapter 10

In 1984, the planning and construction of the new community HUD homes forged ahead. Having people with disabilities living in community neighborhoods was still a new concept. There was initial pushback from some their new neighbors. Although the town of Jefferson had a long, positive relationship with St. Coletta, this venture brought out some skepticism about whether "those people" would be good neighbors. Across the country, as the community living movement began to become a reality, there were a great deal of "not in my neighborhood" objections going on in city council meetings. Fortunately for St. Coletta, Jefferson's city council voted unanimously to approve the housing. As the town began to see the lovely homes being built, and their new neighbors moving in, the initial fears and prejudice began to disappear.

The future of the St. Coletta School continued its slow decline in students. The administration knew the decline was not going to turn around. They began preparing for the eventual transition of the organization to providing services for adults only. The emphasis on adult services kept growing. For the first time, adults who had not been a part of the school were being admitted into a program designed just for them. This program was not undertaken lightly. As the adult clients aged a research project was begun to provide baseline information for the future. The goal was to plan progressive programming so that the clients would not have to move on to other housing options, such as nursing homes, in their last years.

"Aging in place" is now a common and desired solution for both individuals with disabilities and the elderly. This term is defined as "the ability to live in one's own home and community safely, independently and comfortably, regardless of age, income or ability level" (from the U.S. Centers for Disease Control and Prevention.) This concept was almost unheard of in 1984 when St. Coletta made this concept part of their future.

To continue their ongoing efforts of outreach to the local community, a new Thanksgiving tradition was started to welcome lonely residents of Jefferson for a Thanksgiving Mass and holiday dinner. Since many more of the St. Coletta clients were now truly members of the local community, it was essential to show the rest of the community that they were appreciated as neighbors.

Sr. Mary Theodore wrote a new book that year titled, "Developmental Disability: A Family Challenge". It was honored by the Wisconsin Council for Exceptional Children. This book was one of my resources. I read the stories of individual families who had come to St. Coletta and related to their experiences of living with and supporting their children as they became adults. Sr. Mary

Theodore was never content to help only those families that came to St. Coletta. Her goal was to help as many families as she could around the globe.

The book included stories about individuals as they moved towards adulthood and all of the challenges that arose as puberty emerged and progressed. Sr. Mary Theodore focused on sexuality, legal encounters and the crises that families faced. She also encouraged the continuing development of a spiritual life to assist with the challenges that all people face in adulthood. I was impressed with the frankness and honesty in which Sr. Mary Theodore approached these sensitive subjects. Sexuality can still be a taboo subject when it concerns people with intellectual and developmental disabilities.

In 1985, Sr. Margaret Peter, the sign language teacher at St. Coletta, was recognized for her publication of thirty different language workbooks for nonverbal and deaf children with 180,000 copies sold all over the country. They were so sought after that a special education company bought the publishing rights for the entire inventory.

With the funding from the million dollar donation from the Kennedy family, the new Rosemary Kennedy wing for older adults was near completion. An adult day care program for the aging population also began.

The staff and administration has always been cognizant of of the terminology and titles that they use. Not only do they want to use words that reflect respect for those that they serve, but also use them for the staff that serves with such dedication. In 1985, the titles for residential staff were changed from child care workers to Residential Living Assistants and Residential Living Supervisors. This change came about because of the transition to serving more adults within the community. There have continued to be changes in titles, even in the past six years that Daniela has been a part of the community. There is always a drive to find the best way to designate staff titles, duties and responsibilities.

A sign of the times came in 1985 when IBM computers were added for use in all departments. A new telephone system was also installed. St. Coletta had a wide range of services and programming that required accurate documentation, especially for governmental oversight purposes. Communication and record keeping was and, is still, a high priority. The new technology was helpful in making sure that goals were met and information was distributed to all those who needed it. In 1986, photo ID cards for both staff and residents were added to help with security. Because students and adult residents frequently flew back and forth from the campus to visit their families, the IDs were essential at the airports, as staff went to drop off and pick up clients.

In that time period, St. Coletta had established a supported workshop program called the Work Activity Center. It was used by clients with more severe disabilities and also by workers who hoped to transition to community jobs. The Activity Center provided opportunities for people who never thought they would be able to earn money at a job. It provided useful skills and pride for completing their daily projects.

Disability rights were becoming more recognized across the country. People fought the discrimination that had long prevented them from living their lives with the equal rights of those who were considered non-disabled. In 1986, St. Coletta set up a Human Rights Committee to make sure they were protecting the rights of all of their students and clients. The committee included student representatives and set up a Human Rights Policy with grievance procedures to be followed and supervised. Since our family has been involved with St. Coletta, it's become obvious that this is an area that is still highly important to the staff and community. St. Coletta emphasizes self-advocacy for all of the clients and I'm grateful to know that Daniela and her friends are empowered to speak out if anyone tries to violate their rights.

Patricia Lawford Kennedy represented the Kennedy family as the Rosemary Kennedy Wing was opened in June of 1986. Her family's donation had contributed greatly to its construction. Many other client's families have also gone above and beyond in donating to St. Coletta over the years. Without their generous support, the community would not be what it is today.

St. Coletta was featured, along with another longstanding Wisconsin community for people with disabilities, on a 1987 CBS documentary series called "For Our Times". It was a religious series and focused on caring for those with disabilities in a religious setting. At the time, St. Coletta was the largest Catholic organization serving individuals with intellectual disabilities.

After her many years of service at St. Coletta, Sr. Mary Theodore finally decided to retire from her final position as the Director of Public Relations in 1987. This did not end her service completely. St. Coletta was her life's mission and her mission continued. She continued to write and volunteer in as many ways as she could find to make a difference. She began work on a new booklet, for sale in the community gift shop, about the life of St. Coletta, the patroness of the community.

That same year a new program was created for the growing lay staff. It was called "Resident for a Day". Staff members were assigned to shadow a resident for a whole day. It was designed to create empathy for, and experience briefly, the life of those that they cared for. Both the staff and clients benefited from this program. The clients felt pride and became closer to their assigned staff member. For the staff, it gave them new insights into the variety of experiences, choices and the independence afforded to each person that they shadowed. Many of us have been part of shadow experiences, as we were being trained or were training someone in a new job. Shadowing those that you serve provides an entirely different and unique perspective.

The school began to transition to a twelve month program, splitting up vacation time in shorter periods throughout the year. The summer sessions of school had a different focus that both staff and students embraced. Academics were taught in the mornings, but the afternoons were camp-like with lots of physical skills and outdoor time. More time was spent in the community and there was an emphasis on vocational skills, art, music and dance. The program was set up in mini-courses that were designed with careful objectives and lesson plans.

St. Coletta held its first large dinner auction at the historic Pfister Hotel in Milwaukee in 1987. Three hundred guests enjoyed a beautiful evening with the profits going to the Endowment Fund. It was such a successful event that there were immediate plans for another event the next year. This continued for some years before ending. In 2018, this event was revived, as I wrote about in Chapter 7, as the "Lead the Charge" Gala dinner auction and held at the, still prestigious, Pfister Hotel.

1988 brought an event called the Very Special Arts Festival, celebrating the artistic talents of the students and adult residents. Artists who specialized in different media came to share their skills with all who attended. Very Special Arts (now called VSA) is an international organization that was founded in 1974 by Jean Kennedy Smith, one of Rosemary's sisters. It celebrated the creation of music, visual arts, drama and dance by, and for, individuals with disabilities.

As St. Coletta continued to look for new ways to train clients to work in competitive jobs in the community, they decided to build a large greenhouse that could be used to supply plants to local retailers and also employ and teach clients. This was St. Coletta's first venture in marketing products to the private sector. In April of 1988, the Milwaukee Journal Times wrote about the new enterprise. "The fact of the matter is that the St. Coletta staff realizes that many residents, with proper training, can enter normal society and become independent, productive citizens," "Sister Elaine Weber, the school administrator said." "It is our plan that the operation be self-sustaining," Weber said of the greenhouse, "It will create an environment in which St. Coletta residents can gain skills that are usable in the job market, or provide work for those need to be productive but require a sheltered environment."[32]

That same year a new summer program called RespiteCare replaced the former summer program called ReCreation. This program offered a one week camp experience for children with disabilities who were not attending the St. Coletta School. Knowing that their child was having a fun, safe experience

78

with well-trained and enthusiastic staff, many families were able to take a vacation for the first time in years.

A large airy home was built just outside of the town of Jefferson in 1988. It was named St. Agnes. This beautiful, well-designed house has been Daniela's home since 2016. Some of her housemates/friends have lived there for many years. Originally it was built to house 14 young women with goals of becoming more independent. It has since been renovated and now can house up to eight women in their own private spaces. The women are proud of their home and help keep it clean and beautiful.

Daniela loves living there with her friends. She considers them her family. The home allows each client the opportunity for as much privacy or socialization as they desire. Daniela usually needs some quiet and privacy after a busy day of classes, activity or work. She then joins her family for dinner and catches up on everyone's day. They all know and worry when someone has had a rough day or isn't feeling well. They help each other out with chores during those times. While they sometimes annoy each other like any family, they are there to provide each other with support and encouragement.

Another home was opened that year at Capistrano, formerly a group home for adult men. It provided one on one care for individuals who needed a higher level of care. St. Coletta's clients have a large spectrum of different challenges and needs. These needs are individually met, with care and commitment, in the housing and programming settings that best meet their specific needs.

1988 brought an emphasis on evaluating and researching new programs. The Director of Development, Evaluation and Research did just that. The goal was to be creative in finding innovative ways to help each person move forward in reaching their goals, no matter how small. This effort continues. Daniela has a yearly meeting with her supervising staff, from both St. Coletta and the state of Wisconsin. With guidance, she sets her own goals for what she wants to achieve during the coming year. During the year those goals are rechecked to see if she is reaching them and, if not, what creative ways can be found to help motivate her. Every single client has a meeting like Daniela's and is celebrated for the positive achievements they make during the year and encouraged to keep working to pursue new goals.

Sr. Mary Theodore, still striving and writing in retirement, wrote her book called "A History of St. Coletta School" in 1989. This book was expanded in 1995 for an updated version titled "A History of St. Coletta 1904-1994." She wrote on the cover that she "compiled" the book, but she was far too modest. I honestly don't think I could have written this book without her meticulous documentation and attention to detail. I have relied on it, heavily and gratefully, for all of her research and the heartfelt portrayals of the events in the life of the community.

Chapter 11

As 1990 began, the community of St. Coletta began a decade in which they would experience some of their largest transitions since the school was first established in 1904. Before the beginning of the new millennium the school, which had been founded almost one hundred years before, would close its doors for the last time. Its closure would not, with God's Grace, mark the end of the community.

Two pieces of federal legislation that became law in 1990 would permanently change the trajectory of both children and adults with disabilities in the United States of America. I remember distinctly watching the news as President Bush signed these Acts into law. At the time, while I was really pleased to see these changes, I watched without feeling a connection to them. I wasn't then personally involved with anyone who had a significant disability. I didn't know that there was a baby in an orphanage bed in Romania that would soon be entering our lives. I didn't know that the baby would need those new laws to help her negotiate her education and her life. The laws, while not perfect, have positively impacted Daniela's life and millions of other lives.

The first of these laws, for children from infancy to adulthood, was the IDEA. The Individuals with Disabilities Education Act ensured that all children would finally receive an education that would serve them according to their individual needs. The previous law, the Education for All Handicapped Children Act, was enacted in 1975. It had failed to emphasize inclusive education and services for the very youngest children. This new law ensured that all children with disabilities were eligible to receive a free and appropriate public education in the least restrictive environment, including regular public classrooms. The law governs how states and public agencies provide special education services from infancy until adulthood. While schools can still pay for children to be educated in private special education settings, if they cannot provide the needed services, the emphasis was, and is, for school systems to provide those services themselves.

The other historic Act that passed that same year was the ADA - The Americans with Disabilities Act. This sweeping civil rights legislation would provide protections in many aspects of people's lives, including employment, housing, public access, and protection from discrimination. With these two new laws, everyone working at, and those served at, St. Coletta would be impacted in monumental ways. While they have changed life positively and profoundly for people with disabilities, the IDEA and the ADA have had limitations. They continue to evolve over the years to address issues such as abuse, poverty, and equal treatment for minorities.

That same year, the farming operation received an environmental award from the Jefferson County Land Conservation Department for the way in which it operated. The farm was doing very well and was able to renovate the creamery because of a large donation. It continued to serve the community with healthy food and vocational opportunities.

A new and very popular Wisconsin attraction opened in nearby Fort Atkinson, Wisconsin in 1965. The Fireside Dinner Theater brought in professional actors for wonderful stage productions and also had gourmet dining in a beautiful setting that was overseen by an executive chef. Since its beginning, Fireside has been supportive of the St. Coletta community and has welcomed its adult workers by providing training and employment. In 1990, St. Coletta celebrated a shared anniversary with the theater, celebrating 25 years of working together. That work continues today. Two of Daniela's housemates have happily worked at Fireside for many years. The theater also has many longtime theater goers amongst the staff, clients and families of St. Coletta. Daniela and I attended productions of "Annie" and "A Christmas Story" at Fireside. My husband joined us for "Cinderella" in 2021. We were amazed at the professionalism of the shows and the delicious food and hospitality.

A new strategic plan was developed, featuring five major goals in 1991. It included reaffirming the community's Franciscan values and committing to "a firm future" for everyone they served. The administration also resolved to develop systems to create more independence and integration into society. Part of creating a firm future was in developing resources both financial and human.

I'll quote the fourth goal. "To assure a quality program for the future based upon the School's historical strengths and current and future trends in society through collaborative participation with internal and external public's." (That goal, in referring to "the school" referred to not only the children, but also the adult clients being served. St. Coletta School was still the name of the organization, though its services had long expanded beyond serving children.) This goal says everything about who St. Coletta was then and who it is now. It uses and applies its remarkable heritage, while interweaving today's ideology and technology on disability services. They rely on their own ideas and also incorporate the ideas of others.

Their fifth goal discusses making a long term impact upon disability legislation, "particularly in ethical and moral concepts (concerns) and empowerment of persons with handicaps." This too is something St. Coletta has been involved in since its early years. It is why they have been invited into both state and federal policy making decisions.

The newly created job of Director of Human Resources was created in 1991. As the transition to lay staff gained momentum, a new focus was placed on recruiting highly motivated staff and training them to provide and supervise the kind of care that would reflect the high standards of the Strategic Plan. The new director also made sure the staff was fairly compensated. This is something that continues today in a very competitive workforce. Recruitment, retention and promotion of staff is essential to provide high quality care and continuity for clients.

St. Coletta's emphasis on the environment continued to grow with an annual celebration of Earth Day and an emphasis on recycling. Everyone pitched in with collecting recyclables to help protect the earth and the environment.

In their promotion of maintaining and strengthening the families of students and clients, and also in assisting in research that would help better understanding of those family relationships, St. Coletta participated in a sibling relationship study with the University of Wisconsin in 1991. The areas addressed were several, including the types and qualities of relationships and the expectations of family members for their St. Coletta student or client. The community felt an obligation to help individuals with disabilities and their families to make progress in both their education and their family stability.

In this time period, the names of people who I have come to know in the community started appearing in St. Mary Theodore's writings and in newspaper accounts of St. Coletta. One of those people is Mario Dealca. Like other long time staff members, Mario has worked in a number of different positions. In the early nineties, Mario had become the Vocational Coordinator. His department was responsible for coordinating between the work programs and the school, and helping clients develop and maintain their work skills.

Since that time period vocational services for all clients who are capable of and interested in working have been encouraged. It was these services that provided the final push needed to get Daniela into the workforce. Without their continued encouragement and training it would be very difficult for Daniela and many others at St. Coletta to keep their jobs. We are very appreciative of the combined efforts of everyone who has reminded her of her responsibilities and the benefits that a job brings her. (In 2020-21, many clients, including Daniela had to temporarily stop working because of the COVID-19 pandemic.)

In their efforts to lead and educate those working and living with people with disabilities, in 1991, a conference was held titled, "Ethical Issues for Persons Who Have Developmental Disabilities (Empowering Rights and

Responses to Fullness of Life)." It was well attended by caregivers and professionals from across the country.

In 1991, the pastoral team renewed its effort to be sure those of any faith community were able to pursue their religious practices. They involved churches from the local communities to assist them in their efforts.

In that same year, a national organization began a local chapter at St. Coletta. Best Buddies had been developed two years earlier at Georgetown University by Anthony Kennedy Shriver (Eunice's son and Rosemary's nephew). Still active at St. Coletta today, it is a program designed to unite individuals with developmental disabilities in friendships with peers who do not have disabilities. Its goal is to prevent isolation and encourage independence, inclusion in living, employment and self-advocacy. There are now nearly 2900 chapters worldwide. Daniela was nervous about being a part of the program but is now an enthusiastic participant. At St. Coletta the program has been run, since its beginning, in coordination with students at the University of Wisconsin-Whitewater.

Sr. Mary Theodore Hegeman celebrated 60 years of service in 1991. Her dedication and contributions to St. Coletta were already beyond measure. And still she continued to serve.

As clients moved off the campus and into community housing and employment, there was a new demand for consistent, safe and accessible transportation. In 1992, a Transportation Department was added to the organization. Its responsibility was to maintain the vehicles, hire drivers and coordinate rides to the campus, jobs, church and into the community. Transportation remains a vital part of the community, now with a large number of accessible vehicles. As an effort to provide assistance to the local community, the Transportation Department offers its (paid) services in providing accessible rides.

Sr. Elaine Weber resigned her Presidency at St. Coletta in 1992. A lay person, Thomas Atkinson, became the Acting President while a search began for a permanent leader.

Sr. Margaret Peter, who had been a Sister for 52 years, developed a religious education video series that year that was available to be shown on the campus TV channel.

In 1993, a decision was made to move the Golden Options Adult Day Care Center from the Alverno building to St. Francis Hall. At the time, there was a staff day care center in that building. A plan was put in place to coordinate intergenerational activities that would create positive interactions between the children and older clients.

The search for the new President led to the selection of Dr. Henry Meece Jr. to be installed as the President and CEO of St. Coletta in the fall of 1993. At the beginning of 1994, Dr. Meece began to lay the groundwork to restructure the staffing and programming in a way that would best serve each student and client. The new plan was put into action throughout the rest of the year. The goal of the plan was to provide services that would continue to encourage development and independence for each person being served.

The plan divided living areas into groups called "neighborhoods" and each neighborhood had its own supervisor called an Individual Service Coordinator. This person was responsible for 12-16 clients and the staff that worked with these clients. These coordinators were put in place so that decision making issues could be addressed in a more timely and personal level. This person would also help with budgeting and communication between clients, their staff and the administrators.

These new directions that were put into place 26 years ago were the beginning stages of St. Coletta as it is today. Over the years there have been changes in the names and the structure of leadership and programming, but the basic premise was set in place. The ability to adapt and to be open to new ideas has continued to serve and enrich the entire community.

New federal legislation was influential in the changes and services provided. The ISP - Individual Service Plan (for adult services) and IEP - Individual Education Plan (for students under the age of 22) came into play for the first time. They remain at the center of service plans for every child and adult who is entitled to disability services nationally. Annual plans and assessments make sure that these plans best serve each person. These are required and strictly regulated. While IEPs dictate a student's school life only, ISPs involve each person's entire life - home life, health services, recreation and vocational services.

Daniela's IEPs began when she entered the public school system at age 3. Our meetings involved her teachers, school therapists, administrators and her family. When Daniela was 14, she also became a valued member of the IEP team. The meetings evolved over the years, depending on her level of services. In middle and high school, she went from self contained classrooms to inclusive ones. When she was in high school, transition services came into play and gradually became the main focus of the meetings until she left the school system completely at age 20. (We decided to move on to postsecondary services outside the school system at that point. She could have remained until her 22nd birthday.)

ISPs first entered our lives when Daniela became part of the St. Coletta community in 2015. Daniela is a vital part of her ISP team, along with me, her lead support staff, her vocational coach and her state case manager.

Daniela and I were very nervous about our first meeting with her team. Her school IEP meetings had often been stressful. The reminders of those meetings weighed heavily on us.

We were in for a big surprise at her first ISP meeting at St. Coletta. These meetings, run by very experienced and caring professionals, are just the opposite of stressful. The meetings are designed to address issues that might be causing challenges in the individual's life and they focus on what is needed to help the client progress. Daniela's meetings always start with everything that she has accomplished in the past year. She literally basks in their praise. Everyone is sincere and upbeat, even when addressing difficult issues. Daniela is encouraged to take the lead and to give her own suggestions on the goals she wants to focus on in the coming year. Unlike her IEP meetings of the past, I take a backseat in the meetings, only occasionally providing information or asking questions. Daniela is respected as the adult that she is. When Daniela walks out of her ISP meeting, her head is held high and her determination to continue learning and growing are strong. St. Coletta takes what could be a frightening experience for clients and families and fills it with hope and strategies to move their lives forward in a positive way.

Computers were already a part of making the community run smoothly by the mid-nineties. As technology advanced and the internet became commonplace, St. Coletta concentrated on training all of the staff in the latest ways to facilitate communication, keep track of records, and plan the best way to coordinate their vast and diverse network of services. Everyone came together to accomplish the same goal - providing for each individual that they served in the most competent and compassionate way possible.

A Family Association was formed in 1994 to increase the interaction and community for all of the families who had someone living in the St. Coletta community. They included a newsletter to provide news and information about activities.

Although at some point this association ended, in 2019 two new family groups were formed. The first group, the "St. Coletta Family Advocacy Association", was led by fellow parent and my good friend, Mary Jo Shackelford. Its focus was on making sure families were informed about Wisconsin and federal legislation regarding disability funding and encouraging all of us to have a voice about issues affecting our family members and the continuing stagnant, less than adequate funding for home and community based services.

That same year the St. Coletta organization also started the "St. Coletta of Wisconsin Family Alliance". It focuses on a variety of things, including communication, events, volunteer opportunities, advocacy and more. At some point in the last two years, it was decided to end the Advocacy

Association since the Family Alliance was also strongly promoting advocacy opportunities. The Alliance sends out emails and also updates in the St. Coletta magazine, Homelights.

Many of the longtime families of St. Coletta have been involved in events, advocacy and volunteering for many years and know each other well. For those of us who are newer families, it has been really nice to be become part of the family community, and to support each other and our St. Coletta family members. Our love for them and St. Coletta is the common bond we all share.

As St. Coletta continued its focus on providing lifetime care for adult clients, it was increasing its initiative to provide a more holistic approach to services. They were seeking to provide care for each individual in all areas of their lives, including their physical, mental and emotional health. Recreational activities are essential in providing people joyful outlets to express themselves. To that end, a new position was added - the Director of Recreational Services. They also added recreational therapists. Each client was evaluated to find their interests and abilities for recreation and leisure skills. A grant application was made and fulfilled by the Ronald McDonald Foundation to initiate this important program.

The variety of recreational opportunities that St. Coletta continues to offer make it stand out from other disability communities. Recreation brings joy, mental and physical development, and most importantly, social engagement with each other and the wider community. Since Daniela has been at St. Coletta, booklets were sent out every few months with many activities for clients to choose from (for an extra fee). As I wrote these words in 2019, Daniela was off on a daylong boat trip/tour in downtown Milwaukee with several of her friends. The next week she went horseback riding in Lake Geneva. Every week provides new opportunities for all of St. Coletta's clients to look forward to.

The pandemic in 2020-21 temporarily curtailed most community recreational opportunities. In the summer of 2021 with almost all of the clients vaccinated, a yearly catalog was sent out for them to choose from of a large variety of trips, day outings, classes, sporting events, Special Olympics sports, Best Buddies and many other activities. Daniela joyfully signed up for a variety of activities, including a weekend trip to a horse (dude) ranch. Life at St. Coletta   continues to be an exciting adventure and the clients' lives are enriched by the opportunities.

In 1993-1994 volunteers contributed 50,000 hours of service to St. Coletta. Volunteers have always been an important part of the community. From local school and university students, to church members, sports teams and family members of staff and clients, each person provides priceless services that increase community involvement and provide positive benefits for everyone involved. They are involved in holiday performances, parades, sporting events and fundraisers. The variety of their contributions are endless and greatly appreciated.

1994 marked the 90th anniversary for the St. Coletta School. This was a multi-day event. An original play called "Visions of St. Coletta", about St. Coletta's history, was presented by the students. The next day the main event was a Liturgy of Thanksgiving, attended by the Governor, Tommy Thompson. Staff, students, clients and everyone's families attended, along with 250 Sisters of St. Francis of Assisi. A public reception followed with 1000 guests. The President of the school, Dr. Henry Meece, gave a speech which included these words, "May God continue to bless St. Coletta's as we begin our next 90 years of service to developmentally delayed persons and their families".

There were clients then who lived farther away from the main campus. They resided an hour away in Madison. The building being used was part of St. Coletta. It was called the Coletta-James Home. It had started as the transitional residence in 1980 for women who had graduated from the Vocational Rehab program. Later those women were transitioned to a more independent lifestyle and looked for employment. In 1986, the local county surrounding Madison had entered into a partnership with St. Coletta. Only local residents from that county were able to live in the home because of local funding. In 1992, the home became a "long-term residence" and then finally in 1995, it changed again to a new "Supervised Apartment Living Program". This program required a high level of independence but still offered support. Sr. Grace Schauf was, as she had been since the first clients moved to Madison in 1980, in charge of the program.

The organization decided on a name change for themselves in 1995. Since its focus as a school was slowly coming to an end, the name "St. Coletta School" no longer envisioned the adult program that was becoming its primary focus. St. Coletta of Wisconsin became the new title. This name was in line with the two other affiliate organizations that the Sisters of St. Francis of Assisi had created, St. Coletta of Massachusetts and St. Coletta of Illinois.

Before the name change happened and as the gradual change in direction was being planned, the administration requested a study to be done by an outside professional team of consultants from Seattle. The study was titled the "Report of the Program Review at St. Coletta School, Jefferson, Wisconsin, January-July, 1993." The study reflected the need for clients to have more living space and to continue to strive for their life off of the campus and into the wider community. Sr. Mary Theodore noted, "The consulting team found a higher level of functioning among St. Coletta residents than they had seen in any other residential setting during the past decade."[33]

New staff and continuing staff education, and the opportunities for staff promotions, were a priority in maintaining the staff's skills and providing sustainability in the high quality services and care provided for each client. Emphasis was placed on the individual needs and interests of each client, as was realistic goal setting. St. Coletta increased the number of lead professional staff to guide the staff working directly with clients.

One way St. Coletta continued to bring in new ideas and perspectives was the program called the Special Studies Program. Started in 1971, it had brought in international students from all over the world to do one year internships (with free room and board). They came from places like Kenya, Borneo, Brazil and Guyana, as well as many countries in Europe, plus Australia and Canada. The interns worked beside staff in many different areas. Imparting and gaining knowledge, their energy brought joy to everyone. The biggest hope for this program continued to be for each intern to return to their country to help start their own programs for individuals with disabilities. It was important to St. Coletta to share their knowledge of what could be accomplished in the area of disability education and adult programs.

Sr. Mary Theodore Hegeman finished her book, "History of St. Coletta 1904-1994" in 1995. She was 86 years old. In that book, except for the epilogue, she only spoke of herself in the third person. She had humbly tried to downplay her many accomplishments and the critical role she had played in creating the character and direction of the organization.

In the epilogue, she freely gave praise to many other Sisters, lay staff and the administration, detailing their achievements with gratitude. She especially expressed her appreciation for Sr. M. Anastasia Mueller, who came to St. Coletta in 1909. She wrote about the Sister being met on her arrival by a horse and buggy. Sr. Mary Theodore says this about Sr. Anastasia's arrival - "At the time, there were twelve Sisters, a chaplain, and three lay employees, with an enrollment of 33, many of them severely retarded. From the first day, Sister devoted herself to the mission that would become her lifework."[34] Sr. Mary Theodore could have also certainly made that last statement about herself.

There were so many Sisters who devoted their lives to their mission at St. Coletta, and elsewhere, over many years. Reading about them and their contributions made me want to know more about the current Sisters of St. Francis of Assisi . The next chapter shares just a few of those voices whom I was privileged to listen to and record.

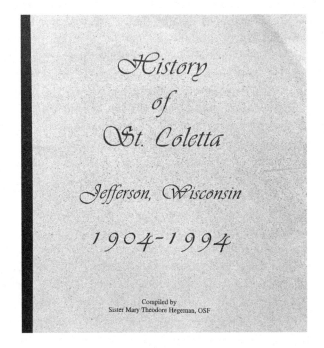

The books of Sister Mary Theodore
Hegeman, O.S.F.

Chapter 12

The Sisters

In the spring of 2018, when I first made the decision to write a book about St. Coletta of Wisconsin, I knew that I wanted to bring in the diverse voices of the individuals within the community. I have been able to find many voices through media such as newspaper accounts and through the writings of Sister Mary Theodore and other Sisters. I also have conducted interviews - in person, by phone, and through email exchanges.

I was easily able to get stories from current and past staff and from clients and their families. People were eager to share their love of the community, and their lives as part of the St. Coletta family. There was another important group of voices that came to the forefront - the living Sisters of St. Francis of Assisi. I knew that I wanted to interview them first. Finding and adding their voices to this book became my very first project. Most of the Sisters are now in their retirement years and many are in their late eighties and nineties.

To find   Sisters who would be willing to share their lives and involvement with St. Coletta with me, I went to the only Sister that I knew in 2018, the remaining working Sister at St. Coletta - Sr. Grace Schauf. Of course, her voice was the first one that I requested. She readily agreed. She was also instrumental in helping me find three other Sisters who had been involved with St. Coletta in various ways. One of the Sisters that I interviewed was a sister to a longtime St. Coletta client. She was also on the Board of Directors of St. Coletta (as was another of the Sisters I interviewed). One Sister had been a teacher at the school and one had developed educational programs for the school. All shared a common love for the St. Coletta mission and the people that it served.

Sr. Grace Schauf

I started my conversation with Sr. Grace by asking her how she came to be a Sister. Sitting across from me with her hands clasped together and her eyes gazing into the past, she began.

Her story began when she was attending St. Mary's Academy as a high school student in Milwaukee. When she was a sophomore, at the age of 14, she became an aspirant. Young Catholic women, who showed an interest in becoming a Sister of the Order of St. Francis of Assisi, could begin a dedicated program to "aspire" towards a spiritual life.

After completing the two year aspirant program, Sister Grace graduated from high school in 1953. She had decided at that point not to return to the convent. After she returned to her family's home she received a letter from the Motherhouse requesting her to come back. They wanted to send her out to be a teacher. She was only 16 years old. She said to her mom and dad, "I've got to go back." She returned to the Motherhouse and immediately began teaching at St. Gertrude's Parish in Franklin Park Wisconsin. The Order had decided to have all their teaching Sisters become accredited teachers with college degrees. That decision left them with a severe shortage of teachers. They asked the new postulants, including Sister Grace, to fill in the open teaching positions.

She began teaching in a second and third grade classroom. She was supposed to have the assistance of an established Sister. She said this about the Sister, "But poor Sister Cynthia had been transferred from third and fourth grade to teach 60 little first graders." She said that Sister Cynthia was under a lot of stress. So, of course, was Sister Grace. She was basically on her own. She taught 49 children in her class. I told her I could not even imagine taking on such a monumental task when I was 16. She said, "I got through the year. I set the room up like my grade school. I don't know if I did a good job or not."

One of the most touching parts of this story was the fact that she later found out, while she was attending college, that she had a challenging learning disability in math. What bravery and determination she must have had to take on a teaching position at age 16 with her undiagnosed disability.

Two years later, in 1955, Grace was professed as a Sister. She was assigned the name Sister Eucharia. After she was professed she was missioned to St. Coletta of Wisconsin. She told me, as she breathed out a big breath, "That was a big sigh." She had actually come before to St. Coletta, while in high school, to attend movies on the weekend. She said, "I was scared to death of the population." She was assigned the first time that she worked at the community from 1955 to 1962. She was assigned to the Villa which was a new group home for 24 girls. She was group mother to 24 women, with 7 women being older than her. (She was 19). She didn't know what to do with them. Two women in particular "were very much a handful". She worked there for 3 years until she became brave enough to work with older clients who had more challenging disabilities and who lived at the Alverno Cottage.

In 1962, Sr. Eucharia moved on from St. Coletta and spent two years at the Motherhouse. From there she was transferred to a sister school, the Kennedy School in Illinois. She remained there until 1980 when she returned to work for St. Coletta. Sr. Elaine Weber, who was then the superintendent at St. Coletta, had begun changing the living conditions to a more community based and progressive standard. She wanted all of the clients to make their own choices in clothing and food. Sr. Grace said that Sr. Elaine was a builder like Sr.

Anastasia. (She said Sr. Mary Theodore and Sr. Sheila were more concentrated on education).

When I asked her to relate any memories of working with Sr. Anastasia, Sr. Grace spoke of an early experience with this esteemed Sister during her first year at St. Coletta - She was tasked with canning bushels of vegetables. The Sister normally in charge was having surgery. As then a very young Sr. Eucharia, she timidly asked Sr. Anastasia "What am I supposed to do with these? I don't know how to can. " Sr. Anastasia looked up from her desk with a serious face. 'Can you read?', she asked. 'Yes, Sister', I replied. I went down to the Villa and called my mom. 'Mom', I said woefully, 'how do I can beans?' So mom told me how to do it. I learned. And I loved it. I loved working with the clients."

There were 104 Sisters working in the community when Sr. Grace arrived at St. Coletta. She said, "After I left St. Coletta the first time in 1962, it seems like they were down one or two Sisters every year." She stated that part of the reason for that was Vatican II.

Vatican II was the Second Vatican Council held from 1962-1965. It brought about massive reforms within the Catholic Church, including in the lives of the Sisters. Many Sisters left their Orders because of the changes. She noted one big change for the Sisters. When Sr. Grace began her life in the Order, the Sisters were missioned to their assignments. After Vatican II, the Sisters had to find their own positions within the Order.

By 2018, there were approximately 170 Sisters left in the community of the Sisters of St. Francis of Assisi. Out of that number only 50 were under age 70. (At their highest number, Sr. Grace estimates there were 900 Sisters.) The Order now no longer takes any new Sisters.

Sr. Grace has gone on to serve the rest of her life working with clients with disabilities, including a long period working in Madison Wisconsin with the young women working on their independence skills. As I am writing in 2021, that service - her mission continues. I hate to think of a day when Sr. Grace isn't the first person I see when I walk onto the main campus. Wherever she is, her spirit and dedication, along with the spirits of all of the Sisters, will always be part of every aspect of St. Coletta.

Sr. Julianne Koch

Sr. Julianne's connection to St. Coletta is quite different than Sr. Grace's. She never actually worked in the community, but her connection to St. Coletta is just as strong. She grew up in Jefferson and belonged to the parish of the St. Lawrence Church. The church has had a strong alliance with the St. Coletta community for many years. As a child, she came to the St. Coletta picnics every year. It was a big area event with hundreds of people in attendance. Sr. Julianne was also familiar with the Sisters of St. Francis of Assisi from her school. She grew up admiring them as models. She gradually decided that, like them, she would devote her life to God.

Like Sr. Grace, Sr. Julianne became an aspirant at a young age, after 8th grade. She lived in the Motherhouse at St. Francis while attending high school and graduated in 1962. After graduation she entered the Order and then went directly to Cardinal Stritch College to continue her education. She spoke to me about the options that were available to women when she was young. She said that being a Sister gave her, and other young women, opportunities for higher education. They could be leaders in ways that they may not otherwise have had. Sr. Julianne said, "Sisters were heads of hospitals and hospital systems and CEOs, long before women were generally able to do that. So, in a sense, we were really forerunners in that regard for women. Education for Sisters became a real necessity."

While Sr. Julianne never had a direct mission at St. Coletta, she was assigned there one summer in 1969, while on break from attending university. While there, she was assigned to help in the sewing room to help clean all of the many ancient old curtains. She washed and repaired them in the basement of Serra Home, hoping they wouldn't fall apart in the process.

She also helped with the garden one summer, to assist Sr. Demetria "in the deep freeze" and, like Sr. Grace, in preparing green beans for canning. Sr. Julianne said that it seemed like it would never end. I shared with her that I knew exactly what she meant as I spent my long childhood summer days helping my older sister pick and can green beans on her farm in Ohio.

She told me that the adult clients were very involved in the running of the farm. She said, "I don't know how that would be understood today, but it was definitely helpful to the clients back then. They could do many things, whether it was in the dining rooms, in the kitchens, out in the gardens or the orchards - they were doing all kinds of things." I agreed with her that in that time period it was appropriate to have clients be involved. In the outside world there had been so few opportunities for individuals with disabilities to feel part of a community. She continued, "You know the whole thing with people with disabilities is to figure out what they can do and then give them the opportunity to do those things and that gives them purpose."

Sr. Julianne's main connection to St. Coletta came in a different aspect. Growing up, she had a younger brother, George, who had intellectual disabilities. He didn't become part of the St. Coletta community as a child, or even as a young man. He lived with her parents until he was 40 years old. Like many families who have an adult child living with aging parents, they knew they had to soon find another living situation for George where he could live in a safe and supportive atmosphere.

Fortunately for them, they didn't have to look far away. George, at 40, became part of St. Coletta in 1980. At the time, Sr. Julianne was assigned to a mission far away from Jefferson in another state. Even so, she immediately became part of the St. Coletta family. In 1990, she moved back to Wisconsin to a mission a few hours away from Jefferson. She wanted to be able to help her mother after her father passed away. A year later, in 1991, she became her brother George's guardian. In 1998, she was able to move to Madison, only an hour away. She would come on the weekends to visit George and attend functions at St. Coletta, including the annual family meetings.

I asked Sr. Julianne how she, and other St. Coletta families, felt about the clients gradually moving off campus and into the community. She said there was a lot of anxiety amongst the families as the clients started to move out. There was also fear of the loss of the close connections that had developed between all of the clients and families. She said there was a loss in one sense, but that there is also now a community connection in a different way, especially with the smaller groupings of clients.

As we brought our conversation to a close, Sr. Julianne told me that Sr. Elaine, then the superintendent, was instrumental in pushing for the community transition. She said "It's been amazing. The transformation to community based housing is huge. It's philosophical, it's physical, it's everything. There's a whole different psychology and philosophy why we're doing things the way we are doing them now." She said that clients are now treated more individually as people, which allows them to grow.

Sr. Julianne has also become part of St. Coletta as a member of its board of directors. As a Sister of St. Francis of Assisi and also a loving family member, she has brought her unique perspective, her faith and her knowledge to help all of the clients and families of the community. I'm certainly grateful for her contributions.

Sr. Coletta Dunn and
Sr. Ruth Marie Soens

My last interview that week was done jointly with two Sisters. It required an hour long drive from Jefferson to visit the Motherhouse. The Motherhouse is located in the city of St. Francis, just south of Milwaukee and directly west of Lake Michigan. The city took its name from the St. Francis Seminary, which was first founded in 1845 by Archbishop John Henni, the first Archbishop of Milwaukee. It was here that the original Sisters had arrived from Bavaria to begin their mission in 1849.

Many of the remaining sisters are now fully retired. The retired Sisters who are now living in the Motherhouse range in age from 82 to over 100 years old. Clare Hall, which had originally been built in 1956 as housing for seminarians, became the home for retired Sisters. This building is where I came, in August of 2018, to listen to the sage words of Sr. Coletta and Sr. Ruth Marie. During my visit, I found out that the Sisters were excited about the construction of the St. Francis Convent, that would soon replace the old Motherhouse. It would have ample space for the aging Sisters, including those who needed assisted living and memory care. After living their lives so completely dedicated to serving those in need, I was pleased to hear that they would soon have all of the comfort and services they certainly deserved. The new building has a chapel and also a space for archival storage. It is very important to the Sisters to preserve their history and all that they have achieved in the past 170 plus years.

Daniela came along with me for my interviews with the two Sisters. She was very interested in listening to them speak and seeing the home where the Sisters lived. Also joining us was Sara Foerster, Daniela's wonderful Case Coordinator. Sara was one of the very first people I told about my interest in writing a book. She expressed instant enthusiasm for the idea because she has also become fascinated by the Sisters and St. Coletta's history. She speaks to new staff members about the history of the organization. I invited Sara to come with Daniela and I for the interview. She wrote down some questions that she asked, which definitely added to our conversation.

As I did with Sr. Grace and Sr. Julianne, I asked both Sisters about their entry into the Order and their involvement with St. Coletta.

Sr. Ruth Marie's story -

Sr. Ruth grew up in nearby Kenosha Wisconsin, forty miles directly south of Milwaukee. She became a young postulant after high school in 1956. When we spoke in the summer of 2018, she had just celebrated her 60th year as a Sister. Like Sr. Grace, she started teaching as a novice. She had a long career of teaching first grade. After 23 years, she decided that she wanted a change. "That was enough." she said emphatically. By that year, Sisters had much more autonomy in deciding where and how they would like to serve.

Sr. Sheila Haskett, the administrator of the St. Coletta School at the time, invited Sr. Ruth to a convention with the St. Coletta Sisters and then invited her to help out in the community during the summer. She worked in the vegetable room with the "nicest crew of clients, just great girls and guys". She also helped out at the vacation lake house at Padua Point with the older clients. She said they didn't have families and so would spend a week at the lake for vacation. After those experiences, and since she had decided that she didn't want to teach first grade anymore, she decided to teach at St. Coletta. She trained under Annie Schmidt. She worked first with the St. Joseph junior boys, and then she took over with the senior boys. She said, "A great group of guys." "I did love it." She worked with the high school boys for two years and then moved to St. Anastasia Hall. This is where the girls lived. She said with a laugh, "I didn't last too long with the girls. The boys were easier." "Then I moved on to an adult program with men which was nice because they didn't graduate and leave." "We had such good times." On Sunday afternoons they would pop "wonderful huge tubs of popcorn with butter from the farm." "It would disappear quickly."

She said this about the St. Coletta teaching system, "That whole education program that St. Coletta set up, they wrote all those manuals for all the different subjects." The program, as I have indicated earlier in the book, was groundbreaking. Many other school systems used those same manuals to initiate their own special education programs. Sr. Ruth also talked about the changes that occurred at St. Coletta when the state and federal government first became involved for funding purposes. She mentioned that they had to lessen the amount of religious icons and there were many more inspections. She proudly told me that they always passed the inspections at the highest levels.

Sr. Coletta Dunn's story -

Sr. Coletta was an aspirant at age 14. She was not a Wisconsin girl. She, very bravely, came alone to St. Mary's Academy, traveling on a train from South Dakota during World War 2. After her 3 years as an aspirant, she graduated from high school. She then followed the normal course to enter the Order of the Sisters of St. Francis of Assisi. She was a postulant for one year, then a novice for two. Because of the great demand for teachers (caused by the baby boom that started after World War 2), like Sr. Grace, she was sent out to teach without having a college degree in education.

Sr. Coletta came to know St. Coletta while she was teaching in nearby Johnson Creek. She would go to the St. Coletta community on the weekends to work. She did whatever was needed during her visits. She would help out at Serra House, washing dishes and cleaning up the hotel that had been built to house visiting families. She worked a total of fifteen summers, including filling in at the summer respite camps that were held in the 1980s. She loved working at the camps with the college student counselors who were hired to help run the camps. (She noted that, to this day, some of the former college students still correspond with her.) She said that it was exhausting work and that she thought it might kill her. She said with a smile, "If I died, there would be no time for a funeral and then Sr. Sheila would have to work by herself!"

Sr. Coletta told me that increasingly, the outside world looked to St. Coletta for guidance. She commented that she remembers the time that the man in charge of special education for Wisconsin visited and said this about St Coletta, "I want to know what is happening there, the tip of the iceberg, the newest things". She said, "I come to St. Coletta to learn the newest and best care for people with retardation."

Sr. Coletta, who eventually received her doctorate degree in religious education, co-wrote the "Journey with Jesus" religious education program in 1969. She said, "In the 1960s we were publishing curriculum for every other area (in special education). After the Second Vatican Council, we decided to look at what was happening in the teaching of religion. I had just finished my doctorate in that area." She worked with Sr. Sheila Haskett, who had finished her doctorate the year before, to develop the new curriculum. The determination of these women to change the sphere of education for individuals with disabilities was fierce. Sr. Coletta said that Sr. Sheila had worked her way up from a child care worker at St. Coletta to become the superintendent of the school. Sr. Sheila and Sr. Coletta also served together on the St. Coletta board of directors.

Both Sr. Ruth Marie and Sr. Coletta said that St. Coletta definitely changed who they are as people. They are both openly thrilled with the way St. Coletta is operating today. Sr. Coletta said, "The current CEO[35], Ted Behnke, is a miracle." She said "It's a long legacy and not every decade was without problems.' She admired Ted for his role in the great advances that the community has made since he became the CEO. Sr. Ruth Marie also expressed her admiration and said, "I think it's wonderful. Thank God that they have him. (Ted)."

After I was finished with my questions, Sara Forester had a few questions she wanted to ask. She asked about what it was like when clients began living and working in the community - Sr. Ruth Marie remembered that when the clients started preparing to move out into the community, that she noticed there was more loneliness amongst the clients who moved, alone, into their own apartments. They had been used to having many more friends around. It was a big adjustment for them. She also said that for the individuals who first started working and living in the community, she remembered a lot of support in the local community. She said this was especially true at the Fireside Dinner Theater and the local grocery stores who hired clients. She said "There were a number of success stories." Sara commented that in the current work atmosphere, having companies take on an employee with disabilities has been more challenging.

Sara also asked about the challenges that the Sisters had experienced with family members. Sr. Ruth said that there had been a lot of support and that they always loved to see the families be involved. She said it gave the staff a whole new perspective about each client (including finding out that one of her clients spoke French when his grandfather called him!). The hardest part was when there was no family left. Then the staff truly became family to those clients.

Sr. Coletta said that families sometimes found it very hard to give up the total control of their family member, especially for the young children of the school. (As a parent, I think that must have indeed been very difficult.) Sr. Coletta said that families would sometimes miss their adult child so much that they would want to take them home for long periods. This was a difficult situation because it made it hard to keep that spot (housing) open for the client. There was such a demand from other waiting families to find a living situation for their adult child, that they tried to be sure that every opening was filled. Both Sisters said letting go was just extremely hard for families, no matter what the age.

Sara asked what made St. Coletta stand out from the other organizations and institutions that were working with individuals with disabilities over the years. Sr. Ruth said St. Coletta was a leader in the field of disability education and care. She said that it was important that teachers, staff and Sisters came to St. Coletta from other organizations, schools and Orders. They took away so much new information on education and the treatment of the disabled that it made a huge difference across the country.

Sr. Coletta spoke about the time, so many years ago, when Sr. Anastasia and Sr. Madeline went to the Vineland Institute in New Jersey. She stated, "They said, 'we want to learn about what's happening someplace else.'" She said that the Mother Superior reluctantly let them go. When they came back, they told her about all of the wonderful things they had seen and learned about new methods. The Mother Superior, said bluntly, "Do it your way." Sr. Coletta threw her hands up in the air to show that the Mother Superior just gave in to their enthusiasm. She yielded to the two young Sisters and to their ideas that the students could learn academics. They could learn more than just life skills, religion, virtues and better behavior.

Sara asked what they would want to tell new employees at St. Coletta.

Sr. Coletta said. "Every life matters." "Everyone belongs to a family, even if their natural family is gone."

Sr. Ruth simply said for the staff to remember that for some clients, "St. Coletta is their only home." They are their family

My interviews with the Sisters were absolutely one of the highlights of writing this book. Their lively enthusiasm for their faith, their missions and their lives have inspired me in ways that will stay with me as long as I live.

Sister Grace Schauf (formerly Sister Eucharia)

Sister Grace Schauf today with President Ted Behncke in front of St. Coletta's historic bell.

Sister Julianne Koch and her brother George

Sister Coletta Dunn and Sister Ruth Marie Soens

Chapter 13

There was a twenty year period between 1995, when Sr. Mary Theodore ended her writing. and 2015, when Daniela and I first landed on St. Coletta's doorstep. I knew from the beginning that I was going to have to branch out to find more avenues of research for this very critical time period. This was an important time span, St. Coletta had, again, faced another battle and had to fight for their very existence.

So many times this community had faced challenges that would have devastated and closed many other organizations. I don't think that St. Coletta ever came closer to falling off the cliff than they did in the ten year period between 1995 to 2005. Before I began my research I already knew the basic facts from speaking to staff who had weathered the crisis. I asked several current, and one past, staff members about their recollections. You will hear their voices as I write about this time period. I also wanted to find some neutral coverage of the crisis. For several weeks in the summer of 2019, I searched newspaper archives for many hours and read every newspaper article about St. Coletta, and disability history that I could find. There articles were about, not only the 1995-2015 time period, but from St. Coletta's earliest days in the 1900s.

The research sent me so deep into the past, that St. Coletta, the Sisters, and everyone I read about began to enter my dreams in a very real way. When I woke up in the morning I had to pull myself back into the present day. I found myself deeply missing people who I had never met and experiences I had never been a part of. I felt a growing responsibility to them to tell their story in a way that would make them proud.

By the late 1990s, a number of factors came crashing together causing St. Coletta to face a financial crisis. Through judicious money management, they had created a large endowment. They tried diligently to use only the interest of that endowment for ongoing costs. Because of a number of recent changes to the community and school, that had become almost impossible to do.

Many people assumed St. Coletta was well funded by the Catholic Church. When we first came to the community, I also thought that was true. It is not. From the very beginning, St. Coletta has always had to raise its own money to fund all of its programs. Through the years, those methods have evolved and changed with the times. Finding the funds to keep the organization alive has been a constant and challenging effort since 1904.

People also assumed that the Kennedy family was providing huge and constant sums of money since the time when Rosemary moved into her home on the campus. This is also not true. While the family had provided a few large and generous gifts, they were for several specific projects, and they were not an ongoing source of major funding. There have been other large benefactors over the years as well, but it is much more critical to have a consistent and adequate - steady and safe stream of income, especially when faced with unknown negative factors - such as facing a worldwide 2 year pandemic.

One very large factor that caused a gradual worsening of finances was the retirement of the Sisters of St. Francis of Assisi. Their lives of devotion and unpaid work had made the community able to survive and, even grow, during the depression and two World Wars. In 1963 there were 103 Sisters at St. Coletta. By the year 2000, there were only 14 (most over the normal retirement age). Many of the Sisters had served into their eighties and even their nineties. When they were physically able to, they worked in multiple positions, even contributing to the hard labor on the farm and in the kitchens. Often two or three lay persons had to be hired to replace one Sister. Having to consistently pay salaries and benefits for over 600 full and part time employees was extremely difficult for the organization.

The very large farm had also been a substantial cost saver. The community raised their own animals for meat, milk, and eggs and they grew their own produce, which was canned and frozen. They had a dairy and a bakery. All of these efforts made the campus almost entirely self-sufficient, even during those times when the rest of the country was struggling. For almost 100 years, the farm had provided not only fresh and delicious meals, it also provided training and employment for the adult clients who worked alongside the Sisters to provide for themselves. It was a different time.

By 2000, St. Coletta announced that the majority of the farm was for sale. (They have continued to own and use the vegetable gardens and their orchard.) It was sad, but also necessary. The clients were now able to find better work in the community, a longtime goal that everyone had been working towards. Clients were also moving off campus at a steadily increasing rate. They were shopping for, and preparing, their own food. The mission had changed for positive reasons but these changes did not come without problems.

Another critical factor in funding was the closing of the St. Coletta School. While the focus had by then shifted to working with adult clients, the change in the dynamics and staffing had a financial impact. After changing the lives of thousands of children, the school had gradually stopped accepting new students and the number of students grew smaller and smaller. The school graduated its last two students in May of 1998. While Wisconsin and other states had once contributed to paying for educating students at St. Coletta, and other private special education schools, by the late nineties that was rarely an option. By then, most schools had well established their own special education programs that could handle almost all types of students (except those with the most severe behavioral or physical needs).

I recently asked a longtime staff member, and a former teacher at the school, Diane Pinnow, about the general mood at the school's closure. She said this, "I think it was viewed with mixed emotions because it was sad, but joyful in other ways. While here, the school program students had the chance to be on the basketball team and cheerleaders and the prom king and queen and many other things they might not get to experience in an integrated school, but in another way it was hard to see young students living far away from home so there was joy that they'd be closer to families (or living at home with families)."

Although everyone at St. Coletta loved the school and they were proud of all they had accomplished (including educating hundreds of teachers), they were incredibly happy that it was now possible for children to stay with their families and be educated at home. They applauded the new legislation and the opportunities that it could provide. The people of St. Coletta always have the best interest of the population that they serve as their goal, even when it means changing the entire focus of their mission.

St. Coletta knew that it still had a vital purpose after the school closed. That purpose was now solely involved in providing housing, support and services to their adult clients. As large state institutions began to close, this need was becoming critical. The organization was prepared to continue to grow into this opportunity, knowing that the challenges and costs were substantial. Federal and state funding for adults with disabilities was rapidly changing, with a priority of moving people out of congregate settings and into their local communities. St. Coletta enthusiastically believed in this concept. They had been transitioning their clients to community homes as quickly as they could raise the money to provide housing.

They also knew they had to move their clients off campus to receive this funding. By 1997, 92 adult clients had moved into community homes in Jefferson and three surrounding counties. That still left 372 remaining clients on campus, some with no families and no funding. It was a daunting prospect to quickly have to build or buy accessible, appropriate housing for so many people. It was even more challenging to build or buy that housing in the small rural county of Jefferson. The cost to build the accessible was immense. There was also issues getting the zoning they needed and convincing local citizens they were going to be good neighbors.

And so it was, with all of these financial and other challenges, that St. Coletta tried to figure out how to move forward. In January of 1997 Henry Meece, the president of St. Coletta at that time, did an interview with the Wisconsin State Journal. He announced some cost cutting measures, as well as new efforts in fundraising. He said that non-essential spending would be cut

103

and wages would be frozen. He also said vacancies would not be filled.[36] In the summer of 1997, the local newspapers continued to cover the issue. Mr. Meece announced a layoff of employees, possibly up to 100 people, among the staff of 656 people. He said that some clients might be asked to find other accommodations. The layoffs would be needed because there would be less clients to serve. In the Capital Times, an article quoted Bruce Bennin, a member of the St. Coletta board of directors. He said "The overall financial situation is not immediately dire but we cannot continue to operate with the same staff when the number of residents decreases."[37]

The newspaper articles cited the fact that federal, state and local funding were not covering the costs of a number of the clients still living on campus. Add to this the fact that some clients' families were not paying for their family member's costs of care. In the past St. Coletta had been able to fund some clients and students with "scholarships". Sr. Mary Theodore, then 90 years old, said this, "We never turned anyone away except those whose needs we could not meet. We took in anyone, no matter what their religion, race, creed or their ability to pay."[38] With all of the changes that I noted above, this was sadly no longer a feasible option. As more clients were moved into housing that met federal criteria, the hope was that the funding would increase and ease the shortfall.

St. Coletta planned, in whatever way they could, to assist the clients and their families affected by the changes. The original local counties and states, where the clients had once lived, became involved in the possible transitions as they were the ones responsible to fund their residents with disabilities. It was a time of stress for everyone involved.

By January of 1998, the diligent and difficult efforts of the board and staff seemed to be paying off. The staff reduction and other measures had reduced the deficit almost in half. Only 39 employees had actually been laid off, out of projected 100. 40 other positions were simply not refilled when employees left. The Wisconsin State Journal stated "Working with state and county officials, St. Coletta has obtained $500,000 in federal money and cut staffing costs, giving the institution a little breathing room."[39] The newspaper articles did not say how many, if any, clients had to be transferred to other living options.

The community knew that they had to continue to make changes in their structure and to increase the pace of moving clients off the campus. They had to constantly reassure the clients, their families, staff, and supporters that St. Coletta would survive. They also had to offer reassurances when the long anticipated school closing occurred in the spring of 1998, and again, when the decision to sell the farm was made public in 2000.

St. Coletta was certainly not the only organization in Wisconsin, and around the country, that was having to deal with the huge changes in disability education, services and funding. Some organizations had to completely shut down. Those organizations who did not close, including St. Coletta, have had ongoing struggles with periodic changes in legislation and constant shortfalls in funding. There was another large and dedicated disability organization in Jefferson County who has had many challenges. They have also offered housing and many services to individuals with disabilities since early in the last century. This organization provided Daniela with job coaching services at her job in the local community. That organization has, sadly, closed all of its homes and programs in Jefferson County.

Since Daniela moved to Wisconsin in 2011, she has been involved, in different aspects, with four large disability organizations, including St. Coletta. The other three organizations have all had major financial funding issues that have caused them to have to restructure the way they offer services (including having to end or drastically reduce their residential services). Any person or disability organization that depends on government funding to survive is vulnerable to the political winds that change and blow in different directions. It is only through the dedication of families, disability activists, disability organizations like the Arc, and like St. Coletta, that the most vulnerable people in our country are able to continue to receive the residential and support services that are vital to them.

Annual family picnic Illinois

A football clinic with the University of Wisconsin
Warhawks

4th of July fun

The True Colors Festival

Chapter 14

By the beginning of the new millennium, the pace had quickened in moving clients off of the campus and into the community. In an article from the Lacrosse Tribune in March of 2000, a reporter stated this, "St. Coletta supports adults with disabilities and 207 of its 407 clients live off campus in homes and apartments as far away as Madison, Janesville, Waukesha and soon, northern Illinois. Many of St. Coletta's 600 employees are out in the community as well, supporting the clients in their jobs and independent living."[40] That was quite a jump in numbers from 1997 when 92 clients lived off campus.

As the article mentioned, St. Coletta had also ventured across the border into northern Illinois. There had always been clients from Illinois. This new venture offered residential and day services to clients who were Illinois residents (and they were funded by the state of Illinois). In 1991, the families and friends of those clients had formed a strong advocacy group for their St. Coletta family members called the "Illinois Friends for St. Coletta WI/IL". This group became more organized and dedicated as the homes and services in Illinois were established. They continue now to advocate strongly for St. Coletta of Wisconsin and its mission. They have raised over $650,000 to use for programs and services for the clients in Illinois.[41] (By 2022, they have raised almost $875,000) The group keeps a close eye on Illinois legislation, which is entirely different than Wisconsin's, in how they distribute funding. The group actively communicates with their state legislators to make sure their family members' voices are heard.

In the spring of 2000, St. Coletta decided to make another sweeping change to the community. The school had closed two years earlier. The community was embracing the focus on supporting adults with disabilities, and having them live and work in the community. With these changes, the long held farming operation had become a lovely, but outmoded, part of the organization's history. When the decision was made and the news broke, some long-time supporters and members of the community found it difficult to understand.

The new President of St. Coletta, Robert Stern, wanted to make it very clear that this decision did not mean an end to St. Coletta of Wisconsin. He stated for the Wisconsin State Journal, "We don't want people to think that because we're closing the farm that St. Coletta is closing too. St. Coletta as an organization is growing, the closing of the farm will allow us to continue our mission." Bruce Whitmore, who ran the farm for the previous 12 years, said this, "It's hard, dirty and sometimes smelly work. Our people are a lot more

107

accepted in the community than they were in the past."[42]   Because of their training and education at St. Coletta, the clients were able to find jobs in the local community, which fit in exactly with the mission of St. Coletta. Acceptance and inclusion were now a goal both at St. Coletta and nationally. As I mentioned earlier, St. Coletta still maintains ownership of the orchard and vegetable gardens. Everyone continues to enjoy this small part of St. Coletta's past.

In June of 2005, the Wisconsin State Journal wrote an article focusing on the closure of state and private institutions (and intermediate care facilities known as ICFs) for the disabled and the transition to new options of care in smaller settings such as group homes. "At their peak usage around 1970, Wisconsin's three centers for the developmentally disabled held around 3,700 residents, according to the Legislative Fiscal Bureau."[43] (the main state centers were the Central Wisconsin Center, Southern Wisconsin Center and Northern Wisconsin Center.) By June 2004 that number had dropped to 1377 for all three centers.

The intermediate care facilities were also sharply trending downwards in residents. St. Coletta had a licensed ICF at Alverno. It was forced to close and some clients had to be moved to other providers. "The Wisconsin Council on Developmental Disabilities successfully urged the closure of long-term care at the Northern Center. The group also wants the Southern Center closed by 2007, and the group People First, a statewide advocacy organization for people with disabilities, is asking for the state to close Central by 2012."[44]

The transition started with those clients with mild and moderate disabilities, and by 2005, those with the most severe challenges were being required to move as well. All three centers remained open as of 2020, although new admissions ended before the year 2000. Only two centers now provide long term care. The Northern Center ended their long term care in 2006. All three centers currently provide short term and intensive treatment. By 2015, the number of clients living long term in the other two centers was down to 389.[45]

While these moves were welcomed by disability rights activists and many families, at the time these changes were happening, there was also vigorous resistance from some families, the administration and staff of the facilities. Families of the individuals being transitioned (who had the most severe disabilities and who had lived considerable years in an institutional setting) were understandably wary of a community based system. The families noted injuries and deaths along with behavioral problems that local communities were not accepting. Gerry Born, the council chairman from People First, stated "Although parents often resist moving a child from an institution, they're often satisfied after the move has happened." "Many people who historically were institutionalized are now living in the community advocating for their own rights"[46] It was a tumultuous and scary period for families as they tried to negotiate the best possible solutions for their loved ones.

After this Wisconsin State Journal article came out in 2005, one of St. Coletta's parents, Tim Hood, wrote a letter to the editor about the situation. Tim is the current (2021) Chairperson of St. Coletta's Board of Directors. He and his wife Janice have long been two of the organization's most dedicated advocates. It has been my pleasure to come to know them, as well as their lovely daughter Jenny. She is one of my daughter's housemates and friends. Jenny entered the St. Coletta School in 1982. She was one of the original residents of their home, St. Agnes. Jenny and the other housemates enthusiastically welcomed Daniela into their fold in 2016.

Tim gave me permission to share his letter to the editor here. Fifteen years after it was written, I find that it holds up extremely well. State and federal regulators and agencies still dictate solutions and funding that aren't always in the best interests of those that they serve. Those solutions often aren't even the most fiscally responsible ones. The decisions, which are subject to being politically swayed, can lead to well-qualified non-profit organizations that serve the disabled, such as St. Coletta, being severely underfunded. Loss of funding often causes them to reduce their services or even close. The disruptions to the lives affected can be profound.

Tim's article -
'Hybrid' Option AvailableTim Hood, Wisconsin State Journal, June 25, 2005

"Sunday's piece focused on the state centers and the pressure to empty institutions but failed to discuss an alternative, which is under attack by ill-advised public policy and short-sighted fiscal decisions. That alternative is a "hybrid" organization that supports the holistic development of developmentally disabled individuals and retains a strong spirit of community.

My daughter, age 36, is a resident of such an organization, St. Coletta of Wisconsin in Jefferson, where she has been supported for 23 years. Supporting people in smaller, community-integrated homes has been the trend for several decades. Unfortunately, we live in a society where the "one size fits all" mentality rarely works. Though couched in terms of "personal choice", the reality is in order to receive public funding, individuals must live in a manner consistent with federal and state regulations whether or not that is the best setting for them.

At St. Coletta, housing has evolved from a congregate setting to the current community-based housing, where my daughter lives. Yet even with the dispersion to various communities, the most reassuring thing to families is a strong attachment to St. Coletta. There is a genuine sense of community and stability, where people like my daughter have made life-long friends. The residents can readily access opportunities in their communities but they also have the chance to gather with their peers.

Due to underfunding, the state is increasingly using what is best explained as a foster care system with no sense of permanence or stability. We would be better off to emulate places like St. Coletta to support developmentally disabled people in a manner that promotes quality of life but which is also fiscally responsible."

I am in total agreement with Tim's letter. St. Coletta is, and has always been, a fiscally responsible model that combines the best of all worlds - living and working in the broader community, having an internal family-like community and also having a very large and varied support network. While I don't think it is possible for the heart and spirit of St. Coletta of Wisconsin to be replicated, it could and should be emulated across the country - and the world. I asked Tim recently about that letter he wrote 15 years ago, and if he could write an update to his comments. He graciously agreed.

Tim Hood - August 16, 2020

"Unfortunately, in the 15 years since my letter of June 25, 2005 referenced earlier suggesting policy makers consider a 'hybrid' organization to support developmentally disabled individuals, not much progress has been made. The vast majority of developmentally disabled do not belong in an 'institution' and some would be happy and do well living independently in their own home with some caregiver support.

And those needing more care could be very happy in the family's home with care provided by their parents, with perhaps some caregivers provided by a service organization. But there are reasons to consider what I earlier referred to as a 'hybrid' solution, especially those whose parents have tried to care for them at home.

There are two things that drive the decision in favor of a residential facility like St. Coletta. First, most developmentally disabled have a normal life span (the average age at STC is in the upper 40s) and living in their parents' home they would likely live past their parent's deaths. At that point, unless the parents had made private and very expensive arrangements, they would become wards of the state and placed in what are basically foster homes, perhaps moving several times before they die. At a time of great grief with the passing of their parents, they would also lose the home environment in which they had become comfortable and experience a string of caregivers who are strangers to them.

Second, whatever care needs developmentally disabled persons have, they also need their friends. Organizations like STC provide spiritual, vocational, and recreational opportunities <u>with their friends</u> for the people they serve. I have never understood why it OK for

110

seniors to migrate to senior living facilities to be with their contemporaries, while the developmentally disabled are directed by the state to live "as independently as possible" in the community. Perhaps more than any others, the developmentally disabled need their friends, and need a place to call home. As a neurologist treating Jenny told us as she turned 12, everyone needs their contemporaries.

Janice and I have considered our obligation as parents of a developmentally disabled daughter of course to be to love and care for her. But the obligation goes much further; it is to give her a life with her friends and contemporaries, with as much freedom as she can accept, to live as adventurous a life as possible. And also to give her a home where she can continue to experience that life after we are gone, for as long as she shall live.

Residential facilities like STC become that home, and provide a safe, caring environment for them to live their lives with their friends, as well as give their parents comfort during their lifetimes that their child will have a home and friends for their lifetimes. Unfortunately, we seem to still be consumed by the 'one size fits all' mentality."

Janice, Tim, and Jenny Hood

My gratitude goes out to Tim, Janice and all of the advocates and self-advocates who are continuing to fight for themselves and for millions of people in the United States who are living with intellectual and developmental disabilities.

During those years that institutions across Wisconsin were being emptied, St. Coletta's clients were continuing to move out of the old campus and into their new community homes. As Tim's letter said, a huge factor in these transitions is, and continues to be, funding. At one time, St. Coletta could afford to privately fund individuals who had run out of private funding and didn't qualify for state funding. By the beginning of the new millennium that became impossible.

By 2006 there were 45 clients whose futures at St. Coletta were in serious jeopardy. Some had come as children from orphanages. Some had very elderly families or no family left at all. For most of their lives those clients had lived on the campus. They were fed by the farm and were cared for by the Sisters who took no salaries. Even with those advantages, St. Coletta had provided more than $20 million dollars of free care over the years for the clients who couldn't pay. Now all of these clients were living in community housing, with their care provided by paid professional staff. The costs of paying for that care and for housing, utilities and food had grown beyond the means of St. Coletta to be able to continue to pay. There were also growing expenses of some clients, as they aged. These costs threatened the organization and the hundreds of other clients who also depended on its care. In 2006, the costs for the unfunded clients, many of them elderly, was approximately $1.3 million dollars annually.

The dilemma was extremely painful for everyone, including the county of Jefferson who had always worked hand in hand with St. Coletta and the disability community. The County Board was afraid that the Human Services department would end up having to pay $700,000 a year in extra funding from the county budget. St. Coletta had been working vigorously for two years with the Wisconsin state government to have them pick up part of the costs - without results. The local state representative, David Ward, and the state senator, Scott Fitzgerald, were trying to secure the money within the State Department of Health and Family Services budget.

In an article from May 12, 2006, in the Wisconsin State Journal about this challenging situation, Mike Prentiss, a Fitzgerald aide said, "Were not giving up but it's a difficult situation." He said that the expanded Family Care program may provide some relief.[47]

Wisconsin's Home and Community Based Services (HCBS), "waivers" which are funded through Medicaid, set the rules for individuals who were eligible to be served, and the organizations serving them. The waivers are paid

112

for by a combination of federal and state of Wisconsin funding options. "Family Care" was created by Wisconsin in 1999 to manage the Medicaid waiver funding. Starting in one county in 2000, it very gradually expanded across the state. The last county came on board in 2018. The program has two components - 1. Aging and Disability Resource Centers - which is the entry vehicle for families seeking information on all of the resources available to them and 2. Managed Care Organizations - which manage and deliver the funding and services that are designed especially for each individual's needs and preferences. (There is also a separate and unique state program named IRIS which bypasses MCOs and allows clients themselves to directly receive and designate the funds for their needs.)

Obtaining Wisconsin state waivers for the 45 unfunded clients was the goal. As the senate aide stated, it was "a difficult situation." As I continued to research the situation from 2006, I fretted and hoped that a solution had been found - that the clients did not have to leave their lifetime homes and friends. I scrolled and scrolled through newspapers hoping to see good news. Finally I did. In the Wisconsin State Journal on June 24, 2006 there was an article titled "State helps St. Coletta Clients". All of the dedication and hard work done by St. Coletta, the state senator and state representative (and their staffs) had paid off. The state legislature's budget committee had designated state funding which, combined with federal funding, would provide almost 1.2 million dollars of funding for the 45 clients. The funding would continue annually for the rest of their lives.

Andrea Speth, who was then St. Coletta's Vice President of Development and Community Relations, said this in the article "We're thrilled. They've been a part of our family throughout their lives. It's a victory most importantly for our 45 clients." She continued, "This effort was part of us being able to continue being well positioned for the next century. We're always going to be providing more services than we are paying for. It's about the people. We want to be here 100 years from now and in order to do that, we need to be fiscally sound."[48]

Whew! I was so glad to read that article. Andrea Speth also stated that all future clients would have to have funding in place before they were admitted. Funding is too costly for most families privately, but programs like Family Care have assisted in providing funding to many thousands of Wisconsin's citizens who live with significant disabilities. It is a constant battle though to make sure the funding that is given by the state and federal government for client care is sufficient, as the costs for providing high quality care continue to increase.

The funding issue was certainly a major issue, and it was a major focus in 2005-2006. It was not the only one. In the fall of 2005, another decision at

St. Coletta was about to change the community in another very emotional and bittersweet way. In September of the year, it was announced that the 174 acre main campus, with its 20 buildings (some as old as 100 years), was going to be put up for sale. With the closure of the school, and with all of the residential clients now living in apartments and houses in the local community, the huge campus had outlived its usefulness. The previous ten years had brought so many changes and decisions. This one was definitely the largest. From the Capital Times on September 9, 2005, "We are selling the campus because it no longer fits the needs of our operating model and therefore, our buildings are largely unoccupied." Andrea Speth, St. Coletta Vice President said Thursday. "People with disabilities are being supported in smaller homes that are integrated in communities." The article went on to explain that the community was keeping 500 acres just down the road and would rebuild smaller corporate offices in the Alverno building located on that property. The President during that period, Tony LoDuca, said, "St. Coletta remains committed to continuing to be a leader in the provision of quality programs and services for people with developmental challenges and retaining a strong presence in the Jefferson community."

The article stated that the Sisters who spent their lives working on the campus went though a grieving process but understood that things had changed and that the campus was no longer part of the organization's plan. A sign was placed at the campus which read, "Same Mission, New Location."[49]

It took quite some time for the campus to sell. As of the date I wrote this in the summer of 2021, the new owners had yet to move in. The empty buildings sit quietly alone, with the spirits of all of the heavenly Sisters, staff, students and clients keeping watch.

In January of 2005, St. Coletta's most famous client joined those heavenly spirits. With her family by her side, Rosemary Kennedy died at a local hospital. The family gave a statement about St. Coletta and its impact on Rosemary's life. "We are forever thankful to the loving members of the St. Coletta community who cared for Rosemary, loved her, and in a very real sense became extended members of our family."[50] The Kennedy family statement is one that I'm sure has been echoed by hundreds of St. Coletta families concerning their loved one. It is certainly echoed by mine.

Four short years later on August 11, 2009, St. Coletta mourned Rosemary's sister, Eunice Kennedy Shriver. She was a great friend to the community, and to all people with disabilities across the world. Mrs. Shriver had been a very frequent visitor over the years as she spent time with Rosemary. The Daily Jefferson County Union wrote about this friendship with St. Coletta giving a statement in honor of Eunice's life. "The community of St. Coletta of Wisconsin wishes to express its deepest sympathy to the family of Eunice

Kennedy Shriver. Inspired by her love for her sister, Rosemary, Mrs. Shriver was a wonderful friend to our organization and was a tireless advocate for the rights of people with disabilities to be included in all aspects of life." Andrea Speth went on to say in the article, "The Kennedy's were generous to St. Coletta, but more importantly, they have worked on a national scale to make the world better for persons with disabilities." Andrea also noted that St. Coletta's clients actively participate in the various programs created by the Kennedy family. The article specified that the clients of St. Coletta have been very active in Special Olympics. "All over the world people with disabilities experience the thrill of competition because of her vision in founding the Special Olympics, St. Coletta officials said of Shriver. "Her legacy will continue through her lifelong efforts to enhance the lives of people with disabilities. Our thoughts and prayers are with her family at this difficult time."[51]

As the first decade of the century came to a close, the long and intensive project of moving all of the clients into community housing was finally coming to an end. With the sale of most of the old campus in progress, the next objective was to find new spaces for the day programming, the chapel and offices for the staff and administration. They found a solution that saved them from having to build an entirely new structure.

The Alverno building , emptied of its last residents in 2009, was large enough to be adapted and brought back to life for this large new project. It is located along County Highway Y, east of the City of Jefferson. It is diagonally across the road from the original school campus and housing. Alverno needed many renovations for it to be put back into service as an effective multipurpose building. In 2011, the renovations kicked into high gear. The goal was for them to be completed by the end of that summer.

"It is an exciting time for our organization as we complete our transition to fully community-integrated services," said Anthony LoDuca (St. Coletta's president and CEO in 2011). "A lot of hard work and energy has gone into developing accessible community-based housing that can support people with disabilities as they age."[52]

Besides making spaces for the administration offices and the new chapel, there were plans for the building to house two day programs. The first was Golden Options - which began in 1986 for seniors with disabilities and dementia. It would also house one branch of the program named Excel (with the other branch at the University of Wisconsin-Whitewater). Excel offered and continues to offer training in daily living skills, prevocational skills plus social and recreational activities. (The building also now houses the Genesis, Vocational Training Skills Program and Access programs .)

One of the most important aspects of the renovation for everyone - clients, families and staff - was to bring as much of the history of the old

115

campus as possible into this new space. "As we complete the transition to being a provider of community-based services, it was important to us that we retain some of the historical treasures that have been a part of the St. Coletta story," said Andrea Speth. "The new chapel which is literally located in the center of the new building, becomes both the spiritual and physical center of our community reflecting our commitment to providing quality services that support people with developmental challenges."[53]

Daniela and I arrived at the Alverno building just a few years after the renovations were completed. We had no idea then about the many transformations that had happened within the community before our arrival. Daniela was just beginning her journey to begin a transformation of her own. Her journey was made possible by the dedication and efforts of everyone who has been a part of the mission's long history. Her story, and our family's would now become part of the colorful and rich tapestry of St. Coletta of Wisconsin. The next chapter shares the beginning of that journey.

Wisconsin's frigid winters make skiing a great choice.

Since its earliest days sports of all kinds have been an important part of St. Coletta's culture. They increase health and more importantly, self esteem

Sports clinics improve skills, with the much appreciated help of professional sports teams like the Milwaukee Bucks.

Special Olympics 50th Anniversary Celebration at Soldier Field in Chicago.

Sports achievements are another wonderful
way that clients are honored, at many different
abilities and skill levels.

Watching college and professional sports is
always a fun option and there are many to
choose from.

Everyone has their favorite team -

And their favorite sport!

Chapter 15

In the late 1990s I wrote my first book. The book was about Daniela and focused on the challenges that she faced from the time we adopted her in 1991 until she turned nine years old. Since the book was published in 1999, I have shared parts of her story at speaking engagements, in newspapers and in various education, disability and adoption magazines. I took a break from writing about her life during her teen years as we focused as a family on her and her older sister Marcy. Those years were mostly wonderful, but we also dealt with some serious family illnesses and, tragically, some deaths.

I have shared small parts of Daniela's story at St. Coletta throughout this book. Since she is the reason that I have come to know and love the community, I would not be honoring her if I didn't include her story more fully. Daniela has always been very happy and open for me to share her story. She is proud of how far she has come - and - she frequently tells me that she likes "being famous". She is quite interested in being an advocate for herself and for others like her, those who spent time in institutions and those with disabilities.

Daniela is the reason I became a writer and a disability advocate so many years ago. Her quirky, funny, exciting, sometimes stressful but never boring life led our family down a path that has forever changed all of us. She has changed many other lives along the way.

Daniela's Story -

At the beginning of 2015, I had no idea of the big changes in store for my daughter Daniela. The summer before, she had proudly graduated from Shepherds College in Union Grove Wisconsin (located an hour southeast of Jefferson). She had spent three years at the postsecondary program which dedicated to improving the lives of young adults with mild intellectual and developmental disabilities. She found her way to Shepherds after we made an exhaustive search to find the best program that we thought could help Daniela lead her most independent life.

Daniela spent her elementary and secondary years in our county's (Gloucester County, Virginia) special education program. Because of her disabilities and challenging behaviors, her years before high school were spent in mostly self-contained classes. Her high school education gave her the chance to integrate more fully with the non-special education classmates. Her learning opportunities expanded. She enjoyed school, even with the difficult challenges it presented her. The very challenging behaviors when she was younger started to dissipate. Her warmth, empathy and humor took center stage. Daniela had terrific teachers, therapists and doctors who were dedicated to helping her live her best life. Our fears for her when she was younger lessened. We realized that she had many strong abilities that needed to be developed as she became an adult.

After Daniela had graduated from high school in 2009, she spent an extra transition year at her high school while doing some outside vocational training and volunteer work at her former elementary school. She also worked at a local sheltered workshop run by the Arc of Virginia that I hoped would provide her with motivation to work and also provide friends. She absolutely hated it there.

It became obvious to all of us that we wouldn't be able to find any programming long term in our area that would be able to keep Daniela stimulated, fulfilled and moving forward. Despite our best efforts she, like many other young adults with disabilities, "fell off the cliff". In other words, the local educational, social and vocational opportunities fell away sharply once she aged out of her school programming.

In my, often late night, research to find ways to find opportunities for Daniela I found a website called Think College (https://thinkcollege.net). I was happily surprised to learn that there were a growing number of postsecondary programs across the country for young adults just like Daniela. Many colleges and universities had programs, both residential and commuter. There were also programs, like Shepherds College, that were independent.

With Daniela's interest and involvement and being mindful of the costs (these programs can be very expensive), we ended up looking at six different programs - three university and three independent ones. All but one were in other states. The competition for admission to these programs was fierce because most were quite small and only admitted 5-20 students per year. Daniela and I headed out on tours to visit all of the schools we selected. The trip to Shepherds in Wisconsin was last on the list. It had seemed too far away and I had actually ruled it out before visiting the other four programs.

Daniela was accepted at two of the other programs that she interviewed at. Three programs were not a good fit for various reasons. Before choosing which of the two remaining programs she should attend, we decided to look again at Shepherds. Despite it being so far away, it did seem to offer the best fit for what Daniela both wanted and needed. It had academic, vocational, and life skill classes. It also offered a graduated residential program moving from dorm to group home to apartment living.

Daniela and I flew to Wisconsin for the first time in September of 2010. She fell in love with the program, it fit her well. We were able to make it work financially. Getting her acceptance letter, later that fall, was one of the happiest moments of her life and a huge relief to my husband and me. She started at Shepherds College in August of 2011. Although there were huge and often painful transitions for her over the next three years, Daniela grew to a level of independence we never imagined for her. We also fell in love with Wisconsin itself.

During her last year at Shepherds we realized that bringing her back to Virginia would be a big mistake. As I wrote earlier, Virginia's funding and programs for individuals with disabilities were extremely lacking. Daniela became a Wisconsin resident while at Shepherds and had already qualified for their Medicaid waiver funding without a waiting list. I worried initially that Daniela would be upset at the thought of not moving back to Virginia. I couldn't have been more wrong. She was quite happy to continue her independent life in Wisconsin.

Daniela had majored in horticulture at Shepherds. Her horticulture instructor volunteered with a residential life program for adults with disabilities about an hour west of Union Grove. She suggested that Daniela give it a look to see if she liked it. We traveled there and Daniela saw that she could live in her own lovely apartment in a large building. It was a long established program and the staff and other clients seemed very nice. They promised lots of activities and help in finding her a job in the local area. I had a few concerns about their housing model, which was mostly in the one large building, but other than that we decided it would work well for her.

In the end, it didn't - it really didn't.

Like many programs for people with disabilities, funding is a constant battle. As soon as Daniela arrived, the promised assistance in helping her to continue to learn to live independently was cut. The few activities that they had for clients were more suitable for the mostly older and physically disabled clients. Trips away from the campus were very limited. They had contests to win the few excursions available.

Each visit to Daniela became more discouraging. Her obsessive and self-stimulating autistic behaviors escalated to levels that we hadn't seen for many years. She became sadder and angrier. She was completely bored and her main focus each day was being first in the line for lunch and first to get her medications at the nursing station. (It became very competitive.) The clients and most of the staff were lovely and Daniela's studio apartment was beautiful. The atmosphere though was definitely more suited to older nursing home type clients. We knew that we needed to start looking for a new living situation for Daniela and we needed to do it soon.

I talked to Daniela about moving somewhere else but she was hesitant. Changes, especially major changes, were so hard for her. She had experienced so many changes and transitions in her life the past few years and she, understandably, was loathe to have to move into another strange situation.

By the summer of 2015, the situation was becoming untenable. The administrator started making stronger suggestions that she wasn't happy having to manage Daniela and her challenges. She demanded more attention than the older, more settled clients and was causing issues among the younger clients. My husband and I had several long talks with Daniela and she started to consider that another living situation might be better for her. I told the administrator that I was going to start looking for another residential community.

Very late on a hot summer Virginia evening in 2015, I was anticipating another long sleepless night worrying about Daniela's situation. I decided to distract myself with reading the book about Rosemary Kennedy that I had lying on my bedside table. It was written by the niece of one of the Sisters of St. Francis of Assisi at St. Coletta. Her aunt had cared for Rosemary for many years.

In the book as I read that night, Rosemary had just started living at St. Coletta. Knowing that it was in Wisconsin, I wondered if it still existed. I stopped reading, grabbed my iPad and decided right then to stop reading the book and begin exploring St. Coletta. I was very curious to see if it could possibly be an option for Daniela. I was not hopeful. I had already looked at many other options in Wisconsin unsuccessfully. After my research that summer and the year before, in helping Daniela to find a residential community, I knew St. Coletta was probably a long shot. Most organizations and communities had very long waiting lists.

However, what I found that night seemed immediately and surprisingly encouraging. I sat up in bed, very awake now. I grabbed a pen and paper. All night long, I googled every reference about the organization. Before I knew it, it was early morning. On St. Coletta's website, I found the email address of the Manager of Admissions and Outreach for St. Coletta, Elizabeth Bouchard. (She is now the Director of Day Programs.) It was a Saturday morning, but I decided I would go ahead and email her while everything was still fresh in my sleep-deprived brain. At 5:06 am, this was the email that I sent her.

"Hello,

I am interested in finding out about residency options with St. Coletta's. My daughter Daniela is 25 and we adopted her from a Romanian orphanage when she was a toddler. Daniela is a very loving and wonderful young woman who has mild ID with some autistic characteristics. She currently is living (since Sept. 2014) at (*****)54 Wisconsin. While she loves living there (in her own studio apartment) it is sometimes a struggle for her to live and get along with the 60+ other residents of varying ages and disabilities. Sometimes it feels a bit too much like a nursing home.

We are wondering and exploring if it might be better for her to live in a smaller and less institutional type setting. I've been exploring your website and the wonderful history of St. Coletta's. I see you are in Jefferson County which is not too far from where she lives. Daniela receives SSI and has a Medicaid waiver. She participates in Family Care. Does St. Coletta participate with Family Care?

My husband and I live in Virginia and I am planning one of my regular visits for mid August. Would it be possible for me to bring Daniela for a visit on August 14th?

Do you have a packet that you could send out?"

I hit send, got up and sent a small prayer out to Rosemary, hoping for miracles.

Within a week, I had heard back positively from Elizabeth (Liz) and we set a visit for the next month, the soonest I could take time off from work. They sent me a thick packet of information about the community and I couldn't wait to take Daniela to see the program. They asked for as much documentation as I could provide them so that they could get a better sense of Daniela and her needs before our visit.

Before we knew it, our visit to St. Coletta was upon us. Daniela hesitantly entered the administration building and went into the meetings quietly and shyly, shaking with nervousness. She was still very hesitant for making any changes in her life. Our main meeting involved a number of the staff who would be involved in the decisions about whether this trembling young woman would be a good fit for their residential and day programs.

Daniela hid behind me when she could and tried to get me to answer any and all questions. Slowly the people at the meeting, with their cheerful and welcoming demeanors, won her over. She stopped trembling and lessened the death grip she had on my arm. Her bubbly personality began to emerge.

As we toured the day programming and one of their residences that day, her eyes grew wide. Everywhere we went, the staff and clients came up to her, welcoming her, hugging her and asking if she would be joining the program. She told them that she was thinking about it.

Before we left, the staff offered to let her come spend the night in the residence we had toured. She said again that she'd think about it. As soon as we climbed into our car, she began to bubble over with enthusiasm about all that she had seen and heard. I wrote to Liz Bouchard the next day -

"I wanted to tell you and the rest of the staff just how much Daniela and I enjoyed our visit yesterday. They can tell you that Daniela really warmed up. She was amazed at how many opportunities you offer. She went from not even wanting to consider the idea of moving to

very much wanting to explore the idea of living at a St. Coletta home. She met some young men in the program and that also was a positive for her. She especially liked the Best Buddy program, being able to take classes and being able to get out and do things much more than she currently does. She has thanked me numerous times for taking her for the visit. I was also very impressed by your staff and programs."

Liz wrote me back (excerpt)-

"Thank you for your kind words...we very much enjoyed meeting you and getting to know Daniela. She absolutely charmed everyone, and we're always happy to show off our programs...energy and enthusiasm abound!"

I decided to make another trip to Wisconsin the next month so that we could make an extended visit and Daniela could spend the night. She was nervous about staying the night with complete strangers without me nearby. Her challenging behaviors seemed to be escalating and she was making constant complaints about her living situation. She began talking about medical issues that I suspected were driven by anxiety. Liz was very accommodating to my schedule needs and Daniela's fears. She was willing to do whatever we needed to do to make our next visit a success. I continued to send more documents about Daniela's needs.

Emails shot back and forth between St. Coletta, Daniela's managed care manager (that controlled her waiver funding) and myself in the coming days. Right before our visit, Liz sent me a detailed schedule for Daniela's two day visit -

"Greetings, We are very excited to see you and Daniela again tomorrow! Below is an itinerary that I've drafted; it can be amended as anyone sees fit to best accommodate...

Thursday, September 17th

9:30 a.m. – Arrive at St. Coletta main campus in Jefferson; meet with Stephanie McDonald for transport to the Whitewater Excel program

9:45-10:45 – Program tour 10:45 – lunch at Whitewater Student Union with Excel participants; approximately $10 per person (Campus cuisine has gotten quite fancy in recent years!)

11:45 – return to Jefferson campus to socialize, participate in weekly chapel services (all denominations welcome) or alternate activity (computers, cooking, etc.)

2:30 – travel to (residential) home   in Jefferson; evening activities, dinner, etc. Daniela spends the night at the house.

Friday, September 18th - Morning – Daniela takes St. Coletta shuttle to Jefferson Excel and on to Whitewater Excel to participate in activities; departure tbd

Again, this is pretty flexible so if anything needs to be changed, please let me know. Thanks, everyone!"

I was certainly impressed by the care and organization that had gone into creating a fun and informative visit for us.

As I wrote back to Liz, *"I am very touched."*

As all of this was coming together, things were further breaking down for Daniela in her living situation. I was getting more emails and calls about Daniela's behavior and read between the lines that her welcome there was wearing extremely thin. I could feel the tension with the administrator when I arrived to take Daniela for her St. Coletta visit. It cast a pall over my excitement and made me quite worried about what would happen if St. Coletta decided that Daniela wasn't well suited for their community.

I was able to put those feelings on hold as we drove to Jefferson. I knew I needed to calm Daniela's fears about the overnight visit. She again silently hid behind me as we began our visit with a tour of St. Coletta's Whitewater day programming. Stephanie McDonald (at that time the Day Program manager at St. Coletta, now the Recreation Coordinator) was our tour guide and she very quickly got Daniela laughing and hanging on to her every word. Her shyness melted away. She was blown away by all of the opportunities that might be possible for her. After I dropped Daniela off for her overnight, I wrote Liz and everyone else a thank you email from my hotel room. -

"Thanks to everyone for a lovely, lovely day! Daniela and I had such an interesting and positive experience. It was everything I could have hoped for and more. Daniela told me multiple times that she wanted to move there. I was shocked when we went to the house that she showed no issues at all with me leaving after about half an hour. What a beautiful home! The staff made her feel so comfortable. Daniela is very excited about joining the Whitewater group again tomorrow.

I just got a text from her saying she is having so much fun!

Elizabeth, I guess we need to start talking particulars on how this would all work logistically, financially, etc. and if your staff feel she would be a good match for your housing and program. I honestly feel that Daniela would thrive at St. Coletta. I need to talk to my husband in detail when I get home of course, but he always trusts my judgement. I think

Daniela feels the same way. I think she would move next week if she could (I told her, if everything works out, after the holidays might be better.)"

Stephanie, who took us on our tour that day, recently wrote to me with her remembrances of that day and how Daniela has grown since the day she met her. Like so many of the people we met on those first trips, we have come to know Stephanie very well. I can never see and talk to her now without thinking fondly of her cheerfully breaking down Daniela's protective wall of shyness. -

"When I first met Daniela I was going to be giving her and her family a tour of our Day Program in Jefferson. I didn't know a lot about her at the time, but was excited to meet her because I heard she had been at Shepherds College and was eager to hear what she had studied. We met in the lobby by the front desk and, to my surprise, Daniela was very shy. In fact, she was so shy she stood behind her mom and gave me a little peek when I was introduced to her. I instantly got the picture in my head of her hiding behind a doorway peeking to see if she could spot Santa leaving presents. I believe she came out from behind mom to give me a little wave, and she was definitely nervous. We started the tour with me leading and Daniela following behind, close to mom. I engaged with Daniela as much as she would let me and asked her questions in hopes that she would start to warm up to me. She did answer some questions with a nervous tone, but shortly after we started the tour I got to experience Daniela's first excited smile. This was it, I was finally able to break through her shyness. Daniela seemed to really enjoy the tour and by the end of the tour she was talking away! She was happy and full of smiles and even appeared to be excited that she may be joining our program. Daniela and her family said their good byes and she left with confidence.

Since that day Daniela has grown into a confident woman and has even assisted me in many tours. She enjoys sharing the success of her breaking through her shyness and is very encouraging to those we are touring. Daniela has even participated in an Athlete Leadership Program and spoke to her peers two times in a larger group. She really has done a fantastic job over the years opening up."

When I picked up Daniela that next afternoon after her very successful night and the next day of programming, she ran up to me, hugged the breath out of me and said she wanted to move there "right now!" I hadn't seen her so joyous and positive in many months. My mind was made up - if only St. Coletta would admit her to the community. I had lots of questions and knew it would be a lengthy process. I immediately wrote Liz and Daniela's managed care manager a very long email that night with SO many detailed questions.

The care manager sent me back a short email -

Hi Tina, I just want to make sure I am interpreting your email correctly......it sounds like you definitely want to pursue with moving Daniela, providing she is accepted to St. Coletta?"

I wrote her back, telling her how enthusiastic we felt about the programming and housing. I told her about the new pre-vocational program they were developing that they thought would be perfect for Daniela.

I told her - *"Yes - absolutely yes".*

Blessedly, the answer from St. Coletta was also "Yes!" We all set a goal to get Daniela moved to her new community after the holidays. Being the professional and thorough organization that St. Coletta is, the move involved very detailed medical, psychological, legal, financial and every other kind of paperwork imaginable. After a lifetime of doing these things for Daniela, I was prepared. It was still daunting, and I knew it would take every day of the next 4 months to complete it all.

Then, in the first week of October, our organized schedule to move Daniela completely fell apart. Once the administrators of the community where Daniela was living heard she was moving, they pretty much decided that they were done with her. Daniela's managed care manager had to break the news to us that the administrator had called her and wanted Daniela moved out as soon as possible.

I was so upset that they didn't even bother to call and tell us personally. It made me feel hurt, angry, and also much more confident about our decision to move Daniela. Daniela's funding care manager was also very upset by the way things had been handled and told me she was so happy for Daniela that to be moving away to a better community. She had previously worked in residential services and told me if she was still working in that field, she would have taken Daniela into her residential setting in a heartbeat. She vowed to do whatever she could to expedite things.

I was honest and apologetic with Liz Bouchard when I explained the now rather desperate situation. I had no idea if they would be able to move up the schedule by three months. The funding issues in itself were complicated and challenging. Having the state involved did not usually lend itself to a speedy resolution.

What I didn't know then, but surely know now, was that Liz and the whole St. Coletta team were completely empathetic and were on board to do whatever was in their power to welcome Daniela into the St. Coletta family as quickly as possible. This is an excerpt from her response to my pleas for help -

"I'm so sorry things are stressful right now. We think Daniela will fit in well. We are anticipating that there will be a transition process, as there is with anyone moving to a new environment, but we believe it will be very manageable. There may be some bumps along the way, but time, patience and good communication can accomplish a great deal."

"We'll discuss the timing at our next Admit team meeting on Tuesday morning and I'll be able to give some firm dates at that point. We'll do our best to accommodate a move as soon as possible."

From that point on, the faxes, phone calls, and emails were constant. Liz's emailed promise of expediting Daniela's admission came on October 7, 2015. By the next week, Liz let us know that Daniela could move in on October 28th. I was in awe.

She said, "We are so excited to have Daniela join us! We really appreciate your assistance with getting all the forms returned so quickly - its a huge help on our end."

I replied to her, "Appreciate my assistance? You are so funny! You deserve ALL of our appreciation! I have a feeling Daniela's life is going to make a huge leap forward after languishing this past year."

I decided to write to family and friends about Daniela's future life in a letter. This is an edited version -

"BIG MOVE......Last month I posted about some exciting upcoming events concerning Daniela Goldstone. Well, we are finally ready to share the big news. Next week, I'll be flying to Wisconsin to help Daniela move to a new home! She will be moving to a beautiful house in Jefferson Wisconsin, about an hour north of where she is living now. She will share the house with 3 housemates and have help from someone during the evenings and weekends, so that she can continue to grow in her living skills, such as menu planning, cooking, and budgeting. This is all possible through an incredible organization called St. Coletta of Wisconsin. Some of you may have heard of St. Coletta. It was the home of President Kennedy's sister Rosemary for over 50 years. (We saw her former home on our first visit in August.) They have grown over the past 100 years to be one of the nation's leading and most well respected organizations working with people with disabilities. We are thrilled for Daniela to become part of the St. Coletta family. They have been so incredibly welcoming and supportive during this big transition (and we are SO appreciative!). Everyone there thinks Daniela, with all of her strengths AND challenges, will fit in beautifully. If ever we had an ultimate dream for Daniela's future, we could have never dreamed of something this grand. During the weekdays, Daniela will immediately be very busy with classes and many activities

at St. Coletta's program at the University of Wisconsin - Whitewater. Soon she will, hopefully, also be volunteering and working. She will NEVER be bored again! She had the chance last month, during my visit, to spend a night in her future home, meet some of her new friends and classmates, and attend some classes and activities. She absolutely loved every minute. St. Coletta has a new pilot program "Genesis" which is for young adults hoping to work in the community. It focuses on vocational and leadership skills plus academic, social and living skills. The community is also very involved with Special Olympics and Best Buddies, which Daniela is so excited about. The talented and experienced staff are vibrant and enthusiastic. She will have so many opportunities that I can't even begin to list them all. Daniela has really missed the structure, community, classes and activities that she experienced at Shepherds College. Now she has this new remarkable chance to continue to grow on her journey to independence!!"

Daniela moved in to her new home and settled into her new life gradually. There were, as to be expected, a few bumps along the way as she adjusted to a much more structured and busy life. Living with 3 new housemates who were older and much different than her in their interests and abilities was the most challenging aspect for her. We had been forced to rush her move and we couldn't wait for the best housing match for her. It was certainly fine though and a good place for the staff to continue to evaluate what the best living situation for her would be.

By the beginning of 2016, after Daniela came to stay over the holidays with us, she was obviously gaining back her confidence after the previous year's deterioration. She transitioned into the new Genesis program and threw herself into volunteering and many activities. She gained many new friends. She called me enthusiastically every day to recap her life. She was challenged to try new experiences and become a self-advocate - not only for herself but for the entire community. She signed up for some of the many day trips and activities offered (overnight trips are also offered to areas further away, including out of Wisconsin). Her dad and I continually sighed big sighs of relief. Our stress levels from the year before happily became a thing of the past.

By the summer of 2016, a more suitable residential placement became available in a large friendly house known as St. Agnes. The women in the house welcomed Daniela for a visit, and in August, we moved her into her new bigger space. She was able to spread out her collection of shoes (many shoes) and books and all of the things she enjoys. Since that day, St. Agnes and the wonderful women who both live and work there have truly become Daniela's family, home and sanctuary. We have become friends with the other clients' families and we all try to work together to add some "extras" to make life cozy to all who enter the home.

Daniela's life at St. Coletta continually adds new facets. For a while, she worked on campus as she figured out what kind of a job she would like to have. When she found and became successful at her job at the local Kwiktrip, she was congratulated by all who saw her there as they stopped for coffee, gas, or snack. Everybody at St. Coletta knows Daniela. Her vibrant presence has become a vital part of the fabric of the community just like every other person who has lived and worked there since 1904. Her history and ours will forever be entwined in this unique family.

I decided this would be a good place for Daniela to say how she feels about St. Coletta. I asked her questions about her life at St. Coletta. Her answers are in Italics:

"What do you remember about your first day at St. Coletta?"
"I didn't know anybody and I was shy. After a little bit I opened up and they became part of my family."

"What were you most afraid of back then?"
"I was scared about moving to a new house, but I got the hang of it. Just look at me now!"

"What were you most excited about when you joined the community?"
"Meeting new friends, and I was very excited about being in Genesis".

"What do you love about Genesis?"
"I've been learning about math and money skills. Genesis helped me get a job out in the community and they helped me keep my job too. I've taken lots of online history courses that I love. My favorite ones were on Romania and Ireland. Right now we are reading a book called, The Code Girls. They were codebreakers in World War 2."

"What are your favorite things about living in your house?"
"I love living with my housemates. I love going out to dinner with them and going to the movies. We like to have cookouts. We like to play games together.

"You had to quit your job because of the pandemic. What do you miss about it?"
"I miss working. I miss making money and learning new skills. I liked working with the staff. When the pandemic is over, I want to start working somewhere again.

"What are you looking forward to this year?"

"I'm looking forward to going to the Woodside Ranch for a weekend and riding horses.. I'm also looking forward to going bowling, doing track and field and playing basketball. I also like going to hockey and basketball games with my friends.

"What are you most proud of yourself for?"

"I'm proud that I go out in the community on my own. I take taxis to the stores by myself and walk to the ice cream store." "St. Coletta has changed me in lots of ways. I try new foods. I'm not as shy as I used to be. I've learned to speak up for myself and other people with disabilities. It has made me more motivated to try new things."

"Why is St. Coletta special to you?"

"Coletta is my other family. All the people here are special to me. It's the perfect place for me to live. I want to be in my St. Coletta family forever."

The next chapter highlights just a few of the many, many other wonderful family stories at St. Coletta. I wish I could share them all. That would be a multi-volume series of books. All are families who are compassionate, battle-worn and fierce advocates for their loved ones.

2015 - Daniela moves in - Nervous, excited and with no idea what wonderful adventures await her!

She loves being a part of the St. Coletta community. It's in the people.

With Jefferson's finest at the Special Olympics Torch Run - my favorite photo by Noah Smith

Daniela and me. I'm her mom and biggest fan. What a journey we have traveled.

Chapter 16

Family Stories

When I decided to write this book I knew that I wanted to include family stories. Because of the importance of their privacy, I wasn't quite sure how I was going to accomplish that. I eventually was told about families who might be willing to contribute. I decided to write to them, tell them my plans for the book and hope that some of them would respond. Fortunately for me, they did. I am very grateful to all of them.

I gave the participants a few guidelines and suggestions, but I mostly wanted them to feel free to share what they wanted to tell about life at St. Coletta. These are their stories -

Joe Shackelford -

This story is shared by Joe's mother Mary Jo Shackelford. Mary Jo and I have gotten to know each other over the past few years when she decided to help create the Family Advocacy group at St. Coletta. She reached out to me over the phone and I knew from the beginning that we would connect. We shared both a love of St. Coletta and the goal of making sure that the community would continue to thrive for at least the next hundred years. Her story was written by her, and her husband Doug. It contains within it, parts of a story that was put together by the Shackelfords for, and previously published by, St. Coletta. I appreciate their permission in allowing me to use it.

From the beginning, Doug and I pretty much took control of Joe's situation, as we were not finding a lot of support in the Columbus, Ohio area at the time (where we were living). Joe was one of those children that defy any label, so it was difficult to determine what the best course of action would have been. In Ohio, starting at age 3, Joe had positive experiences in two separate programs (through much research, many phone calls and using all the resources we could find at the time).

From there, when Joe was 6, we moved to Milwaukee and he attended St. Francis Activity and Achievement Center which was part of Cardinal Stritch College. While there we were introduced to St. Coletta of Wisconsin. While Joe was attending St. Francis Activity and Achievement Center, he also attended summer camps at St. Coletta. After a move to Ohio and a disastrous attempt at putting Joe in the public school system where we were told the school district had no "special needs" children and placed Joe in a SBH (severe behavioral handicapped program, not good) we made the difficult decision to place Joe (who was then 12) in the residential program at St. Coletta. Joe has now been at St. Coletta for 38 years.

During his time here, he completed the school program, vocational training program, and eventually held a job in the dish room at the Fireside Dinner Theatre for 20+ years, working up to 40 hours per week. In addition to that Joe delivered papers 3 mornings a week in Jefferson. From a social perspective, one of Joe's favorite activities was to walk downtown Jefferson, talking/visiting with the shop owners and sometimes having a beer at one of the local taverns. His friendly, social approach with all those working downtown Jefferson earned him the nickname of "Downtown Joe" among those that he regularly visited. Joe also participated in Special Olympic events and other social activities provided by St. Coletta.

All was going well and Joe was living independently in his own apartment until May 28th, 2016. While riding his bike, Joe was hit by a car and suffered life threatening injuries. Joe suffered a skull fracture (the best type they told us, if there is such a thing) coupled with other injuries and was in the hospital for a total of 107 days. We were living thousands of miles away and were unable to get a flight until the following day. From that first day through the 107th day, it was St. Coletta that made the difference. The day the accident happened, residential staff and Ted Behnke, St. Coletta's President, stayed by his bedside throughout the night. Joe spent 2½ weeks in ICU and was then transferred to a rehabilitation hospital that is certified in traumatic brain injuries. During his hospital time, St. Coletta staff was with him every step of the way, beginning with being at his side when taken to the emergency room at the time of the accident, to visits at his bedside, providing counseling for us, and continued to support him through his hospital stay. The staff and residents at Assisi came to visit Joe while he was in rehab and provided the motivation needed for him to continue to work hard so that he could return to his apartment at Assisi.

Although Joe's recovery is progressing well, we are still working through some of the issues caused by his accident. We made the decision to relocate to Wisconsin so we can continue to support Joe throughout his recovery. They originally told us it would be a 3 year recovery process for Joe. We are into year 3 and still continue to see progress every day, especially in his cognitive functions. Joe has been able to return to his apartment, regaining his independence and is working part time on the St. Coletta campus in the dish room of the elder care center on the campus, as well as attending day programming 5 days each week.

We are blessed to finally have Joe back at St. Coletta, where they have always provided him a safe haven within a real community. St. Coletta stands by their tag line, "It's in the people" and we are grateful for the amazing work they do.

These words are from Joe about his life at St. Coletta - "I really like my apartment and friends at St. Coletta. They are really nice to talk to and I have fun with them. I like being independent and going to work every day. I like to walk downtown, eat at the restaurants and go to the gym to work out."

The Pennington Family -

This story comes from Art Pennington, the father of three daughters who spent part of their lives at St. Coletta.

"The Magic of St. Coletta of Wisconsin"

In 1991, my oldest daughter Terri was 24 and anxious to leave home to become as independent as she could be. However, she was a special needs adult so her options were limited.

We lived in Chicago. I was told the group homes and other facilities in Illinois had a twenty-year waiting list. Not to be deterred, I visited the one farthest from Chicago; in down state Illinois, thinking their list would probably be the shortest. It was shorter – eighteen years! In addition, if I were to make a $40,000 contribution, she could move to the top of the list. So, I quickly learned of their primary objective, and it had nothing to do with my daughter's best interests.

I decided I would just look for a private placement for Terri but do my research to find the very best possible environment for her. Even way back in 1991, that research took an amazingly short amount of time – St. Coletta of Wisconsin was the obvious choice:

- Founded in 1904, based on Franciscan values
- The first school on the nation to offer an education for special needs children
- Offers a comprehensive program of education, work, spiritual values, and community integration
- Pioneered many successful techniques for special needs education
- Measures their success by the success of their clients
- Chosen by the Kennedy family for their own daughter

That is only a short list of the many accolades I found for St. Coletta. Terri moved to St. Coletta in Jefferson Wisconsin within just a couple of weeks. She was so excited to be finally "On her own". She entered a special program,

134

run by one of the Nun's (wish I could remember her name), to practice independent living skills. She was one happy girl!

That began a weekly trip to Jefferson that I made for twenty-six years to visit, until I packed up and moved to Jefferson myself in 2017. On my weekly visits, I took my other two special needs daughters to visit Terri. She would also come home every holiday.

After a few months of this, my youngest daughter Tami decided she wanted to live at St. Coletta too! She saw what a great experience it was for Terri & wanted that too. Within a few more months, they were all three at St. Coletta, after my other daughter Tonya decided to go. What a great testament to the loving, caring, supportive environment of St. Coletta.

At the time, St. Coletta was structured in a campus setting, with all clients living on and around the integrated campus. It was a beautiful arrangement – with clients able to walk between their homes, work, activities, and visit their friends whenever they wanted. They all had a great feeling of being independent and, at the same time, being in a safe, protective environment. That was all about to change, in a big way, compliments of the federal government!

For reasons I will never understand, our government decided it would no longer fund clients who lived in a centralized campus environment. The campus would close and all clients must be disbursed in integrated community housing. St. Coletta had no alternate space available in Jefferson. So, I was forced to move all three daughters to non-St. Coletta group homes in the area in 2000.

I feared that might spell the end of St. Coletta. How could they possibly make such a drastic change to their structure and survive? Little did I understand their history of resilience and brilliance. After all, they had survived, and even thrived, all through the great depression.

From 2000 until just a few years ago, I lost track of what was happening at St. Coletta – assuming they were still struggling through somehow. Two of my daughters developed serious health issues and had both passed away by 2016. So, my focus was on them and helping them through their struggles.

In 2017, I decided to move to Jefferson. My daughters had relocated to a town outside of Jefferson. So, I hadn't spent much time there for many years. I started driving around a bit and noticed many little white shuttle busses with "St. Coletta" on the side. To my amazement, St. Coletta had transformed itself from a campus environment to a disbursed community environment and was thriving even more than before.

I cannot even imagine how that was accomplished. I asked Cathy Roberts, head of St. Coletta admissions[55] until retirement, how that was accomplished. Her answer was characteristically understated; "Just one group home at a time". My head explodes just thinking about the task they had to perform:

- Relocate hundreds of clients from campus to group homes – homes that mostly did not even exist at the time
- Relocating hundreds of Alverno nursing home residents to make room for the main offices to be relocated in the building
- Finding a buyer for the old campus property
- Redesigning all programs and jobs to function in a disbursed setting

I've built four successful software companies during my career – pretty complex undertakings – but I wouldn't even know where to begin the task that St. Coletta had to perform.

I can only surmise that the seed for success that has enabled them to not only survive but thrive, through all of the calamities that have befallen them over the past 115 years is their Franciscan values – values that enable a clearer vision of the real problem and visibility to the right solution – the solution that is best for their charges; our children. Through it all, somehow, they have continued to provide a home where special needs individuals are accepted, valued, nurtured, and enabled to be the very best they can be.

I am proud to now be a part of that magic – working at St. Coletta as a direct support professional*. My deceased children would be so excited to know that I am working there now. And I am so blessed to be able to honor them in that way.

*(Art Pennington is currently the Transportation Manager at St. Coletta.)

Michael McTigue -
The next story was sent to me by Michael's younger brother, Dennis McTigue.

So let me tell you a bit about my oldest brother, Michael. He was born in 1941 in a small town in Iowa and due to an accident at birth he suffered irreversible brain damage. His condition was further compromised when, at the age of 7, he was struck by a car and was in intensive care for weeks. In spite of his significant challenges, Michael developed into a charming person with a great sense of humor and a strong body.

The greatest concern for any parent of a child with special needs is "who will take care of him/her when I'm gone"? Our parents began searching for a place where Michael could continue to learn, be safe and be happy and they found that place in St. Coletta in Jefferson, Wisconsin. Our mother's family was from Racine, WI, and our father worked for Northwestern Mutual based in Milwaukee so St. Coletta was close and convenient. Even more importantly for our parents, the Sisters at St. Coletta provided an environment where Michael could grow spiritually as well as intellectually and he began there in 1954.

Mike made many friends at St. Coletta and our family developed a network with other families who had loved ones living there. On holidays and summer breaks when Mike would come home our parents would often bring other St. Coletta residents who lived in our area. Riding along on these trips I can well remember how interesting and engaging they all were and some of my earliest friends were Michael's St. Coletta pals.

I first came to realize how special St. Coletta was one July day in 1958 when my parents were picking Mike up for the summer. I was hanging out with some of his friends while my parents were talking with Sister Mary Theodore. Suddenly, all of the guys started running down the hall and I tried to catch one to tell me what they were doing. A boy told me that the Milwaukee Braves were outside and they were all going to meet them. I thought, sure, the Milwaukee Braves -reigning World Series champs - are here at St. Coletta today.... Despite my skepticism, I walked over to a window and sure enough, there was a bus with a bunch of Braves - in full dress uniform - getting out and greeting the guys. Without telling my parents I ran down the stairs and outside to get a better look. Among the dozen or so players were All Stars: Henry Aaron, Eddie Mathews, Johnny Logan, Del Crandall and Warren Spahn. I was so tempted to join the throng of kids crowding around the players for autographs but even as a 10 year old, I realized that this was the St. Coletta kids' day and I was so envious of them!

Michael has always been a valued member of the St. Coletta community. Once when I visited to attend his annual service planning meeting, I stopped in to meet the newly appointed president, Bud Meece. After a brief chat he asked if I'd mind if he sat in on Mike's planning session as he hadn't been to one yet and, of course, I agreed. For many years, St. Coletta ran its own laundry to serve the needs of its residents and Michael loved working there. In fact, the staff always noted at these meetings how responsible and task oriented he was, significantly reducing their work load. So imagine how surprised I was when, in front of the new president, they reported having a problem with Mike in the laundry!

The laundry facility was on campus in a ground floor building and it seems that Michael was opening a window every Sunday evening and climbing in to work there, un-supervised. The staff was appropriately concerned and made it clear that this just couldn't continue. Mike defensively replied that he was just trying to organize the laundry bins so that they could get a quicker start every Monday morning.

Everyone in the room knew that Mike meant no harm but this activity had to stop – Michael was crushed. After an awkward silence, Mr. Meece asked if he could offer a solution. He noted that all agreed that Michael was an outstanding worker, very responsible and reliable but climbing in through a window was dangerous and being there without anyone knowing it was unsafe and irresponsible for the school to allow. So he said, "How about this? Let's make Michael the Assistant Director of the Laundry and put a key in his home to check out every Sunday afternoon. That way, he can enter safely and work there for a little bit while his residence staff know where he is." What a solution! It was truly a win-win and Mike continued to work and excel in the laundry as long as it existed.

St. Coletta and Jefferson, Wisconsin, have truly been Michael's home. He has had the freedom to go into town and has made numerous friends in the community, attending their family's baptisms, weddings, funerals as well as a host of community events. Our parents found a gem in St. Coletta and Michael and our family will forever be grateful.

Craig Buker -

Craig's story was written by me after a phone interview with his mother, Karen. We conducted the interview in April 2020 as we were both dealing with life in the middle of the Covid 19 pandemic.

Craig was born in Wisconsin in the early 1970s. He first came to the St. Coletta School as a young man of 17 and in 2020 he celebrated this 30th year in the St. Coletta community. He was born with Down syndrome and his family had to deal with all of the challenges that were present for families of children with disabilities in that time period. The most important challenge was trying to give their son the best education that would help him develop to his greatest potential. Craig's family was successful. He was able to start an early intervention program at the age of 10 months through Cardinal Stritch University in nearby Milwaukee.

While Craig was there, his parents became friends with a family who had a young daughter in the program. That little girl and Craig also became close friends. At the age of three they started in a preschool program together

138

located in a public school. While the two little friends eventually ended up attending different schools, the families remained close. The girl, as a teenager, became a part of the St. Coletta School in Jefferson. Craig's family followed her progress there and gradually became interested in their son also joining St. Coletta's school program. As a benefit of entering the school program, Craig would also be eligible to join the adult program after he graduated. Craig started at the high school at age 17, he was happily reunited with his childhood friend. After graduating from the school at the age of 21, he transitioned and settled into the adult housing and programming.

When St. Coletta opened their new Waukesha adult residential program, the family was very happy to have the opportunity to have Craig move closer to home in the Milwaukee suburbs. As the years progressed, he changed housing there several times. He now lives in a comfortable group home with other young men who have become his close friends. For a long time the day programming in Waukesha was provided by one, and then another, outside agency that both ended up closing because of financing issues. Thankfully by then, St. Coletta had opened its new Brookfield Inter-generational Center, in a town near Waukesha, in 2019. This new center offers the same great and varied day programming as is available at St. Coletta's main campus in Jefferson.

Craig is part of Brookfield's Genesis program and is a very active participant in the St. Coletta community with many interests. He also enjoys spending most weekends with his family so he has the best of both worlds. At his family home, he is the crucifer (cross bearer) at his church and he loves helping with shopping and chores. At his St. Coletta home, he likes to keep his living area very tidy. Craig enjoys drawing and loves a wide range of music from Metallica to Neil Diamond to Johnny Cash. He enthusiastically plays his air drums to accompany the artists. He also loves action hero movies. He has also been a vital member of St. Coletta's Special Olympic team, participating over the years in track, swimming, bowling, and bocce ball.

Craig's main interest is doing research on his laptop. The topic of that research is, surprisingly, Dracula. (I mentioned to his mom during our interview that my daughter was from Romania, where the Dracula myth first originated from the history of the prince, Vlad Tepes. I promised his mom that I would bring Craig some Dracula souvenirs that I once bought on a trip to Transylvania, Romania. I brought it to him in May 2021).

Craig's mom tells me that "he has a great sense of humor and considers himself the funny man! His family, friends and staff can attest to that." Like every client I have been lucky enough to meet at St. Coletta, Craig is a unique and fascinating person who is adored by his family and community.

Ralph Derucki -

St. Coletta of Wisconsin loves all of its clients and treats each one with equal care and respect. There is, however, one client who deserves just a little extra. His name is Ralph and he epitomizes everything that St. Coletta is or ever was. His smile and warmth light up everyone's day. On my most recent visit to the campus, everything stopped and everyone gathered to celebrate his 95th birthday. The following account was written several years ago by Robin Baker, St. Coletta's Vice President of Development and Marketing, and is posted on St. Coletta's website. Thank you Robin for allowing me to include your beautiful tribute to Ralph.

No one at St. Coletta is more steeped in tradition than Ralph. Coming to St. Coletta in 1936, at the young age of 9, Ralph was given an opportunity to live, learn and grow through his experiences with the Sisters of St. Francis and his peers.

Ralph has fond memories working alongside the Sisters in the fields and gardens, canning fruits & vegetables and tending to the chickens. In his spare time, Ralph also cut hair, served Mass, learned Latin, sang in the choir, and held a number of jobs in the community. He went on to learn such practical skills as cross stitch and knitting, which he still practices today at age 91. "My skills allow me to help others. I'm currently making blankets to help Wisconsin's homeless Veterans".

In 1975, Ralph was selected to travel with the Sisters to Rome for a pilgrimage.. It was there he prayed to connect with his birth mother and upon returning from his trip, he was met with a phone message from the nursing home his Mother was at. From there, Ralph spent the next 15 years getting to know his Mom before her passing in 1990. "My trip to Rome changed my life and I'm grateful to the Sisters who helped strengthen my faith in God".

Nowadays, Ralph enjoys spending time with his housemates and attending St. Coletta's Golden Options day program, He serves on the Franciscans committee just like he did for the Sisters in the 1950s and was recently selected to be an official brand ambassador for St. Coletta. "I want to help advocate for my peers, who may not have a voice."

After 82 years of support, Ralph insists this was the plan all along. "When I walked into St. Coletta a young boy, Sr. Anastasia came up to me and said 'this is going to be home for you' and while I may not have realized it at the time, I do now".

Update - June 1, 2022

I received the very sad news today that, last night, Ralph's long, glorious life journey finally came to an end. Just a few weeks ago on May 11 Ralph celebrated his 95th birthday and the next day he posed for this book's cover photos. I'm sure he is celebrating now with many of his family, friends, fans and the Sisters who watched him grow up. Ralph - God blessed so many with your beautiful soul here on earth. May you now find peace and happiness in Heaven.

Ralph Derucki on May 11, 2022 with Ted Behncke

Chapter 17

Staff Stories

The final group of stories that I am including in the book were gathered from the lay staff, past and present. They have worked over decades to make St. Coletta of Wisconsin what it is today. Without the contributions from the lay staff when Sisters retired, the organization would have had to close many years ago. There are so many individuals who have worked in the diverse parts of the community to keep it afloat. Every person at St. Coletta is critical to the mission. Daniela's life and the lives of all of her friends depend on them, their professionalism and their compassion.

Andrea Speth -

Andrea Speth, like many current and past St. Coletta staff members, held several key positions in her work at the organization. Though she is no longer part of the organization, it clearly has made a large impact on her life. I reached out to ask her about her work in the major transitions that happened at St. Coletta from 1995 to 2010.

In Andrea's employment at St. Coletta, she served as a grant writer, development director and as a Vice-President of both Development, Communications and Marketing. She said, "Over the years I worked with 5 Presidents." I asked her about what she remembered from the huge transitions of closing the school and moving clients out into the community. She replied, "I remember that it was uncomfortable! Clients didn't understand, nor did their families. While so many institutions had a bad rap, that was not St. Coletta. Families adored the family/group home setting on the inclusive campus." "I was involved in the changes from a planning, fundraising and communications perspective. There was lots of need for good communications and I often found myself working with individual families."

When I asked Andrea about her memories of the Sisters as their numbers slowly decreased over the years she said, "When I first came, there were several households of Sisters living in the main building. We benefited tremendously from their wisdom as changes were made. I can remember working late in the night and having them come visit in their house robes! They were so kind and generous with their stories, their advice and their care and concern for the lay administration. When enough was enough, they shut the lights off on us....it was time to go home to our families. (Andrea wrote this with a smile emoji.) She also spoke about making sure the community kept an emphasis on what the Sisters had established as it moved more and more into a lay organization. "We established our Franciscan Values which are now seen in so many places. We established the Office of Mission Effectiveness." She also said they began Corporate Ministries meetings and had a Sisters of St. Francis representative on every Board of Directors (for the Corporate Ministries). Those efforts were very successful. Everything that happens at St. Coletta is infused with the Sisters' knowledge and contributions.

I asked Andrea what she was most proud of during her years of St. Coletta. She said that there were so many things. They included organizing Rosemary Kennedy's funeral, working on the new Alverno building (as it transitioned from housing clients to becoming St. Coletta's administration building, chapel, and the center for many of day programs.) She also saw her work on the building and its history wall as her "last love letter to the organization that gave me so much good experience." (She empathized that she had lots of help with the history wall.) She spoke about being involved in the very serious issue of securing funding for the clients in 2005. "Battling for funding for people who were never funded through the state...it was a long battle of legislative advocacy, but it meant millions for those individuals and for St. Coletta. I began my day thinking about who I could bug at the state to bring attention to the issues."

It was obvious to me from every word she wrote about St. Coletta, that Andrea's life was forever changed and impacted by her work there.

I also conducted interviews with three current, long-term, members of the St. Coletta staff. Through the years all three have held a variety of positions and have contributed greatly in making the community what it is today.

Geralyn Dorn -

I first met Geralyn a few months after Daniela became part of St. Coletta in 2015. Daniela had been given a few months to adjust before the staff decided on the best day program for her to join. (Daniela contributed to the decision). After she settled into community life, Geralyn asked her if she wanted to be part of their new program called "Genesis". The program is a pre-vocational endeavor for the community's younger clients. It serves both day and residential clients and covers a broad area of topics. Geralyn became the program's first director and it was she who thought Daniela would fit in very well.

Before Genesis, Geralyn had 35 years' worth of experience at St. Coletta. She started out as a young woman working as a "chief child care worker". The children called her Miss Geralyn and she says a few clients still call her that. Since then, she has worked with a variety of clients, from childhood until the end of their lives. Long before starting the Genesis program, she held a number of important positions. She was involved in St. Coletta's first ventures into community integration and living. She also started as the first coordinator of the Excel program, as well as working in Golden Options (for the community's senior population)and Adult Education and Recreation. She then moved on to managing all of the day programs and services. After getting Genesis off to a great start, Geralyn moved to the Director of Admissions and Outreach.

Geralyn has special memories from early in her career, when she oversaw young men from ages 18 to 21. She said, "One thing I do remember is that everywhere that I went with my group, I counted them - frequently. I was responsible for a group of 24 men with varying support needs - I didn't ever want to leave anyone behind! Yes, there are a number of people who are still at St. Coletta that I worked with so many years ago and it's great to be able to continue to be a part of their lives." Geralyn says she also continues to stay in touch with clients and staff who have moved on from St. Coletta.

She spoke about her experiences in the creation of the Excel program which is the program created in partnership with the University of Wisconsin - Whitewater (located near Jefferson). This program is innovative and beneficial for both the university and the St. Coletta community. Geralyn said, "The program was created to enhance community integration, form a partnership with the university and to provide a day filled with educational, recreation/ leisure and relationships with the students/faculty who provide our individuals with friendships, learning opportunities and fulfilling relationships with each other." The program continues to be a huge success. Geralyn says, "There have been many changes along the way - actually they provide us with more and more opportunities both for Excel as well as the Recreation Program. I think one of my favorites is bringing interested individuals to practice with the UW-Warhawks football team. There are also many other opportunities such as Best Buddies."

I asked Geralyn about what it was like for families when the school and old campus closed. About the school, she said , "Parents had difficulty because they weren't always in favor of their child attending public school for the fear of bullying, teasing and not knowing if the public school system could do what schools like St. Coletta could."

About the campus closure, I asked if it had been a gradual change. Geralyn replied, "It was. It was very difficult for many parents/families. Some of the families found other places with campus living for their loved ones to move to, some individuals went home, but most of the individuals stayed and moved into houses in the community."

144

When I asked about how government involvement changed St. Coletta, Geralyn said this, "I don't think anything or anyone could or will take away from the heart of St. Coletta. I think we adjust to changes and still find ways to stay the same." I asked her about the faith element and if she thought it has diminished. She feels it is as strong as ever, saying "The Sisters are and will always remain as involved as they ever were."

When I asked how St. Coletta had changed her, she said this, "My job helped me to become more responsible, flexible, patient and understanding. St. Coletta has been the best education I have ever had, being able to learn from the people we serve, other professionals and the families. I have made many friendships along the way. I have learned that people are people; each of us have gifts to share no matter who we are. I have been given the most valuable gifts from the people we serve and I will hold them in my heart forever. Life really isn't about anything else except finding our purpose, sharing our gifts and serving others. Serving others is limitless."

Diane Pinnow -

Diane started her career working as a sixth grade teacher in the local community. After a seven year break as a stay at home mom, she had let her teaching license lapse. When her husband had a sudden job change, she knew she needed to quickly return to the job force. In January of 1990, she saw a non-teaching position available at St. Coletta and thought it would work well for her family. She said this about then becoming a teacher at St. Coletta, "In August 1990, a teaching position opened up at the St. Coletta School. Because it was a private school they didn't require a current teaching license. I had started my college years as a special ed major and had experience over the years volunteering with students who had special needs, so Larry Gierach (the principal at St. Coletta School at the time) took a chance and gave me the position."

At the time that Diane began teaching in 1990, Diane says, "the school was in full swing." She wrote that the students ranged in age from 9 to 21. "There were about a dozen classrooms and about 150 students with a wide range from low to high abilities." While the school was arranged in the typical elementary, junior high and high school levels, within that structure the students were divided by abilities, rather than ages, "with 3-4 classrooms at each level". Diane taught high school students age 16-21.

By 1995, Diane was prompted to be co-principal (along with Tom Seifert). When Mr. Seifert left in early 1996, Diane was the sole principal. By late 1996 she realized she did not enjoy working in management and moved away from St. Coletta for the next two years. In the two year period that she was gone, the decision was made to close the school. When she came back to work for the organization in 1998 it was in a part-time secretarial position.

Diane now works at St. Coletta as an administrative assistant. She says, "Personally I have stuck with St. Coletta (when I originally thought I wouldn't even last a year.)....if I have to summarize it in one word....because of flexibility." "I loved my early direct care position because it was third shift and allowed me time with my elementary school aged children. I loved my teaching position because I was off in the summer when my kids were. And after I departed for a couple of years and returned in a secretarial capacity I have totally loved that my bosses understand that I am *not* a morning person." "I get much more done from 4:30-6 when everyone is done, and then I don't have to be stressed by deadlines during the day when others come with last minute requests."

Diane continues, "Although flexibility is a wonderful perk, the best part has to be the people - both co-workers and clients. So many kind hearts, so many funny moments, so much joy, so many personalities. St. Coletta has provided a lifetime of memories and feels like a family. There is always something going on, never a dull moment. Getting a job here has been a true joy and I didn't even realize it when it all began."

To finish Diane's story, I asked her if she could share any stories from her many years in the community. It turns out that she actually kept notes of the funny stories over the years. One involved Brother Boniface (a longtime teacher, now retired, who has a wicked sense of humor) and Tom Seifert, the Principal at the time of the story. For fun, they hid a microphone behind a statue of Jesus in the school hallway. Diane said, "As students walked past they would make comments as if Jesus were talking." When one student walked by they called out her name. "She waved dismissively saying, 'Not now Jesus, I'm late for class!'"

In a story involving Diane, she related this, "One of the clients paid me a visit. After several minutes of small talk I reminded him we were both supposed to be working. He gave me a smart salute and said, 'I just wanted to say hello. So you have a good day.' Then as he walked out the door he turned and added, 'And by the way, I'm sorry I farted in your office.' And away he went."

As Diane said - the feeling at St. Coletta goes beyond staff, clients, and families. It goes beyond friendship. It is indeed one big loving family.

Sara Foerster-

The last staff story is an essay written by Sara Forester. She is a person at St. Coletta that our family has come to know very well. Sara is Daniela's case coordinator. She oversees all aspects of Daniela's life and works with all of the other people at St. Coletta working to help Daniela achieve her highest quality of life. She also coordinates with all the people from other agencies in Daniela's life - such as vocational services, Medicaid, Social Security, her managed care organization and her medical professionals. - And, of course, Daniela is only one of her clients.....

At this point, Sara knows as much about our daughter and what makes her tick as we do. She is smart, compassionate and very funny. I love Sara's laugh. Daniela adores her, values her time with her and respects her completely. Sara can whip through red tape in record time. She always goes above and beyond. When people from other agencies speak to me, they frequently mention how amazing Sara is. They say they have never worked with anyone else on a client's behalf who was as organized and who knew their client so well. Sara Foerster is one of the main reasons that I am able to sleep well at night.

Sara loves history, especially St. Coletta's history. She was the first person I told that I planned to write this book. She has accompanied me to interviews and helped me with research. She also assisted with a very detailed final editing of this book. Her attention to detail was flawless and reflected the same dedication that she gives each of her clients and their families. This book wouldn't be what it is without her. Her encouragement kept me going when I doubted whether people would value it.

Sara's Story -

"When I hear the name St. Coletta, the first thing that comes to mind is "opportunity". Reflecting further on this one word, I realize that this not only applies to the residents and participants in the St. Coletta programs but to the employees as well. When you are hired at St. Coletta you are told that St. Coletta has its own culture, that it is a certain unique "brand"; a family. Hearing this, you might think that this is a marketing attempt to onboard new employees. Being a part of St. Coletta for only a year, I can certainly believe that this is not a marketing attempt, but those words ring true.

When you walk into St. Coletta there is a "feeling" that happens, a transformation of oneself that comes over each one of us. This transformation helps us be what we continue to be today, our own unique brand. Looking back at the St. Coletta history, it's clear to me on why we have this brand and stand out from all the rest. This brand was created and conceived by the founders of St. Coletta and was held steadfast by back breaking work, long hours, and most of all; having immense compassion and love for the ones they served. From the start, St. Coletta has always stood out from the rest. Sisters were completing their Master Degrees, Doctorate Degrees and also assisted the participants in receiving their education and life skills that they needed to be as independent as possible. They challenged the norms of society and gave everyone an opportunity to thrive, no matter how severe their disability. We, as part of the St. Coletta family, have to ensure that we carry on this brand today and into the future. With this pledge, it has allowed the mission of the founders to continue on today. I had the honor to meet with some of the Sisters and when asked on how they were able to make St. Coletta thrive and function, even with scarce resources, they simply stated with a smile, "God always provides".

Each participant at St Coletta is given an opportunity to grow, to strive towards independence and to be a part of the mission of the St. Coletta family. In my 20 years of experience in the human services field I have never seen such person centered services.

For me, St Coletta was my greatest opportunity. Right from the start, I was given the opportunity just to interview for the position. When I put in my application, a former employee of mine, (that currently works for St. Coletta) took my application down to the Director of the case management team, and insisted she interview me. The Director thankfully listened and called me for an interview. I was someone that had a vast experience but only held an Associate's Degree. The position I applied for at St. Coletta required a Bachelor's degree. My supervisor told me when I was hired that I was the first person she has ever even interviewed that did not have a Bachelor's degree. She took a chance on me, she gave me an opportunity.

St. Coletta gave me an opportunity to start over. To proceed in life in a more positive direction and to learn that I am someone of value. St. Coletta has given me the opportunity to grow, to step out of my comfort zone and to be a part of something big. The environment taught me how to be part of a team, to share equal responsibility and most importantly feel okay with asking for help. It has also allowed me to dream again. To be optimistic on what life holds, not only for me but for my daughters as well. In this environment we struggle together, we learn together and most importantly we celebrate each other. There is no line drawn in the sand on who is staff and who is a client. It's all of us trying to figure out life together, all in the same way. I have had the opportunity to go back to school, to meet so many amazing people and to apply myself towards something meaningful. God had a plan for me and drawing me to St. Coletta was for sure one of them.

I believe St. Coletta beckons to people that are broken. We are all broken in some sort of way and here we can be accepted for what is broken and empowered to put back some of the pieces that we are able to. This being said, "It's in the people" is for sure a meaningful statement."

These are the stories of only a few of the many wonderful staff members who work at St. Coletta. There is an embarrassment of riches when it comes to the people who have made this community part of their life. I could have shared so many more stories. I'm grateful for each person who has worked at St. Coletta, the Sisters and the lay staff, and for everything that they have done to enrich the lives of the people that they serve.

No one works harder or is more appreciated than each of St. Coletta's DSPs (Direct Support Professionals). It was never more evident than when they risked their own lives to care for clients during the pandemic.

Daniela with her role model and our hero, Sara
Foerster. I don't think this book would exist
without her.

Diane Pinnow, Becky Weber, Geralyn Dorn -
Their dedication to St. Coletta and their
assistance with this book are very much
appreciated.

Robin Baker, VP, graciously accepting a
donation. Her support and contributions to
this book are too numerous to count.

Noah Smith, who records the beautiful
portrait of St. Coletta's history for
posterity and who helped bring this book
to life. So grateful!

The staff give each other support and friendship.

There are many ways that St. Coletta's talented staff are appreciated and every holiday is celebrated.

Christmas brings the staff a special holiday breakfast (or lunch so that everyone can attend.)

Retirement parties (here for Steve Naugle) celebrate staff who often have worked whole careers at St. Coletta. Steve was also a St. Coletta Presidential Award winner.

Staff Recognition Dinner Illinois 2022

Staff Recognition Dinner Jefferson 2022

Chapter 18

St. Coletta 2015 - 2021

Writing about the St. Coletta that existed before Daniela's arrival has been a very different experience than writing about the community that I have come to know so well. It's been so interesting to see the organization continue to evolve in the past six years. They are open to changes and to new programs, ideas and opportunities. When something is not working well for an existing program, everyone works together to make modifications that will make life better for the clients and all those who work with them.

One of their earliest big changes after Daniela arrived on campus was the creation of St. Coletta's "Project Moonshot" initiative. According to the MacMillan dictionary "Moonshot" thinking is a type of thinking that aims to achieve something that is generally thought impossible. "It motivates people to think out of the box by presenting problems as solvable and encouraging people that "anything is possible".

I first heard about the new program in 2016, at a presentation that is given to families every August, on the Friday before the annual family picnic. The yearly presentations review the past year, the financial status of the community and the changes coming for the next year. It's a great opportunity for St. Coletta to share their continuing vision and let families ask questions.

Ted Behncke, the President, had been working with the administration and the St. Coletta Board of Directors to come up with a new plan to hire and retain the highest quality staff possible. This is no easy task. The level of state and federal funding that is allocated for the purpose of paying direct care professionals, including the DSPs at St. Coletta, has been less than is needed for a number of years.

The inadequate funding that is generally available for this very challenging work often results in a pool of staff candidates that are not always suitable for their positions. The work can be physically exhausting and emotionally stressful. It requires a deep level of commitment, compassion and professionalism. The local service industry, such as fast food restaurants and big box stores, sometimes pay more than the pay that is available for working in a position serving people with disabilities. This makes being a competitive employer difficult. This also leads to a high industry wide turnover of direct service professionals. Most long term care providers are constantly having to recruit, hire and train new staff. Having a high turnover in staff is certainly not conducive to providing high quality and stable care for a population who thrives on consistency.

The Moonshot program sought to alleviate the high turnover rate and elevate the level of training and care provided. Through paying its direct service professionals a higher salary, more benefits, better training and a clear path for advancement than other organizations, St. Coletta hoped the staff that they hired would feel valued and want to make their positions into long term careers. Almost immediately, the plan began to show success. At the family meeting in 2016, all the data was laid out in graphs to show us that, indeed, the program was working. The turnover rate in staff was greatly reduced and they were able to attract professionals that wanted to work for the organization long term.

In 2019, the Governor of Wisconsin created the statewide Task Force on Caregiving to analyze and address the crisis that care providers were facing in funding and providing high-quality care for the individuals they served. Ted Behncke became a vital member of the task force, providing his expertise in addressing the crisis. Because of the pandemic, they discussed all of the new challenges that it presented as well. The task force presented their data and recommendations to address the funding crisis in February of 2021.

The conclusion of the 51 page final report[56] stated that the recommendations they made would "represent significant steps toward reducing the strains on the caregiving system in Wisconsin." The Task Force members pledged to "continue to work with the Governor, the legislature and state agencies to guide implementation of the sixteen recommendations" that they made "and develop additional strategies to strengthen family caregiving and the direct care workforce in our state."

The report came out during the height of a pandemic that created havoc in Wisconsin's disability community. Its recommendations became even more crucial to those whose very lives were at stake. Governor Evers, the legislature and state agencies continue to work to implement changes that can make concrete improvements for all concerned. The battle is far from over. Funding direct care continues to be an ongoing state, national, and often, highly political issue.

St. Coletta's ability to surpass the normal expectations of a disability service provider have continued to bring the community accolades and awards. In 2015, St. Coletta received another three years of the highly coveted CARF (Commission on Accreditation of Rehabilitation Facilities) accreditation - the highest level possible. Multiple surveyors arrived for a complex three day examination that involved combing through policies, procedures and reporting systems. Every department is thoroughly looked at from finances to medical care, accessibility, and human rights. They interviewed stakeholders from across the organization to include family members, staff, and the Board of Directors.

St. Coletta Homelights magazine edition from that year noted that during the exit conference one of the surveyors, John T. Collins, stated, "We are pleased to present St. Coletta with a three year accreditation with no recommendations. This rarely happens and in the 23 years I've been with CARF, this has only happened to me one time. The services and programs here are outstanding and I can see how much hard work and dedication goes into this organization. The mission to serve people with disabilities is taken seriously and the spirit of the Franciscan order is alive and well."

Since that accreditation in 2015, St. Coletta has also undergone successful 3 year accreditation in 2018 and in 2021.

In 2016, BizTimes Media awarded St. Coletta its Nonprofit of the Year Award. "This award honors community-nominated corporate citizens and nonprofits for their ongoing commitment to making southeastern Wisconsin a better place to live, work, and play." (From St. Coletta's website.)

In 2019, St. Coletta was awarded the prestigious Moving Mountains Award from ANCOR - the American Network of Community Options and Resources, NADSP - the National Alliance for Direct Support Professionals, and ICI - the Institute of Community Integration at the University of Minnesota. From St. Coletta's website - "These organizations recognize organizations using leading practices in direct support workforce development that result in improved outcomes for people with disabilities." The award was given for St. Coletta's "innovative recruitment and retention practices through an initiative called 'Project Moonshot'.

The organization's continuing goals of excellence shows no signs of abating. In fact, they just keep setting the bar higher for themselves.

The Programs of St. Coletta of Wisconsin

Each program that exists within St. Coletta is innovative and unique. The community is an intricately designed puzzle made up of many different pieces. Without each piece, there would be a gaping hole that would make the picture incomplete. Years and years of crafting have gone into creating the evolving St. Coletta programs that exist today. Some past projects have gone by the wayside due to ineffectiveness. Others became antiquated as the lives of individuals with disabilities have gained a greater acceptance and integration into society.

Each current program is supported and influenced by all of the others. A quote attributed to the philosopher Aristotle aptly applies to St. Coletta and its many programs - "The whole is greater than the sum of its parts." Because the individuals and groups within the community, including the people that are served, have been interconnected with common goals, they have been able to create many more opportunities and surpass existing goals on a regular basis.

The clients within the community, and their disabilities, have changed over time. A large number of them have lived in the community for many years. Older clients continue to be admitted as their families age, when they can no longer support them within their homes. Their needs are influenced by their ages and levels of disability. Those can increase with aging, including dementia and physical changes.

Other clients, like Daniela, are younger. They also have varying levels of needs and disabilities. New clients can enter after they reach adulthood, often after they finish their high school transition programs at age 22. The types of programming that they require can be very different than older clients, regardless of their level of disability. Pre-vocational and vocational plans are often part of their goals.

St. Coletta has increasingly had a number of admission referrals of individuals with challenging behaviors, including those with autism. There are many more families now who include young adults on the autism spectrum. Many of them are seeking residential and day programming. When their high school program is concluded, it is a common occurrence for individuals to be left just sitting at home with no opportunities. This can cause a deterioration of skills and behaviors. Some individuals have aggressive behaviors that simply cannot be served well within the St. Coletta's parameters. They can require very specialized care that is not available within most disability organizations. It is St. Coletta's highest priority for all of their clients to be safe and served well within the best of their ability to do so.

St. Coletta is putting forth a dedicated effort to help as many of these families as is safely possible. Because there is such a need for this population, there is now a dedicated case management and behavioral health services team at St. Coletta. Two Crisis Intervention Specialists were added in October of 2018 to help meet the behavioral needs of all clients. "As support plans are developed and monitored, proactive strategies are the main focus, however, intervention measures and recovery strategies are also involved."[57] Behavioral health is a critical part of every client's life at St. Coletta.

There are now regular meetings of a club hosted at St. Coletta called "Empower U". This is a group for local families and individuals on the autism spectrum. Daniela enjoys being an active part of the group. Another addition on campus to address emotional and behavioral needs is its new "sensory room". This room is a beautiful large open space that uses calming sounds, colors, lights, and sensory objects for clients to touch and manipulate. Everything in the room was designed for any client who is feeling stressed (for

156

whatever reason). They can go into the room to calm themselves and use it in whatever way that is helpful for them, for as long as they need it.

Finding creative solutions and early intervention strategies helps each client manage the more challenging parts of their disabilities. Every person is capable of growing in their social and coping skills. Each member of the residential and day program staff who interacts with clients knows each of them well. They know their triggers and they are able to monitor and positively de-escalate negative changes in their behaviors. These changes in behaviors can be due to many reasons, including organic changes such as age and dementia or outside stressors such as a death in the family or changes in routine, as happened with the 2020 pandemic.

I have seen staff guide my daughter through numerous situations that have affected her behaviors negatively. They always reach out to families and guardians for suggestions and then work collectively to find solutions. There are checks and follow ups to see if the behaviors are abating or are becoming worse. I have been incredibly impressed by the proactive and good humored techniques that they use. Always - the clients are treated and respected as the adults that they are.

Each person's privacy is also guarded zealously. When there is a conflict between other clients and Daniela, I am never told the other client's name by staff. Daniela's ability to cope with these conflicts has grown a great deal in the past 6 years. She has learned to recognize the situations she has difficulty dealing with, often knowing how to improve them without assistance. She knows when to step away and when to ask for help. She will always need some assistance in these areas, but as time goes by, she trusts that the staff will help her find solutions so that she can enjoy her life to the fullest.

Here is a summary of the current programs at St. Coletta.

Residential Services -

Providing the clients of St. Coletta with opportunities to live as independently as possible, has been the major goal since the early days of the school. Back then, they were only hoping to keep their students out of the large state and private institutions. I'm sure they could never have imagined that individuals with developmental disabilities would ever be able to freely live in homes within their communities and not be viewed as objects of pity or derision. They would be amazed to see the quality of life that these people are now able to have.

Some clients attending day services at St. Coletta live with their families. Some live completely on their own. The majority of clients live in St.

Coletta supported homes and apartments within the local communities that the organization serves. Where each client lives depends on many factors. All of the St. Coletta living spaces in Wisconsin and Illinois provide varying levels of support depending on the needs of the people within them.

Some clients live in their own apartments and only need someone to drop in to check in on them and guide them a few times a week. Staff will come in, take them shopping, and then prepare, or help them prepare, their meals for the week. Other clients will have staff with them only during those waking hours when they are not at work or day programming. Many homes have night staff as well to address any issues that might come up overnight. Some clients have much greater needs - physical, medical and/or behavioral. For these individuals, the client-staff ratio is smaller.

Each person is evaluated yearly, with goals to help each one attain as much independence as possible. This is very important. Providing someone too much care can be just as detrimental to a client as not providing them enough care.

From Karissa Holpfer - (former) the Regional Director of the Jefferson Residential Program -

"The unique thing about the Residential Program from my perspective is it gives myself, our managers, and the DSP's the opportunity to serve our individuals in all aspects of their life. Serving people who have varying needs and abilities the Residential department focuses on meeting outcomes and prompting growth in whatever way possible. Our #1 goal is to create an environment that is truly a home to those we are privileged to serve. Promoting a family culture where we spend both happy times and sad times supporting one another. I feel that the impact that this approach has on the individual as well as their family member is profound. The individual feels a sense of belonging and purpose in their life at St. Coletta. Family members feel reassured that their loved one is being loved, supported, and cared for just as they would in their family home."

Grace Landing - St. Coletta's newest Residential Community

Duane McAllister and his wife Connie had long dreamed of finding a long term housing solution for their lovely daughter Kelly. Kelly is a young woman with developmental disabilities. They had hoped that this new home would be near their home in Brookfield, Wisconsin. As they researched their options, they finally decided to create their own community, for Kelly, and for other individuals with intellectual and developmental disabilities - a community to be named Grace Landing. At the same time they were working to make their dream a reality - finding land, designing the community, and reaching out to other local families who shared their vision, St. Coletta was working on their own dream of creating the Intergenerational Care Center in Brookfield. Duane reached out to St. Coletta to see if they would be interested in partnering with Grace Landing. They knew about St. Coletta's stellar reputation and felt they would be ideal in providing the wraparound services needed to provide residential and day services for Grace Landing. St. Coletta embraced the idea.

In October 2019, the city of Brookfield Common Council passed a conditional use permit for the property that the McAllister's had acquired. The designs had been completed to build three 8 bed CBRFs (Community-Based Residential Homes) and a clubhouse within a community green space that will allow for outdoor activities and gatherings. A total of 24 individuals will live in the community. The other families involved have come onboard with a great deal of commitment and excitement for the futures of their family member with developmental disabilities.

The socially distanced and masked groundbreaking took place in June 2020. Even the pandemic couldn't stop this dream. Kelly McAllister, along with other future community members and their families, were there to celebrate the day. Father Al Velk delivered the blessing. The Mayor of Brookfield, Steve Ponto, issued a proclamation declaring it "Kelly McAllister Day". Ted Behnke said this, "St. Coletta is thrilled with the opportunity to partner with the City of Brookfield and join these families who seek a lifetime of consistent, loving support for their family members." "Thank you to everyone who has played a role in successfully getting us to this point today."[58]

The homes of Grace Landing

Blessing the homes

The McAllister family

Ribbon-cutting

The modular construction of the buildings began offsite as the land was prepared for the arrival of the three homes - named for Sister Maria Crescentia, Father Solanus Casey and Sister Angela Merici. On June 17, 2021, the ribbon cutting ceremony was held to open the three beautiful new residences. Several Sisters, including Sr. Grace Schauf, happily cut the ribbons to open the homes that will serve Kelly and 23 other excited new clients.

It is through these new additions like Grace Landing, that St. Coletta continues its efforts to grow and serve.

Day Programming -

The day programs of St. Coletta are at the heart of everything that happens in the community. I will highlight here the current programs and how they strive to positively impact the lives of the clients and families that they serve.

For the residential clients of St. Coletta, the costs of day programming are included in the total costs (with separate rates) of being part of the community. The costs are covered by HCBS (home and community based services) funding which many clients of St. Coletta receive. Some clients privately pay for both residential and day programming. The day programs also serve a number of local clients who are not part of the residential community. These can be students who have transitioned out of local high schools or other local adults with disabling conditions who live independently or with family.

Golden Options -

This longstanding day program focuses on the needs of the emerging population of seniors with developmental disabilities, including those with dementia. This highly underserved group has unique needs that often can't be served in typical senior day programs. With its long history of serving individuals for their lifespan, St. Coletta is well qualified to provide the best support available. It allows these seniors to continue to stay in either their St. Coletta or their family homes and "age in place" for as long as possible. I asked Beth Alexander, the Golden Options Program Coordinator, to tell me more about the program. I asked her several questions that I thought might help others understand why this program is so special. This interview happened at the height of the COVID pandemic when programming was restricted because of quarantines.

I first asked her, "How does Golden Options improve on the quality of life for its participants?"

She responded, "Golden Options is a gem in our community and has been providing services for over 25 years in Jefferson County. Staff and clients work together to both maintain and/or improve their quality of life. There have been many families that I have worked with that are hesitant, at first, to send their loved one to Golden Options. When a family comes to tour, I describe our focus in Golden Options - as keeping the mind, body and soul active. We offer a variety of activities throughout the day that are meaningful, exciting, and gives the individual a sense of purpose.

Mind: When I say that we program the mind, we provide a variety of trivia games, game shows, such as Wheel of Fortune, Deal or No Deal, and Price is Right. – We also incorporate music and many more activities. We aim to keep the brain active and engaged as long as we can.

Body: For the body this tends to be our exercises, however we like to create activities that do not feel like exercise to the individuals that attend but that are fun.

We offer drumming, floor hockey, balloon volleyball, kickball, and the normal stretches or chair exercise. We also travel to a few nursing homes and have Balloon Volleyball competitions. There is even a traveling trophy up for grabs. (Because of COVID-19, we currently have not been doing this, and we can't wait to start it again).

Soul: We offer a variety of spiritual opportunities throughout the week and month. This includes Rosary, Bible Stories, Franciscan Values, Chapel Services, and other spiritual activities throughout the year. Our Franciscan Values and Mission Director, Mario, was able to make it possible for St. Coletta to bring in a Grief Counselor who will come in once per month to those that would like to attend.

Another aspect of our program is our outings. Outings are offered daily (except on days of inclement weather) for group participants and staff. These outings could last all day or for a couple of hours in the morning. During the nicer months, we go to a lot of parks and have picnics. Two outings that everyone enjoys are going out for lunch to a local restaurant or coffee shop."

I asked Beth "How does Golden Options impact their families' lives?"

She said "In regards to the individuals that we provide respite care for during the day, we truly impact their families' lives. When they bring their loved ones to us they are able to live their life without worry. Families are able to continue working, attend their own appointments, meet with friends and families, and are able to rest. They are able to do all this and then bring their loved one back home at the end of the day. Sometimes it is a stepping stone to

162

getting the individual and their family ready for a transition to an assisted living facility or a skilled nursing facility.

One of my most memorable families was a couple and the husband attended programming with us five days per week. During his first week with us I would receive hourly calls from his wife to see how he was doing. It took a lot for his wife to trust us, but we built that relationship with her, made her feel comfortable and informed her of all the things that he was doing. His wife needed comfort to know she was doing the right thing for both of them and was not failing her husband. We were able to do that for her and she often referred to us as her 'real life angels'."

As I have asked other staff in writing this book, I wanted to know how working with these individuals impacted Beth.

She told me, "Working with the senior population is my passion. When I was younger, during the summers, I would often go with my mom to the nursing home where she was working , and would visit with the individuals. Little did I know how much of an impact that would make in my life in regards to my career. I started working at St. Coletta when I was 18 years old. I worked in a group home of 16 ladies and today, I get to work with five of them in Golden Options.

Dementia was not something on my mind when I started as the Program Coordinator at Golden Options. As time went on, Dementia became one of my passions. At Golden Options, about 40% of our population has been diagnosed with dementia or Alzheimer's. As the percentage increased, I knew I needed to start learning more. I started doing more research and decided to become a member of the Dementia Network Community. Through this community, I became "Dementia Friendly" and became an instructor at St. Coletta's in regards to Dementia Friendly Communities. I discuss what it means to be dementia friendly and how to interact and provide support to those with dementia.

All in all, my life has been forever changed by getting to serve the individuals at St. Coletta as a whole and especially in Golden Options. I have grown as a person and my knowledge on the aging population is ever growing as I want to provide the best program possible for all individuals."

It is because of people like Beth and all of the devoted staff at St. Coletta that the clients they serve are able to continue to fully experience joy and dignity throughout their entire adult lives.

Some friends from Paddy's Paws visit
Golden Options for National Dog Rescue
Day

Excel -

Excel is one of the bedrock programs at St. Coletta. It has long provided a wide variety of social, educational and physical activities to clients who vary in age and abilities. Each person's needs are evaluated and approached individually so that they can gain the most benefits appropriate to their needs. In this way, each client is able to move positively forward, growing independence and responsibility. Each accomplishment, no matter how small, is celebrated.

On its brochure, these are the goals and interests that it strives to address with each person - Emotional, Spiritual, Physical, Educational, Community Inclusion, Social, Creativity, and Nutrition. As in all of St. Coletta's programs, a strong emphasis is placed on getting everyone out into, and becoming contributing members of, the wider community. Their wishes and needs are respected as adults no matter the level of their disabilities. Lifelong learning in functional academics is part of the programming, as are communication skills. Goals include training in safety and mobility skills. Daily living and social skills training are also very important. Each St. Coletta client helps set their own personal goals to be re-evaluated yearly.

There is an Excel program on St. Coletta's main campus as well as the long-standing Excel program at the University of Wisconsin-Whitewater. There is also an Excel program at St. Coletta's new Intergenerational Program building in Brookfield - to serve clients from Waukesha and Grace Landing in Brookfield.

Excel is a lively and fun experience that is enjoyed by each client. I have often walked by its programming areas during my visits to St. Coletta. The smiles are always big and the laughter is loud and infectious. The respectful and caring staff are invested in each person that they serve in the program.

An Easter egg hunt at Excel

Genesis, VTSP (Vocational Training Skills Program) and Access

Postsecondary and vocational programs for young adults with disabilities have exploded in the past 10-15 years. As Daniela entered high school in the mid-2000s, no one at her school mentioned anything about Daniela possibly moving on to a vocational or "college" type program. It would

165

certainly have given me so much hope. Even as she was finishing high school, no guidance counselor or special education teacher seemed to know anything about these possibilities, although they were already growing across the country. Internet research was what led me to find the website called "Think College". Now there are hundreds of opportunities at universities, community colleges, and independent schools. Daniela's life changed dramatically when she started Shepherds College. When we toured St. Coletta in 2015 and discovered they would give Daniela a continuing opportunity to learn and move forward in the Genesis program we were thrilled.

In the beginning, there was only one class group in Genesis. As participation grew, classes split into Genesis 1 and Genesis 2. All participants have ongoing person-centered functional assessments and participate in personal, social and daily living skills training. Genesis 1 focuses on introducing students to exploring their options and interests for employment or volunteering. Participants have classes in pre-employment skills, functional academics and technology education and receive individual and career counseling. Community safety skills training is essential for clients as they become more independent. Each person is periodically assessed for their readiness to be successful in a career.

In Genesis 2 some students may work on pursuing specialized training available at a local college and on preparing and taking the tests required to attend the training. For other students, it involves learning the skills needed to interview for a job in the community.   It also focuses on learning and maintaining the skills needed to keep a job. Some new Genesis students may have already received sufficient skills in the high school transition classes to be able to skip Genesis 1 and enter directly into Genesis 2.

Job placement is accomplished in partnership with the Department of Vocational Rehabilitation, which is a state agency. For those clients who want to pursue higher education, tutoring is available to them. St. Coletta actively searches for internship opportunities that will assist individuals in finding vocations that they are interested in. For day clients, support is provided in helping secure appropriate living arrangements in the community. Referrals are also available to other services and agencies.

Some clients may need job modification or assistive technology to succeed in a job. Genesis works in partnership with community employers to make sure the client is able to be successful and safe within their environment.

When clients start any training, volunteering, or job, Genesis does not end for many clients. Since most of the above are not full time situations, their are still days, or parts of days that clients can come to Genesis to continue to receive support and classes. This continuity of support is very important. Many employees with disabilities need continuing and varying levels of support.

Genesis is also, happily, a part of the new Intergenerational Care Center in Brookfield.

Daniela has definitely blossomed in her participation in Genesis. It has continued to benefit her in countless ways. Daniela's disabilities cause her to lose ground if she is not given the opportunities to keep learning and moving forward. This is common for many individuals with disabilities. Every participant is continually challenged in Genesis. For Daniela, it not only gave her the motivation and education needed to obtain her job in the community, it helped her to keep it. It supported her when working in the community occasionally overwhelmed her. It was a key part of the team, with working with her job developer, coaches, and her supervisor at her job. It was such a blessing to know that they would be there to help her over the stumbling blocks that would periodically impede her.

In the spring of 2020, Daniela had to take a break from working in the community because of the COVID pandemic. Working in a public environment, no matter what precautions her employer took, was simply too dangerous, not only for Daniela, but for the many vulnerable clients and staff that she came into contact daily. It was a tough decision for everyone involved including her terrific work supervisor.

In a zoom meeting (because of the pandemic) involving Genesis, her St. Coletta support team, her job developer, her funding care manager and her job supervisor, everyone let Daniela gently know that she would be dismissed from her position. Her supervisor assured her that she would be rehired if she reapplied after the pandemic has receded. The wrap around support Daniela received helped her handle this news with dignity and hope. Genesis is now there for her and the other clients so that they don't regress in their skills as they wait to return to community jobs.

VTSP -

The VTSP program is a program for qualified individuals with disabilities to receive paid on-the-job training. It focuses on job specific training and work experiences in five occupational areas: grounds, mail, maintenance, records and housekeeping. The goal is to help participants develop, improve, and maintain work skills, behaviors and attitudes that would lead to positive employment outcomes.

To qualify for this program, each participant must meet certain criteria for admission. These include the ability to work daily and to be punctual. They also need to have the physical capability to maintain a fairly consistent work pace and meet the expectations of their job. They need to be able to comply with one or two step instructions and complete tasks with minimal cueing.

They need to be able to maintain safety guidelines and the proper hygiene and grooming habits necessary.

Motivation to work is very important. They should also be able to understand the concept of working for pay. A continued interest in working as well as being able to benefit from participation in the program is vital. Each participant also needs to have adequate social skills to communicate work needs and basic needs that might interfere with working such as illness or injury. An ability to work harmoniously and cooperate with coworkers is important as is respect for others property. They cannot be dangerous to themselves or others.

The program helps participants learn work ethics and social expectations specific to their desired career. They learn time management, safety, and the program also helps clients to build work stamina. VTSP is designed to help each person acclimate and succeed in their new job and to get along with their coworkers and supervisors. In a climate where there is still prejudice against individuals with disabilities in the workplace, these clients have the opportunity to show they are capable and help end the stereotype for themselves and others.

Access - Community Employment Program

The Access - Community Employment program is another work related program available to St. Coletta clients. Its purpose, as stated in the Access Guidebook, "is to provide employment opportunities for persons with significant barriers to work". Their primary goal is "to provide individualized person-centered planning, job development, job placement, training, and support services to facilitate program participant's success in integrated, community-based employment settings."

The program utilizes job coaches to attain the employment goals of each person. The level and length of support varies according to need. They provide services to individuals who are capable of competitive employment, in which the job coaching gradually ends. They also provide services in supported employment to those who will always need some of level assistance and supervision to stay employed.

Each participant is assisted in choosing a vocational path in which they have interest and in which they can succeed. They are given opportunities to job shadow, and work in paid temporary and intern positions.

Access has a cooperating relationship with WDC, the Diversified Workforce Development Center which is located in Jefferson. They are a great resource in providing computers, work development information and other literature.

Access also provides job and task analysis so that job training can be broken down into step-by-step tasks. They also figure out job modification techniques to increase the clients' ability to succeed at their job. Sometimes assistive technology is needed and sometimes there needs to be modification design improvements to increase accessibility. Participants are provided with mobility and orientation training to figure out hazardous obstacles and provide ways for them to move around safely and efficiently in a socially accepted manner.

Admission into Access is done on a case by case basis after reviewing their completed admissions packet and a 10 day assessment process. Outside participants are also accepted usually after a referral. The admissions process is very thorough and designed to make sure that each person who is accepted into the program has a very good chance of success.

The educational and employment programs at St. Coletta provide a wide variety of opportunities for individuals with disabilities to grow and to lead their most independent and enriching lives. The clients who are served display a justifiable sense of pride in being a part of society and to be a strong and positive presence in their community. They also make their local community better. Children who are able to see individuals with disabilities as valued citizens, working and providing needed services, grow up to be more accepting and less likely to look down on people who are different than them. Everybody wins. The Sisters knew that back in 1904 and it is even more true today.

Achieve -

For St. Coletta's clients in Illinois the day programming is called Achieve. Serving a much smaller population, it is designed to provide programming for a wide level of ages and disabilities. I had planned to visit the program this past summer to see it for myself but, unfortunately, the pandemic caused me to cancel my travel plans. Instead I asked (former employee) Bridget Owens, Achieve's then program coordinator, to give me an overview of its services. She very kindly wrote the following -

"Achieve is a vocational day program based through St. Coletta of Wisconsin that serves client's with intellectual disabilities. We currently serve clients from St. Coletta as well as a second provider for two other clients here. Achieve is a program of sixteen inspiring and wonderful individuals that attend day programing <u>Monday through Friday</u>. The Achieve Program aims to provide a full and comprehensive program that both inspires and assists our clients in becoming as successful as possible. Our staff here at Achieve are innovative and deeply passionate about helping our clients achieve independence in various tasks. They continue to strive to make this program as comfortable and assistive as possible so clients are excited and encouraged to attend. We aim to focus on client choice, productivity, independence, and community integration through a curriculum that offers variety and excitement.

A day out with Achieve

Our program each week will focus on an opportunity, event, or skill that we are working on. For example, one week may involve participating in social skill activities such as; group exercise, group games, pet therapy, and interactive crafts that involve the participation of multiple parties. Another example would be community integration and volunteerism (something Achieve very much enjoys taking part of). The activities may involve but are not limited too; presenting Thank You cards and items to first responders, learning about community signs and norms, volunteering with members of the community such as Helping Hands, and engaging in community outings. We work towards assisting clients in becoming more familiar and independent in skills such as independent living skills (i.e. baking activities, financial skills, and relationships. We also aim to work towards learning skills such as math skills, reading, and arts and crafts. Lastly, we also aim to work towards independence in mobility skills through fine motor and gross motor activities. This can involve

170

exercise, intricate arts and crafts, beading, as well as community activities such as bowling.

Achieve is a compassionate and active program that works to inspire our clients to reach their fullest potential. Our clients here continuously motivate myself and my staff to explore and engage in activities that are both productive and fulfilling for our clients. I am blessed and honored to be the Program Coordinator for the wonderful individuals that attend and I hope to continue to provide exciting and inspiring programming."

The Intergenerational Care Center -

As I have mentioned previously, Genesis, Excel, and Golden Options have become part of the Intergenerational Care Center (IGC) in Brookfield. As with Achieve, this center serves a smaller population than the main St. Coletta in Jefferson. I was fortunate enough to have the chance to visit the new program shortly after it opened in a decommissioned elementary school.

The programs, clients and staff have large open spaces to work in with lots of opportunities to grow. Because they are a smaller group, they also have the chance to share programming and opportunities between the three programs. As in Jefferson, community programs and participation are a vital and varied part of this more urban/suburban setting. I enjoyed meeting some of the clients and was glad that I already had the pleasure of knowing the director, Becky Netzler-Hohisel and asst. director, Laura Dyer, who had previously worked with Daniela at her home in Jefferson. These professional and caring women were enthusiastic about creating something very special in this new center.

In 2020 St. Coletta and the IGC took a new adventure. With the pandemic straining all parents with young children, families who have a child with disabilities felt this strain much more intensely. Virtual education became a part of almost all educational settings. With this situation, the costs of daycare for working parents became exorbitant and scarce. The availability of day programming for children with disabilities is extremely hard to find, no matter the cost.

Like it always has, St. Coletta decided to assist the unmet needs of families of children, with and without disabilities. Elizabeth Bouchard, now the Director of the Intergenerational Care Center - the Greater Milwaukee area, said this about the new program in the summer of 2020 - "It's a very exciting development that we were finally able to offer this fall after almost a year in the planning. It's a program for children who may have special needs (although it's open to all kids age 7 and up) who need care before and after school. Since St.

171

Coletta's was founded to provide supports to kids, it's nice to return to our roots!"

The program is providing wrap around childcare for the school year. Available from 6am to 6pm during weekdays, it has an accessible setting with areas for socialization and physical activities. They are also providing homework support and snacks in a warm and fun setting with lots of attention designed to meet their individual needs.

The opening of the Intergenerational Care Center

St. Coletta of Wisconsin and its day programming continue to prove that they are a vital and innovative organization. They continue to reach out to serve individuals and families where they are needed and in ways that break the current norms. They strive to never rest on their laurels and to, instead, continue to break the mold.

Elizabeth Bouchard writes here about all of the day programs, including the striking challenges presented by the Covid pandemic.

"I am so proud of our day programs and the teams. Working in day programs is a non-stop activity, but in a structured and organized way. The teams create detailed calendars with a schedule and theme for each day, with modifications that can be used as needed depending on the strengths and abilities of each individual - it truly is person-centered.

Every day incorporates academics, socialization, health and wellness, faith formation, movement, art, music, community integration...everything that brings joy to our lives. We get to see people accomplish new things and encourage their peers, and we have the best photo opportunities! I always enjoy taking a walk through the program spaces to rejuvenate my spirit, but the pandemic keeps me in my office more than I'd like...this has been the hardest part for me, and I know that our persons served miss each other and the exciting things they used to be able to do."

All of the core programs described in this chapter are also supported by other services that are integral to the success of the mission. Without Transportation Services the goal of community activities and integration would be impossible. Without Maintenance Services nothing would be safe, maintained and running smoothly. Without the Administration the lack of leadership would cause the community to fall apart. The list goes on and on - Recreation Services, Finance, Human Resources, Admissions, Nursing, Fundraising, Information Systems and Technology, the Board of Directors, Volunteers - each branch is vital to the mission. The people of St. Coletta hold its mission statement in their hearts as they come to work each day to humbly serve God and every individual that they value as part of their own family.

A day at the Wisconsin State Fair

Going fishing!

Spring planting at Genesis

Giving back to the community

Chapter 19

A Tour -

In August of 2018, during the very first steps of my research for this book, Sr. Grace and Mario Dealca, St. Coletta's Senior Director of Franciscan Values and Mission, took me on a tour. We visited pieces of St. Coletta's historical journey, starting with the chapel and focusing on its renovations over the years. We viewed its use of cherished religious objects from the original chapel on the school campus. Afterwards, Sr. Grace took me to a hall in the administration building where the portraits of all of St. Coletta's administrators are hung. She knew most of them personally from her long presence in the community. I loved hearing her insight about each one. Mario also accompanied me as I walked along the History Wall.

This is my account of what I learned and saw that day. (I recorded our walk on video so that I wouldn't have to rely on my memory.) That day left me with so much inspiration and a drive to make this book become a reality.

As I waited to start my tour, I stood in the reception area of the Alverno building just outside of the chapel. I took the time to examine one of the most iconic and cherished artifacts in St. Coletta's history. A large bell sits proudly in a place of honor welcoming everyone who first enters the building. It was created in 1879 to hang above the original convent building. It has been a witness to everything that has transpired since then. I think the bell's proudest moments were in the early days of the school, as it welcomed every new brave student. Each child was celebrated by the bell's enthusiastic ringing, heralding their new lives of acceptance and education. I took a last glance at the bell as Mario and Sister Grace appeared and led me into the chapel.

St. Therese "The Little Flower" Chapel -

Like the bell, the chapel is at the center of St. Coletta and all that it has stood for. It is used for regular church services during the week and special ceremonies, both religious and not. It is also used as a multifunctional space for meetings and gatherings. The first objects that your eyes are drawn to as you enter the chapel, are the beautiful and colorful stained glass windows that reflect St. Coletta's Franciscan heritage. The windows were part of the Alverno building's original chapel. Mario guided me along. He described what each window means in the life of St. Francis and all those who follow him, especially the Sisters of St. Francis of Assisi. Facing the altar, there are four windows on the left. The first three are based on faith, hope and charity. The last window depicts St. Francis. Faith, hope and charity are the "graces" received from the sacrament of baptism for the devoted followers of St. Francis to pursue their vocation.

On the right side of the chapel are five more windows. The first two reflect humility and temperance. Mario stated that these are the first two virtues that are "the hinge" connecting the three graces to the virtues that are reflected in the last three windows (which depict obedience, poverty and chastity). All the followers of St. Francis have to commit to these virtues in their final vows.

Behind the alter, at the back of the church, are the gold mosaic Stations of the Cross which were designed and built in Europe. They were very carefully transferred from the original chapel located on the old campus. Also found at the back of the chapel, near the Stations of the Cross (and original to the Alverno building), is a hanging statue of St. Francis. The statue depicts Francis, after 40 days of fasting, receiving his stigmata (marks of the crucifixion of Christ) on the top of Mt. Alverno in central Italy. This event happened on September 14, 1224. Francis died two years later in October 1226. He was canonized in 1228.

On the other side of the alter hangs a statue of St. Therese of Lisieux. On Christmas Eve in 1886, at the age of 14, Therese had a conversion that changed her life. The next year she entered a Carmelite convent to give her entire life to God. She lived a simple devout life and died at age 24 of tuberculosis. The world came to know her through her autobiography, "Story of a Soul". She believed in doing the ordinary with extraordinary love. Her love of flowers gave her the nickname "The little flower". She was canonized in May 1925.[59]

Sister Grace said this about the statue, "This statue was in the school building, which was also named St. Therese." The statue had to be removed from the building when the school became certified by the state of Illinois (many students came from Illinois. After the school was certified, it received funding from Illinois for their tuition). The state government stated that, in order to receive certification, no religious artifacts could be present in the school. With much sadness, the statue was moved to the attic. Major donors to the chapel renovation asked that the new chapel be named for St. Therese (who had been important in their lives). Happily, the statue was brought down from the attic and was hung again in a place of honor.

Mario took me over to a small room on the right side of the chapel, up near the alter, that I hadn't noticed before. Mario said it was the Porziuncola Chapel and that it was named after the chapel with the same name in Italy. Mario said, "Porziuncola is in the heart, mind, and the life of the St. Francis Order. It is the birthplace of the St. Francis Order." The chapel is the tabernacle in which the blessed sacrament is stored. Mario explained, "For St. Francis, the tabernacle is like the womb of Mary because that's where Jesus is." Porziuncola is considered to be the place where St. Francis started his spiritual journey and where he met St. Clare. It is also the place where he died.

It was during this discussion in the Porziuncola Chapel that I asked who St. Coletta was. I had done a little research about her but was unclear as to why the school and organization were named for her. Mario told me, "She was a reformer. She was called St. Colette of Corbie (in France where she was born). She was like a hermit in the beginning. But then St. Francis appeared to her and asked her to reform the Franciscan order." After both Francis and Clare had died, the Catholic hierarchy had relaxed the stringent rules of the order. Mario said with a smile, "He obviously didn't like that so he appeared to St. Colette to bring the order back to the same rule of poverty."

Mario also told me that St. Colette was "a little person", "someone with a disability, though also a spiritual giant." For all of these reasons, the school and the organization were named in her honor. As we stepped outside of the main chapel into the entry room of the Alverno building, Mario used his arms in a sweeping motion as he said this about the building. "Alverno is a reminder to us, the staff, that what we say, we should live." I think this is a reminder for us all.

A walk with Sr. Grace -

As we left the chapel, I expressed a little confusion about the early leaders of the school - who did what - and when. Sr. Grace offered to take me to see their portraits. Mario, Sara Foerster, and Daniela followed behind us. We walked along a hallway until we reached a row of portraits (grouped three to a frame) - they featured all of the leaders of St. Coletta - from the beginning of the school in 1904 to the present day.

The first three Sisters came into view, all looking very similar in their starched habits, wearing almost identical wire rimed glasses and stern faces. Sr. Grace began to tell me about them as she pointed to each portrait, "Sr. Emerentia (Ozar) was from 1904 to 1907." I asked her "She was the original superintendent (of the St. Coletta Institute for Backward Children)?" Sr. Grace said simply, "Yes." (Sr. Theophila Nussbaum was the original Sister Superior. She put Sr. Emerentia in charge of the school program.) Sr. Grace continued, "Then there was Sr. Mathilda (described as motherly and genial) from 1907 to 1910, then Sr. Emerentia again from 1910 to 1919." (Sr. Mathilda also took over from Sr. Theophila as Sr. Superior. In 1910, Sr. Emerentia took over the direction of the St. Coletta Institute.) Sr. Grace then said, as she pointed to and describes the last Sister in the first frame, "Then we come over here to Sr. Spes Knott, from 1910 to 1925. When Ted (Behncke, the current CEO) speaks to new staff, he quotes Sr. Spes, as to what she saw we should be doing in taking care of our people." At this point I commented about the first set of photos, "They all look SO serious. Were they?" (Lots of laughs came from Sr. Grace, Mario and Sara). Sr. Grace answered, still chuckling "I asked one of our ladies,

177

who is now deceased, if she knew Sr. Spes. She said, 'Yes'. I asked, 'What was she like?' She said, 'She was strict!'" (More laughs from everyone) I commented again - "They all look strict." I'm sure those dear Sisters had to be strict. Those first children must have needed a lot of loving, but firm instructions as they entered into their first school situation. Children with disabilities were treated in that time period as infants, who were incapable of instruction. The Sisters had no books to teach them about how to show these children that they were capable of so much more.

We moved on to the next three portraits. Sr. Grace said, "Then we come to Sr. Anastasia who came here in 1925 as the secretary to Sr. Spes. She was here from 1925 to 1932 when she went to Vineland with Sr. Madeline to learn how to teach our people. (Their pleas to the Sister Superior are described earlier in the book). Then she returned in 1933 to 1940. She was ill for a few years and returned in 1943 until 1964. She was a LONG timer. In between Sr. Anastasia and Sr. Madeline, in 1940, Sr. Jerome Heller was CEO. Then Sr. Madeline took over for the rest of the time that Sr. Anastasia was ill, until 1943 when she returned. Sr. Madeline then became our Mother General at the Motherhouse. She returned to St. Coletta after she retired and became the Superior at Alverno." (Sister Anastasia's leadership is described in detail earlier in the book.)

We moved on to the third group of three Sisters. From Sr. Grace, "When Sr. Anastasia retired in 1964, Sr. Mary Theodore became the CEO until 1970. She stayed here after 1970 and she developed the store, she wrote her books, she did many things. Then we had Sr. Sheila who was 'the educator'. She was here from 1970-1981. She taught here for many years. She got her doctorate and taught at the University of Wisconsin-Whitewater and at Cardinal Stritch University. When she left, Sr. Elaine Weber (who was the only Sister in the photos not in a habit) came in 1981 and stayed until 1992. Sr. Anastasia and Sister Elaine were 'the builders'. They built many buildings." Sr. Grace added, "Ted Behnke is also a builder."

The next group of three portraits include the first two lay leaders. Sr. Grace continues, "We come over here to Tom Atkinson, who was an interim leader while we were looking for a new CEO in 1992 until 1993. The first permanent lay leader was Henry Meese and he moved the community from a medical model to a CBRF (community-based residential facility). After he left in 1997, we had another Sr. - Anne Mary who was an interim CEO for two years. She reformed the management team and started 'cleaning up' the running of the organizations."

We reached the last three portraits. Sr. Grace said, "We had Bob Sterns who started our program in Illinois. He was CEO from 1999 to 2003. After he left, we had Tony LoDuca until 2015. He was interested in vocational training.

178

He also was very focused on the financial side of the organization." I commented, "So everybody that came into leadership basically added a new facet to St. Coletta - which is wonderful." Mario answered, "Correct. They came when their skill was needed by St. Coletta." I replied, "So it sounds like it all happened with divine intervention." Mario again answered, "Exactly." Sr. Grace moved on to point to the last photo, "Ted Behncke and his wife moved here to Jefferson after being in the Army for 29 years. He saw an ad in the paper for a 'Transportation Person' at St. Coletta." She said with enthusiasm, "So he hired on!" "Little by little Tony (LoDuca) and the management team recognized his skills and moved him up - and moved him up - and moved him up (with Sr. Grace demonstrating the moves with her rising hand). And since then he has been the developer - and reformer - and the rebuilder." Mario added, "And he is very spiritually oriented." Sr. Grace heartily agreed - "Yes!"

Sr. Grace added, as we all looked in admiration at the Sisters' photos, "If it wasn't for the Sisters, we wouldn't be here!" I told Sister Grace that I certainly believed that. I think often of all of the dearly departed Sisters - the leaders, teachers, reformers, builders and caretakers. I sometimes see them in my dreams. I picture them together in heaven, guiding and cheering on the community. I'm also sure that the lay leaders have prayed often for their guidance. So many difficult challenges and transitions have transpired from so many directions. It could have only been through the intervention of God, Jesus, the Holy Mother, St. Francis, St. Clare, St. Colette, St. Therese - and the wonderful Sisters of St. Francis of Assisi, that the mission has been able to thrive and continue to grow over the decades.

The History Wall -

The History Wall runs down the long hall of the first floor to the left and just past the reception room and chapel. Walking along it, you would easily think you are in a museum. It includes many treasured moments and accomplishments, along with photos and memorabilia from St. Coletta's long past. Each period of time depicted the wall also reflects what was happening to people with disabilities in the rest of the country. Especially in those early days of the organization, there was a wide disparity between the treatment of individuals with disabilities in the general population, and their education, care and acceptance at St. Coletta.

I won't give a detailed description of the wall here, but will give a few highlights. (If you visit, you should definitely visit the wall yourself.) The history of St. Coletta depicted on the wall begins with a class photo of the first class of students. It features Mary Noone, the first student that was enrolled. (Mary is buried in St. Coletta's cemetery.) It also has a photo and description of St. Coletta's first Eucharistic class in 1910, as they were being prepared for the sacrament of Holy Communion. It was the first such class in the nation for children with intellectual disabilities. An early newspaper clipping from the Jefferson Banner declares this fact about the building of the school and the class, "This event will always be remembered as one of the noblest undertakings in the history of Jefferson." In comparison, other photos show the painful treatment of people in draconian institutions around the country.

In the section depicting the time period around 1930, the wall describes the reasons for changing the name of the school from "The St. Coletta Institute for Backward Children" to "The St. Coletta School for Exceptional Children". As the years go by, the wall features the expansion of the school both in Jefferson, and then in Colorado and Massachusetts.

Rosemary Kennedy's arrival is highlighted in 1949, right before the start of the civil rights movement in the 1950s. This period began the slow start of a new era, when the rights of all U.S. citizens and residents came into focus.

In a section featuring 1960, a statement from James Melcher, the director of the Wisconsin Bureau of Handicapped Children is featured. "The educational program at St. Coletta ranks in the top five educational institutes in the country. Currently over 40% of our state's special education teachers received some or all of their training here."

From December 4 1967, there is a description and a photo of Sister Mary Theodore with President Lyndon Johnson. It was taken at the White House ceremony for the signing of H.R. 6430 - which extended, expanded and improved the public health law related to people with disabilities. The actual signing pen presented to Sister Mary Theodore is also featured.

As the sixties and seventies continue, St. Coletta's progressive steps in bringing inclusion and community jobs to their students and clients are shown. In the wider world, the disability rights movement is depicted as it continued to grow in strength and speed.

In the eighties and nineties, the wall features the building of homes in the local community for adult clients, as the school program grew smaller and finally came to a close. The end of the nineties show a new partnership with the University of Wisconsin in Whitewater - that featured vocational training, and activities of health, recreation, socialization and community access.

2000 to 2010 were the last decade featured on the wall when I took the tour. (See the epilogue for an update). It describes the new program in Illinois. It also shows the organization receiving its first three year CARF accreditation - at the highest level possible. The wall reflects with gratitude and sadness, the retirement of the last Sisters of St. Francis of Assisi. In 2006, it proudly tells of the successful two year advocacy and legislative effort on behalf of the 45 clients with no funding. The last entries on the wall describe the last of the

180

clients moving off campus, and into community housing. The description of the renovation of the Alverno building brought my tour to a close.

I was able to find out more about the Alverno building renovation. CEO LoDuca said this, as the renovated building was preparing to open, "While it is important that the building reflect our rich history, we are also very focused on today's opportunities, and meeting the needs of people with developmental and other challenges utilizing our organizational commitment to excellence and all the other aspects of our community that make us unique."[60]

By February of 2012, the building renovation was completed and everyone moved into their new spaces. Jonathan Berger, a design and communication specialist at St. Coletta, said this about the successful efforts, "One could say that St. Francis himself was an original pioneer of the green movement through his practices in recycling and his stewardship toward the environment. Glancing around our new headquarters, you can see a number of historic pieces from the campus integrated into our new facility with a modern twist." "Over the years, the school became its own community with an apple orchard, farm, power plant and hotel, but as society evolved, so did St. Coletta. While our mission to serve through compassion, dignity, and respect remains the same, it's the 'how' we serve our clients that has changed."[61]

With clients intermingling with the staff and administration daily, all now in the same building, it is easy for each individual to stay in touch with how everyone else was faring on a regular basis. Hugs and hellos are exchanged hourly. Clients are encouraged when they are struggling and cheered when they have accomplished something new.

The warmth extends to visitors, new staff, new clients and their families. Daniela's and my first visit in 2015 brought curiosity, hugs and smiles from both staff and clients. It overwhelmed Daniela on that first morning. Almost immediately though, she and I felt we had become a part of this warm camaraderie. We had, so quickly, become a part of this place, which was so uniquely special, that she cried when we had to leave that day. What she had experienced brought a new light to her eyes, a light that has continued to burn brighter with each passing day.

It is a fascinating experience to slowly walk the History Wall and read about the people and accomplishments who have made St. Coletta of Wisconsin what it is today. I continue to walk along the wall on almost every visit to the building. It inspires me every single time.

The wall, along with the chapel and all of the efforts to preserve the organization's history, are what awoke in me a desire to know more - about the Sisters, the school, the staff and the clients. I knew that I wasn't the first or last person who has felt that way. These feelings, that wall and the people of St.

Coletta kept driving me in my efforts to write and complete this book. It's been a journey of love

Sisters from the Motherhouse visiting the History Wall in 2011

Chapter 20

The Pandemic

As the pandemic closed down most outside activities in the community, the Transportation Dept. gathered some of the vans into a heart.

With no outside day programming, the homes and apartments became in house programs with lots of fun activities.

The local communities reached out in abundance with supplies that were hard to find, including masks, sanitizer and cleaning supplies. They saved lives with their generous actions.

Safely distanced walks in the surrounding towns became vital for providing exercise.

Since clients couldn't travel home to see family, a masked Santa and his elves brought gifts, food, and other surprises to every single client.

Puzzles, crafts and baking became popular pastimes, along with everyone's regular learning routines.

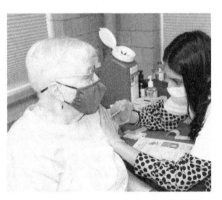

Sister Grace stepped up to receive her Covid vaccine as a role model for all the clients and staff.

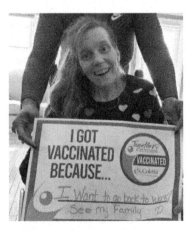

Most clients and staff were thrilled to be vaccinated. It meant a return to work, normal activities, and most importantly, seeing family.

The nurses of St. Coletta

Dan, Shelly, Diane and Terri played a lifesaving role during the pandemic. We are all so grateful to them for keeping everyone healthy everyday.

Thanks so much to Ted Behncke for leading St. Coletta through one of the biggest challenges it has ever faced. Thanks also to Ted for contributing to this chapter.

There are likely very few people in the world who do not know about, and whose lives haven't been changed by, the global outbreak of the COVID-19 virus. The community of St. Coletta of Wisconsin, and the town of Jefferson, certainly have had to deal with the crisis since it first hit the US shores in early 2020. Like all of us, they had no idea what lay ahead of them. Those of us who know and love the people of St. Coletta all hoped that the pandemic wouldn't affect its staff, clients and their families in any significant way. We prayed that it would be a fleeting virus and that it would pass them by - like God passed over the Israelites in the book of Exodus. Unfortunately, as we all now know, this virus became entrenched and has affected every family and community on earth.

This isn't the first time that St. Coletta has had to learn how to protect itself from a major pandemic. The Spanish flu epidemic of 1918-1920 was known as one of the deadliest pandemics in human history. It hit the population of Wisconsin hard. I have found no records on how the Sisters of St. Francis of Assisi dealt with that crisis. I don't know if there were any deaths within the community. What I have learned in my research about St. Coletta in that time period is this - no matter how it affected them, they survived - just as they continued to grow and thrive through two World Wars and the Great Depression. Now they have had to face another great crisis -

When the COVID-19 infection landed in Wisconsin in early 2020, the staff, administrators and St. Coletta Board of Directors immediately gathered to form their battle plan. With such a vulnerable population in their hands, they knew they had to act strongly and quickly. Outbreaks were growing, with severe illness and multiple deaths in group homes, nursing homes and assisted living facilities across the world. Many of St. Coletta's clients are older and have worrying comorbidities. Besides having all of the diseases that the general population deals with, they also have diseases and conditions that are common within their range of disabilities. It has been documented that individuals with Down syndrome[62] are especially affected by the virus, causing increased hospitalizations and deaths. Those with cerebral palsy, brain injuries or disabilities caused by certain genetic mutations are also extremely vulnerable.

There was immediate concern about St. Coletta's staff. Their ages run from late teens to senior citizens. Some of them have their own health vulnerabilities and/or have elderly or frail family members. In just living their normal lives, they could bring in possible exposure to the clients from the general public. Many St. Coletta clients require close up and intimate care. Social distancing is not practical in caring for them. The clients' abilities to practice safe hygiene practices are challenging and mask wearing for them can be extremely difficult. The way forward for the community was littered with terrible possibilities.

In the spring of 2020, everyone grew more anxious. The pandemic began to show signs of spreading rapidly in both Wisconsin and Illinois. I became more worried about Daniela. She was working at her wonderful job in the local community. She was constantly exposed to the public. Her position included cleaning the convenience store that she worked in. I knew that meant her being possibly exposed to the virus on a daily basis. I began conversations with her St. Coletta support team about her taking a leave from her position until things were less scary. Daniela is young and healthy so may not have been as severely infected, but that also meant she could have unknowingly carried and spread the virus to her housemates. She is only one of a number of St. Coletta's clients who work in the community. The virus now threatened them all.

Complicating the situation at St. Coletta was the early nationwide shortage of personal protective equipment and sanitizing products. Once it was determined that masks were essential in fighting the virus, there was a massive effort to try to procure what they needed to keep everyone safe. In the early days that was a daunting and expensive task. The call went out to families, supporters and the local community. That call did not go unheeded. Donations of homemade and medical grade masks soon starting pouring in, along with other PPE and sanitation products. To provide the hundreds of staff and clients with the continuing amount that they need, this had to be an ongoing effort.

Following the changing state and national guidelines, the decisions at St. Coletta had to become ever evolving. As the disease in Wisconsin and Illinois continued to head up sharply, the infection rates in these two states became national news. According to Ted Behncke, the past twelve months (in 2020-2021) probably represented the greatest denial of rights for persons with disabilities in the past 50 years, as persons served were locked down in their homes without even the ability to venture outside or visit with family members. He said, "Both State and Federal guidelines governed this and organizations like St. Coletta had little choice about it."

Within the detailed policy plan created by St. Coletta to guide them, and as things grew more dire, a decision was sadly made for non-residential clients to take a break from daily programming on campus. Those clients who worked and volunteered in the community, like Daniela, had to take leaves of absence from their jobs. Eventually most of their employers had to let them go permanently.

Out of necessity, visits to the outside community and client visits home became almost nonexistent. Strict guidelines were enforced to include testing and quarantine upon their return. St. Coletta's involvement with the outside community has always been vital and strong and this was a very difficult but lifesaving decision. My family's planned spring, summer, and holiday visits to Wisconsin, and also Daniela's visits to see us in 2020, were delayed, delayed again and then finally cancelled. It was not only a risk for my husband and I to travel, but also a risk of what we could possibly bring to Daniela and her housemates.

As the pandemic continued to progress, it finally came to a point when all day programming for residents had to be done within the client homes and not in the regular classroom set-ups on campus. Most meetings with staff (other than the house staff) were done virtually. There were no outside trips, except for medical visits and car rides. There were no more outside church services or meals out.

For clients who can understand the situation, like Daniela, this has been a very challenging transition. For those clients who can absolutely not understand, and whose lives demand regular routines honed over many years, this presented unknowable amounts of stress and change. Their worlds could have easily been turned upside down.

Fortunately - for them and for all of our families - there are the dedicated and loving people of St. Coletta who care for them every single minute of their lives. They took on the challenges thrown in their path with both courage, ingenuity and good humor. Ted Behnke said, "Our approach was to find balance in guidelines and the freedoms we could still safely offer. We kept programming open as long as safely possible and by cohorts so as to not mix homes and individuals. When lock downs were ordered we continued day programming again by cohort, but this time in the home." He called this "reverse community integration", the process of bringing the same staff in by cohort and using the internet to bring in the community. He also instituted a process to export some houses by cohort to the larger program space in Jefferson, Brookfield, and in Illinois to compensate for cabin fever in the homes. He added, "Homes were rotated and again, with risk mitigation accomplished by not mixing groups."

The staff accomplished an incredible feat, continuing to create joy and hope for each person in their care. They uplifted each other as well. Each holiday, and actually every day, was celebrated in innovative ways. Crafts, music, and special treats were provided to every client in all of their living situations. Day programming continued unabated in their homes. Online services expanded. Lessons continued as did needed routines. There was, and is, still fun and excitement. Daniela called me daily with the new and creative adventures and surprises that she partook in. This became a unique growth experience for everyone. A large and successful effort was made to raise money to buy iPads for each home so that clients could FaceTime with their loved ones.

Besides dealing with all of the emotional, physical and health challenges, St. Coletta has also been stressed financially and strategically. Besides having to stock costly and difficult to find supplies, they have also had to deal with employees being out sick and quarantined. They have had to redeploy staff to keep the homes staffed during extra weekday hours and find places for staff who normally work in day programming. Any client who had possible symptoms had to be quarantined and receive more special care until their tests came back. If tests were positive, then the quarantine was extended and the clients were carefully monitored and treated as necessary. The organization has always had a policy of making sure every person on staff was flexible and cross trained for different positions. This current situation has certainly put that policy to the test.

This could have been a much more tragic situation for St. Coletta than it has been. While there have been both staff and clients who contracted COVID-19 and some who became ill, at the time that I am writing in July 2021, there have been zero deaths. Everyone has recovered. That is both a miracle and a tribute to the quick and extraordinary steps that were taken. And as Ted Behncke pointed out, "I believe we were very fortunate and certainly had God's protection in the pandemic so far. We did not furlough or layoff one staff throughout, the entire St. Coletta family was in the workplace conducting the mission. While most of the world was working from home or shut down, we were all here. Although over 70 members of the St. Coletta family acquired the virus (approximately 30 were persons served), no one got seriously sick and we lost no one to the virus."

Part of St. Coletta's strategy for keeping everyone safe and well-informed was to be as public and open as possible about how they were managing this crisis. Since the beginning of the pandemic, the St. Coletta website was updated frequently with any changes in policy. They created a new section called "COVID-19 Information and Resources". There were different pages concerning any area that we as families might be concerned about. The community developed a system called the "St. Coletta Protective Posture Levels". This system moves back and forth from zero which employs standard pre-pandemic precautions upwards to Level Four which employs a full quarantine. The community remained for a long period at Level Three which included a residential lockdown, programming in the homes, no visitors, no client travel or home visits. Regular meetings of the COVID-19 Response Team determined the levels and when they should be moved up or down.

The website included regular updates about the levels, the situation at St. Coletta, as well as in Wisconsin and nationally. The number of infections

189

were updated as well as the recoveries. It has been such a source of comfort to read all that is being done to protect Daniela, her friends and the staff who we have come to love. Each change has been explained thoroughly, openly and honestly. The strict measures have, of course, frustrated everyone involved but each measure has been put in place for a very simple and important reason - to save lives. That they have certainly done.

Ted Behncke describes the COVID-19 Response Team as "an ad hoc committee organized and chartered early in the pandemic to provide a multidiscipline approach to the challenges facing the organization during the pandemic." He said, "Meeting weekly and with membership from every department, the committee dealt with serious issues involving the safety of persons served and staff. Approaches to staff shortages, quarantines, adequate PPE, adequate food and supplies were all discussed, war gamed, and solutions reached.

Questions by families and staff were discussed, answered, and were part of the communication plan to all. Positions on the pandemic differed widely, with some in denial of the threat, and others on the other extreme where no safety measure was enough. We were in the middle swimming in between two shores. The Response Team looked at the virus, news, strategies, the vaccine, and how to allow St. Coletta to be itself. Events were rarely cancelled but modified instead. Even though we could not have the normal religious services with larger numbers, we are humbled to say we had services every week including 14 weeks we conducted services without clergy. Communion was distributed. We never gave up, and thanked the Lord weekly for his protection."

Finally in the late fall of 2020 a faint hopeful light appeared on the horizon - a vaccine. As soon as the Covid-19 vaccines were released to the public, beginning in December 2020, a strong and steady education and advocacy effort was conducted at St. Coletta to make sure the clients and staff were informed and prepared to receive the vaccinations as quickly as possible within the state guidelines. Their main goal was for individuals with disabilities to be prioritized from the very beginning. These priority decisions have been left up to each state. In some states, people under 65 with disabilities were not elevated at all on the priority list. St. Coletta was not about to let that happen to their clients in Wisconsin and Illinois.

The website kept us informed on all of their efforts and timelines. They added a vaccine education page that was better than the ones I found on state and national COVID-19 websites. In preparation for the vaccines, they initiated informed consent immunization forms for staff and clients. They wanted to be completely ready the minute the vaccine was available. It was a celebrated day in late January 2021 when the big news of availability finally came. Dates were released for vaccine clinics for staff and clients to be held on campus in both states. My family was beyond thrilled and relieved. That vague hope on the horizon shone brighter.

In early February the first clinics were held. The joy in the photos, that were released to the public on vaccination day, was palpable. Four weeks later, the second clinics were held. Ted Behncke noted, "An astonishing 98 percent of persons served have taken the vaccine, and 51 percent of the staff. (All clients were mandated to get the vaccine and it is a requirement for new admissions.) With those added who had the virus and who now have immunity, we may be the only organization to have reached "herd immunity" inside of ourselves."

As the clients were vaccinated, plans were put in place to begin to drop down the protection levels in late March of 2021. Daniela and her friends were so excited to be able to return to campus to their day programming and their many friends. Masked trips to the store and other local places were carefully planned. Clients could begin to cautiously make home visits again. (I made my first trip to visit Daniela in well over a year and she visited my husband, her sister and me in our new city of Port Orchard Washington. We couldn't wait to be together again.

I knew in my heart from the beginning of this crisis that Daniela would be kept as safe as was humanly possible in her community. Knowing the organization so well, I had complete faith in St. Coletta to not only take care of our daughter but, as they always have, to also set the example for the rest of the country. Daniela has had many more safe and enriching social interactions with her housemates and home staff than she would have had at home with us. To know that we could absolutely trust everyone at St. Coletta made us so grateful and relieved.

As of August 2021, the pandemic isn't over - and won't be anytime soon. The world has likely changed permanently because of this historic crisis. Through it all, like it has since 1904, St. Coletta of Wisconsin has - again - tenaciously and gloriously survived.

Financially though, the impact of all that has happened has been tough on the community. It has been a crisis for most, if not all, nonprofits working with individuals with disabilities. As evidenced by the Governor's Taskforce on Caregiving, the best and only real long-term solution for making sure that St. Coletta and these other organizations survive is to ensure that they have more permanent and equitable federal and state funding to support their work. Funding has been stagnant for many years leading to many organizations closing their doors. Most simply cannot attract and pay staff enough to do their very challenging work.

This leaves many thousands of families in desperate situations. They only want what we all want - decent, secure and happy lives.

It hurts when very qualified staff, and potential staff, have to choose working at a fast food restaurant or big box store because they pay more. As much as they might want to have promising careers with organizations providing disability services, in the end people have to take care of their families and they work where they are able to do that. St. Coletta mightily tries to provide their staff with bright futures, equitable wages and benefits. They believe their highly valuable staff deserve it. Even without the COVID-19 crisis, that has become more and more challenging to achieve.

It is long past time for the United States government, along with Wisconsin, Illinois and every other state to prioritize people with disabilities and the people who care for them. It will only be because of strong community, state, and federal support and because of strong advocacy efforts, that St. Coletta, and all organizations providing disability services, will be able to power through this crisis (and the next) and continue to thrive. It is up to each of us to do what we can. The nation is surely a better place for all of us with organizations like St. Coletta of Wisconsin leading the way.

Advocacy at the Wisconsin State Capitol by
clients, staff and families

Ted Behncke with Wisconsin State Representative
Francesca Hong advocating for ongoing
opportunities to achieve better Medicaid funding for
clients based on fair market-based rates

Life at St. Coletta of Wisconsin

Sleigh used by the Sisters of St. Francis of Assisi from early 1900s to the 1940s. Brought out of retirement for the 2021 St. Coletta Christmas greeting

The St. Coletta Christmas season can't start without freshening up and placing its iconic nativity scene (with Mario Dealca)

Christmas is just one of the many times that St.Coletta celebrates its dedicated staff.

The community also enjoys their living nativity scene with both staff and clients.

And, of course, there has to be a Christmas dance

40 years at
St. Coletta!

Fun and
Mischief!

Striving for
excellence!

The Polar Plunge!

Music

Blessing the animals

Friendships

Blessing of the Fountain

Faith, Hope, Love, and Charity

Sisters'
Jubilee

Palm Sunday

Nativity

Charity

Celebrating St. Coletta and Life

95 years old!

Client Recognition
Banquet

Being
together

199 Love and compassion

St. Coletta then, now and into the future

Through all of the changes, St. Coletta of Wisconsin has continued to grow and fine-tune its mission. Every change is guided by the mission statement and Franciscan values. These principles are, and have always been, at the core of every decision that is made. On the Sisters of St. Francis of Assisi website, they give these values as their mission.

~ Fostering Christian community
~ Relating in mutuality with others
~ Extending hospitality
~ Balancing a life of prayer and action
~ Reverencing all of creation
~ Embracing the option for the poor
~ Working for Justice through systemic change[63]

I believe it is because of the continuing dedication to these core principles that St. Coletta has survived and thrived. It is also the reason they will continue to survive for generations to come.

The work of Sr. Mary Theodore and Sr. Anastasia (and the all of the other Sisters) and what they were able to accomplish with their advocacy, writing, speaking, and research efforts were remarkable by any standard. That they did all of this while personally and individually caring for so many children and adults   is almost unbelievable. Their work has certainly been well respected, as is evidenced by the many awards and praise given to them over the years. Because they were Sisters of St. Francis of Assisi, they believed their mission was their reward and that being humble was important. I hope that, in a small way, this book pays tribute to them and everything that they accomplished, not only for the many children, adults and families whose lives were improved beyond measure, but for all of the knowledge that they imparted to generations of disability leaders, advocates and the rest of the world.

Epilogue

Every year, just as the hot Wisconsin summer begins to ease into the coolness of autumn, St. Coletta celebrates one of the most special days on its calendar - Founder's Day. On September 10th 1904 the Sisters of St. Francis of Assisi began their ministry with the arrival from Missouri of two little girls, Mary Noone and Pearl McCune. That date has been revered and remembered with prayers and reverence.

In 2020, that date fell in the midst of the pandemic. No one would have faulted St. Coletta for taking a pass on creating a celebratory day for its 116th birthday. For everyone in the community though, it was more important than ever to remember their humble beginnings. Just like every year, on September 10th 2020, they held their annual Founder's Day Celebration.

The event was attended by a much smaller crowd than usual and everyone wore masks and followed all the safety guidelines. All who attended the Tea shared a very simple meal consisting of only baked potatoes, salt and tea. This meal was to honor the first Sisters who arrived at their modest farmhouse in 1864 to begin their new mission. The Sisters' meager beginnings and meal (which they repeated for the next three days because that was all that they had) set the tone for the sacrifices they were willing to make - to follow the life and mission of St. Frances - as they made their way forward.

There was actually something else to be excited about at the celebration in 2020. The history wall had just completed its update from 2010 to 2020, reflecting the continued bond and recommitment to Franciscan values. To mark the unveiling of the the wall and Founder's Day, his Excellency Bishop Donald J. Hying gave a blessing. The following paragraphs were written from the ceremony (featured on St. Coletta's YouTube channel). [64]

The Bishop expressed his "profound gratitude" for the work that St. Coletta does, which he said was not just a job but a "vocation and a calling", "to form a communion of love and and goodness and of mercy and of human dignity." He stated that St. Coletta had always been in the leadership and forefront of that vision (to serve individuals with intellectual and developmental disabilities). The Bishop said that, though the methodology and circumstances change, St. Coletta has been "radically faithful to the original vision".

He gave a reading from the Bible from Paul's letter to the Philippians and asked the Lord to bless everyone, especially in the challenging year that they and the country had just had. He stated that "God would always be with us." He asked the Lord "to bless you, to sustain you and to pray for all of the beautiful people that St. Coletta serves and loves. That together we build this community of faith, of charity, of mercy, of peace and that it becomes a model for the world today, that more than ever needs reconciliation and hope, mercy and forgiveness."

He ended his remarks with "Lord hear our Prayer."

From the Bishop, from myself, and from all those who serve and are served at St. Coletta of Wisconsin -

"Lord hear our prayer."

Bishop Donald J. Hying reading from the Bible at the 2020 Founder's Day Celebration

February 10, 2020 (credit Stephanie McDonald)

Donations

Donations to St. Coletta of Wisconsin are vital to continuing their mission. 100% of the profits from this book will be donated directly to serve St. Coletta's mission. Please consider making a donation that will greatly impact the lives of the hundreds of current individuals served by the organization and all of those who will be served in the future. There are many ways to contribute. These include -

Cash donations
In-kind donations (goods, services, or your time)
Volunteering
Legacy donations (including the organization in your estate plan)
Gifts of Stock and other Appreciated Assets
Corporate Gift Matching
United Way
Thrivent Financial
Cars for Coletta

Go to St. Coletta's website under the tab - Get Involved - for more details. To contact St. Coletta of Wisconsin:

Address:
N4637 Co Rd Y
Jefferson Wisconsin 53549

Website: www.stcolettawi.org

Email: info@stcolettawi.org

Facebook: https://www.facebook.com/stcolettawisc

Phone: 920-674-4330

Thank you so much!

Acknowledgements

I am the author of this book and have spent four enjoyable years researching and completing it. However, this book has truly been a collaborative effort. There are a number of people who love St. Coletta of Wisconsin, its people and its history, who have been instrumental in the completion of this book. I am indebted to them and could not have finished this project without them.

The first person I want to thank is the person who I first told about my dream to write a book about St. Coletta's inspiring story. It was nerve racking to say it out loud to someone, because that felt like making a commitment to actually write it. I had the courage to tell her because we were together at a large, heartwarming St. Coletta Gala in 2018. I was feeling especially emotional. Sara Forester embraced my idea completely. Her face brightened and she immediately shared her own love of, and curiosity about, the history of the Sisters of St. Francis of Assisi and their creation of St. Coletta.

Since that evening, Sara has been there every step of the way, helping to conduct interviews, going on tours of the campuses (old and new), writing her own story and motivating me to keep moving forward. Her meticulous editing efforts consumed much time out of her very busy life. This book would not be what it is without her.

In her professional life, as my daughter's case coordinator, Sara been a huge part of Daniela's life and support in almost every aspect. Sara cares for all of her clients with empathy, good humor and expertise. She has impacted our family's life in so many ways. Saying thank you to Sara seems entirely inadequate.

Ted Behncke, as St. Coletta's President, encouraged and supported this project from the beginning, giving me free reign to pursue my research within the organization wherever it led me. He provided important facts, suggestions and corrections along the way, and as Ted is also an author, I have valued his guidance immensely. His Foreword for this book was so gracious that it made me cry (in a good way). The most important reason I want to thank Ted is for continuing to shepherd and lead St. Coletta, its staff, and, of course, the clients. Since he became President he has weathered governmental shortfalls in funding and battled a pandemic. He dedicates his life to improve the lives of the clients at St. Coletta - and individuals with disabilities across the state of Wisconsin and beyond. His efforts and initiatives have made great strides to move Wisconsin and, hopefully, this country forward. His sacred task is to make sure St. Coletta continues to thrive into the distant future. So many of us are grateful for his dogged persistence to make sure that is a reality.

Robin Baker, St. Coletta's Vice President for Marketing and Development, has also been a crucial source and advocate for this book. Her encouragement and support have been essential. As a busy mom with two small children, along with her endless work for St. Coletta, I have greatly appreciated the time she has taken to constantly answer questions and provide resources. She also, like Sara, was an astute and professional editor and helped to correct errors and make the book fluid and accurate. She is also the person assisting me to get this book published. Thanks so much, Robin.

I want to thank Diane Pinnow, who as a longtime staff member of St. Coletta, gave me so many stories, resources and suggestions. As one of my three main editors, she jumped right into the project and helped my words and sentences make sense. I also thank former staff member Cathy Roberts for her great editing assistance. Thanks to former Vice President of Development, Communications and Marketing, Andrea Speth. You gave me great insight into a period of time after Sr. Mary Theodore stopped writing. Thanks to all the other former staff who assisted with stories and information.

At every event, Noah Smith is there documenting it all for the organization's historical records (and everyone's enjoyment). Many of the modern photos in this book are Noah's artwork. When I asked him to take the cover photos for the book, he graciously agreed. He wonderfully captured each person's unique personality. Thank you so much, Noah!

A number of staff have been supporters of this book and promptly gave me resources, stories and information whenever I asked. Most have also been terrific supporters of Daniela. Since the day we first stepped on campus, they have made her life engaging, fun, and independent. They have encouraged her on tough days and applauded her successes. To Stephanie McDonald, Elizabeth Bouchard, Geralyn Dorn, Mario Dealca, Becky Weber, Nicole Styles, Carrie Fox, Rhonda King and Bob Schmidt - thank you so much for your wonderful contributions to this project and to my daughter's life. Though I wouldn't be able to name them all here, I have to include all of St. Coletta's day, nursing, maintenance, office, transportation and residential life staff through the years. How you are able to meld strong personalities together to create such a fun, loving and educational atmosphere is completely beyond me. You have the patience of saints! Thanks to everyone for making my family part of St. Coletta's family.

To all of the Sisters of St. Francis of Assisi, here on earth and those who have gained their reward in Heaven, how could I even begin to express my admiration and gratitude for all that you have done for my daughter and for the thousands of other sons and daughters whose lives you impacted so greatly.

To Sr. Mary Theodore Hegeman, your inspirational documentation of life at St. Coletta, and your life of service dedicated to the children and adults

206

in your care, formed the basis for my research and writing. You spoke out across the globe in support of the value of individuals with disabilities. Your message changed the world.

To Sr. Coletta Dunn, Sr. Julianne Koch and Sr. Ruth Marie Soens, thanks so much for agreeing to speak to me about your dedicated lives and work. I enjoyed every minute with you. Sr. Coletta passed on to her heavenly home on February 14, 2020. Her legacy like all the Sisters, is reflected by all her accomplishments in serving others. To Grace Schauf, I feel incredibly fortunate to know you, the last working Sister at St. Coletta. My interview with you brought St. Coletta's past and people to life. Your humor and knowledge about the community make every visit to campus worthwhile. I love hearing your stories each time that I see you. May God continue to bless you and keep you strong.

To my fellow St. Coletta families who contributed stories, I feel a camaraderie with all of you. Bless you all.

To Mary Jo Shackelford, Doug and Joe: your dedication to your family and the community inspire me. Thank you so much for your advocacy, stories and also for taking my lively daughter out for lunches! We are so much alike in many ways. You keep me sane in this crazy world. To Art Pennington: with your life as a St. Coletta parent to three lovely daughters, Terri, Tami and Tonya, and now an integral part of the St. Coletta staff, you see life there from many viewpoints and I appreciate all of your contributions. To Dennis McTigue: your love and devotion to your brother Michael was so lovely to hear. Thanks for being a great sibling and sharing your story. To Karen Buker: thanks so much for sharing Craig's story and life as his strong advocate. To Tim and Janice Hood and Jenny: your constant advocacy and support of St. Coletta for so many years are greatly appreciated. Thanks Tim, for your book contributions. It's been a such a pleasure to get to know your family.

To all the Sisters, staff, Board of Directors, family, clients and supporters, past and present: Your lives and histories are each part of the tightly woven fabric of the community that is St. Coletta of Wisconsin. You each made and continue to make contributions that enrich all of our lives. It has been a great honor to learn about and know so many of you. Your struggles and your accomplishments will forever be cherished and respected.

And to finish, I give all my love and gratitude to my family who continue to support me in all of my endeavors - my stoic and steady husband John and my two unique daughters - strong, brilliant and inspirational Marcy - and Daniela, that effervescent spirit, who changed our family's life with your resilience, stubborn independence and your quirky humor.

Endnotes

[1] Virginia Association of Community Services Boards, Inc. - letter on 2019-2020 budget priorities

[2] http://missingkennedy.com

[3] Minnesota Dept. of Administration Council of Developmental Disabilities - Parallels in Time

[4] Minnesota Dept. of Administration Council of Developmental Disabilities -Parallels in Time

[5] https://en.wikipedia.org/wiki/Willowbrook_State_School

[6] 'In our Care' - with host Ray Stewart WOI-TV Ames, Iowa with Iowa State University 1952

[7] from the book, "By God's Providence - the Sisters of St. Francis of Assisi 1849-2001" by Doris Pehowski, OSF - 2007 - pages 18-19

[8] from the book, "By God's Providence (see above) page 25

[9] from the book, "A New Assisi", by Sr. Mary Eunice Hancock O.S.F. (Order of St. Francis of Assisi) - 1947 - page 55

[10] from the thesis, 'The Development of St. Coletta School for Exceptional Children 1963-1970 Inclusive" Sister Kathleen Jansen O.S.F

[11] from the book, "A New Assisi" (see above) - page 128

[12] Roma Rudd Turkey, "School for Saints", Information, Dec. 1955, p. 34

7 Wisconsin State Journal - December 11, 1927 - the entire article "Jefferson Nuns Guide Stunted Minds Toward Normal" by Catherine Colburne

[14] from the book, "History of St. Coletta - Jefferson Wisconsin - 1904-1994" complied by Sister Mary Hegeman, OSF - page 11

[15] Wisconsin State Journal - February 10, 1938 - from the article "St. Coletta School, Nationally Famous, Adds $125,000 Units - no author given

[16] from the book, "History of St. Coletta" (see above)

[17] from the book, "The Challenge of the Retarded Child" by Sister Mary Theodore O.S.F - 1963 - page 17

[18] Wisconsin State Journal - January 10, 1951 - from the article "St. Coletta Makes Life for Mentally Deficient Children Happy, Full" by Helen Matheson

[19] Saturday Evening Post, September 22, 1962 - "Hope for Retarded Children" by Rosemary Kennedy Shriver

[20] Chicago Tribune, January 26, 1976 - "The one Kennedy who has found peace" by Joan Zyda

[21] This information was obtained from the Special Olympics website at: specialolympics.org

[22] Wisconsin State Journal - January 10, 1951 - from the article "St. Coletta Makes Life for Mentally Deficient Children Happy, Full" by Helen Matheson

[23] Wisconsin State Journal - July 1, 1953 - from the article "New St. Coletta Chapel Blessed" by Helen Matheson

[24] Wisconsin State Journal - August 2, 1959 - from the article "She Serves God's Little Ones" by Helen Matheson

[25] The President's Panel on Mental Retardation 1962, pg. 108

[26] Herbert Goldstein, James W. Moss, and Laura J. Jordan, "The Efficacy of Special Class vs. Regular Class Training on the Development of Mentally Retarded Children" Cooperative Research Project No. 69 US Office of Education, 1964

[27] from the book "History of St. Coletta" (see above)

[28] from the book "History of St. Coletta" (see above)

[29] From - independentliving.org

[30] from the book "History of St. Coletta" (see above)

[31] Wisconsin State Journal - July 23, 1983 - from the article "Kennedy's give $1 million to St. Coletta" by Susan Lampert Smith

[32] The Journal Times (Racine, Wisconsin) -April 11, 1988 from the AP article "Greenhouse Sows seeds of future for handicapped" - no author given

[33] from the book "History of Coletta" - see above

[34] from the book "History of Sr. Coletta" - see above

[35] Ted uses the term "President" instead of CEO

[36] Wisconsin State Journal January 26, 1997 - from the article "St. Coletta home faces money crunch" by Richard W. Jaeger"

[37] The Capital Times July 1, 1997 - from the AP article "St. Coletta to send patients home" AP article - no author listed

[38] Wisconsin State Journal June 22, 1997 - from the article "Increasing costs threaten institution's open-door tradition." by Richard W. Jaeger

[39] Wisconsin State Journal January 19, 1998 - from the article "St. Coletta buys time by halving deficit" by Meg Turville-Heltz

[40] The LaCrosse Tribune March 19, 2000 - from the article, "First the school, now the farm" by "Smith"/Lee Newspapers

[41] ilfriendsstcolettawi.org

[42] Wisconsin State Journal March 19, 2000 - from the article "St. Coletta is turning in it's plowshares" by Susan Lampert Smith

[43] Wisconsin State Journal June 19, 2005 - from the article "Local care is the thing" by Tim Sheehan - Lee Newspapers

[44] Wisconsin State Journal June 19, 2005 - from the article "Local care is the thing" by Tim Sheehan - Lee Newspapers

[45] wisconsinwatch.org/2015/03/wisconsin-cuts-back-on-long-term-institutional-Care-for-the-disabled/

[46] Wisconsin State Journal June 19, 2005 - from the article "Local care is the thing" by Tim Sheehan - Lee Newspapers

[47] Wisconsin State Journal May 12, 2006 - from the article "Sad for St. Coletta, tough for county" by Susan Lampert Smith

[48] Wisconsin State Journal June 24, 2006 - from the article "State helps St. Coletta clients" by DJ Slater

[49] The Capital Times September 9, 2005 - from the article "St. Coletta to sell Jefferson campus" (AP)

[50] Wisconsin State Journal January 8, 2005 - from the article "Rosemary dies in Wisconsin" (AP)

[51] Daily Jefferson County Union August 11, 2009 - from article "JFK's sister great friend to St. Coletta of Wisconsin, disabled" by Ryan Whisner

[52] Daily Jefferson County Union June 8, 2011 - from the article "St. Coletta revamping Alverno" (no writer listed)

[53] Daily Jefferson County Union June 8, 2011 - from the article "St. Coletta revamping Alverno"

[54] I prefer not to give the name of this community to protect the clients.

[55] Cathy was Director of Licensing and Quality Assurance when retired.

[56] www.dhs.wisconsin.gov/gftc-report.pdf

[57] stcolettawi.org

58 stcolettawi.org

[59] from the website - littleflower.org

[60] Daily Jefferson County Union June 8, 2011 - from 4th article "St. Coletta revamping Alverno

[61] Daily Jefferson County Union February 16, 2012 - from the article "St. Coletta all under one roof" by Karyn Spory

[62] https://www.yalemedicine.org/news/down-syndrome-covid-19

[63] lakeosfs.org

[64] https://www.youtube.com/channel/UCn_bL7zs8fkJL7QYfCG7Rmg/videos

Made in United States
Orlando, FL
31 August 2022

21776766R00124